A Parents'
A-Z of Education

The Authors

Hilary Mason is a Cambridge honours graduate with experience of teaching in England and in the Middle East. She has worked as a journalist and contributed articles to *The Guardian*. She was one of the team of writers on *The Green Book* (Hodder and Stoughton, 1991).

Tony Ramsay is an honours graduate and former lecturer who has taught both in this country and South America. He is the author of *The Language User's Handbook* (Nelson, 1989). He has also written for a number of periodicals including *The Times Educational Supplement*, *The Guardian* and *The Independent*.

As writers, parents and former teachers, the authors are ideally placed to interpret the rapidly changing educational scene for a non-specialist audience.

A Parents'
A-Z of Education

Hilary Mason
Tony Ramsay

Chambers

Published 1992 by W & R Chambers Ltd,
43–45 Annandale Street, Edinburgh EH7 4AZ

British Library Cataloguing in Publication Data

A catalogue for this book is available from the British Library

ISBN 0-550-18078-8

Cover design by Art Dept, Edinburgh
Typeset by Butler and Tanner Ltd, Frome
Printed by Clays Ltd, St Ives plc

Dedication for
Marilyn

Preface

This book was begun — at least partly — in self-defence. Coming back to Britain after a period spent teaching abroad we found ourselves plunged into an educational scene that had been transformed. We returned to a world of SATS, Key Stages, Profile Components and the whole paraphernalia of the National Curriculum. Parent power had arrived. Schools were becoming more like small businesses. The newspapers were full of stories about Opting-out and falling standards.

After talking to other parents, it quickly became clear that confusion was widespread. It seemed to us there was an urgent need for an accessible, non-specialist guide to the educational scene. When we couldn't find the book we wanted, we decided to draw on our experience as parents, writers and teachers to produce our own. *A Parents' A-Z of Education* is the result.

From the very start we were concerned that the book had to be more than a mere A-Z of the education system. As parents we knew how useful an understanding of recent changes could be, but as teachers we were also aware that in all the high-profile newspaper coverage of new funding and assessment procedures, more important things were getting lost.

What has not changed as a result of recent reforms is the importance of the parent's role in bridging the gap between home and school. That is why making the most of the partnership between parent, teacher and child is a central theme of the book. In addition to basic information about the system, you will find direct practical advice on how you can offer support both at home and at school.

Hilary Mason and Tony Ramsay

Note: The information and advice we offer is relevant to all British parents. There are however significant differences between the way the education system operates in England and Wales, Scotland and Northern Ireland. Where these differences affect the wider picture a separate entry is included.

Acknowledgements

Without the patient support of Ken, Ben, and Joseph Mason, Maggie, Diccon and Josie Ramsay this book could not have been written. Stephanie Mudd's professional expertise and her generosity have been invaluable.

Thanks are also due to: Vera Hughes for her initial support in the garden in Villanova and help with the Scottish research; Masons News Service for professional and technical support.

How to use this book

Each entry provides a summary of individual topics. Cross-references in bold indicate topics which have their own entry. The **How to** sections, scattered through the book, offer direct practical advice on helping with specific subjects at home.

How to . . .

A

abacus

A counting frame consisting of rows of beads on rods or wires which is used for simple calculations.

A cheap, colourful abacus is well worth having amongst your child's play things.

Simple versions of the device are often used in classrooms and **mathematics schemes** to introduce children to the idea of 100s, 10s and units.

(See also **How to help with maths**.)

Academic Board

A committee in **Higher Education** institutions, such as universities and colleges, with responsibility for planning and running courses.

accent and dialect

Two separate features which result in a distinctive speaking voice, usually associated with different parts of the country or different social classes.

Many parents and **teachers** still see having the right kind of voice as an essential mark of a good education. This attitude—based on a half-truth—is understandable, but it can cause needless difficulties for children. Most of these difficulties can be avoided through an understanding of the simple difference between accent and dialect.

A dialect is a version of the language that has features not found in the kind of all-purpose, neutral English used in educational circles, the version known as **standard English**. These features might be unfamiliar words ('mistal', 'godown', 'pammet') or unusual **grammar** ('him that belongs that Ford Escort', 'it frit me!'). If you saw the words written down, you would be able to identify these oddities quite easily.

Accents, on the other hand, have nothing to do with these non-standard features. An accent is concerned only with the way words sound on the tongue. 'The cat sat on the mat' (a familiar example of standard English) could be said in a whole range of different accents.

The important point for parents is this: by all means encourage your children to master standard English and use it in the appropriate situations, but do not make them self-conscious about their accent. Standard English is still standard English whatever the accent you are using. Most educated English-speakers have an accent which shows signs of their linguistic roots. Rather than see this as a flaw which has to be eradicated, it makes much more sense to think of it as something like a watermark in quality paper: a sign which promises individuality.

(See also **language differences**.)

access courses

Courses designed to prepare students without formal academic **qualifications** for entry into **Further** or **Higher Education**.

(See also **mature students**.)

ACE

See **Advisory Centre for Education**

admission policies

See **choosing a school**

adolescence

A period of emotional and physical change experienced by young people as they move towards adulthood.

Most parents will not need a full checklist to recognize this turbulent time in the life of their children. Here are a few of the more common characteristics of adolescence:

A period of rapid physical growth for both girls and boys. Girls tend to reach this growth spurt earlier than boys, usually around the age of 12. Boys arrive at this point up to two years later. Many girls also menstruate for the first time during these years. Young people are often extremely self-conscious about these physical changes and may indulge in faddy diets in an attempt to modify their appearance. In exteme cases this can lead to eating disorders such as anorexia. Remember that everybody is different and your child may not conform to these averages. Generally, you can expect your daughters to grow very quickly anytime between 10 and 14 and your sons between 12 and 16.

There might be a period of emotional and social confusion which spans the whole of the secondary-school years. Around the age of 11 many young children begin to feel more independent of their family. They identify much more with peer groups and friendship can come to seem more important than family ties. They may also enter a period of hero worship: of pop stars or sporting personalities.

Between the ages of 15 and 16 there is, for many children, a surge in intellectual growth and capacity for concentration. If you are lucky, this period coincides with their first public examinations, such as **GCSE** or **Standard Grade**.

There might be an identity crisis: not only do teenagers spend ages in front of the mirror wondering why they are so ugly or admiring their natural good looks, they may also ask themselves: 'Who am I?' or 'What's the point of school?' This phase can last beyond the years of compulsory schooling and into the early 20s and is sometimes characterized by aggressive and rebellious behaviour.

Living with moody, rude and unmotivated offspring tries the patience of most parents. Teaching them is no mean feat either. How to keep teenage children motivated is one of the most frequently discussed subjects at parents' evenings.

Some suggestions for parents

Remember that adolescence represents a step along the way to independence, which is the aim of effective parenting and schooling alike. Underneath all the negative attitudes and changes in behaviour there is an individual trying to come to terms with the complexities of life.

Try to keep the channels of communication open. Although it can be very tiresome to hold a conversation with your 14-year-old child about the importance of getting home on time when all that comes back is a series of sighs or grunts, it is extremely important to keep trying. Your child needs something to rebel against; you and the school are the most obvious targets.

Try to support your child's school experiences. It is very difficult for many adolescent children to see the relevance of school work when their emotions and their hormones are in turmoil. Make sure you are really well informed about what is expected at school and be on hand to help with **homework** if you can.

Try not to appear judgmental. Criticizing your teenager's friends, even if you think they are a bad influence, is likely to push your teenager further away. It is during the latter stages of adolescence that many children experiment with sex, drugs and anti-social behaviour. When all else in your child's life seems to be in complete disarray, home needs to be a refuge and a place of stability.

(See also **How to help with older children, Sex 'n' Drugs 'n' Rock 'n' Roll.**)

adoption

See **children in care**

adult education

A general term used to describe a wide range of educational opportunities available beyond the minimum school-leaving age of 16. Options range from basic literacy and numeracy to bee-keeping classes, or a **science** degree. Courses are often run on a part-time basis. Adult education is known increasingly as 'continuing education'.

Educating adults makes good sense economically. There is a major skills shortage in industry. At the same time unemployment is high, there are large numbers of women anxious to return to the labour market after child-rearing, and people over 40 who find themselves unemployed. Providing the necessary educational opportunities for these people could go a long way towards answering industry's needs: as well as contributing to their own feelings of self-worth.

Adults are often intimidated by the prospect of going back to school. The feeling also persists amongst some adult learners that by continuing their own education they may be depriving youngsters of their fair share. Others simply lack confidence. They fear they may not have as much to offer as their younger counterparts: that their brains are rusty and they will not be able to keep up. These fears are largely unfounded.

Most courses take place in local **Colleges of Further Education**, community centres, and in **evening classes** at local schools. There are some very good examples of schemes which teach adults side by side with secondary-school children. In Strathclyde, in Scotland, around 10 000 adults, 80 per cent of whom were women, joined secondary-school classes to learn a wide range of subjects, from technology to **modern languages**. Fifteen per cent of the adult school returners went on to **Further** or **Higher Education**. The scheme was an imaginative response to the problem of empty school places and subject viability, but was soon to become a casualty of reductions in educational spending.

It may not be easy to find a course that fits your needs but it is worth investigating all possible routes. If you are interested in taking an academic or vocational course at a College of Further or Higher Education, do not be put off by the fact that you have no public examinations behind you. Many colleges and polytechnics welcome the input from **mature students** and may waive normal entry requirements. In Scotland the Wider Access Programme was set up in 1988 to encourage more adults to enlist on courses.

The best way of finding out about courses is to visit the educational establishment you are interested in and ask what is on offer, or send for a **prospectus**. Alternatively, contact your **Local Education Authority (LEA)** through your local council.

This may not be so easy for the many thousands of adults in Britain who are in need of help with basic skills such as reading, writing and maths. Around 4 million people need help with basic literacy: reading and writing. Added to this are 6 million who have problems with basic numeracy (**mathematics**). This means that as many as one in 10 of the population is in need of help with basic skills. Many adults in need of basic education are too embarrassed to ask for it or too poor to afford it. There is a stigma attached to being unable to read or write and people go to extraordinary, but understandable, lengths to conceal their plight.

Adult education is in a very vulnerable position because provision is left entirely to the discretion of Local Education Authorities (LEAs). These are subject to serious restrictions on public spending. The law only stipulates that there must be 'adequate provision' generally for adult education, and that those with special needs (the handicapped, for example) must be catered for.

Interpretations of what constitutes adequate provision and special needs vary from authority to authority. Beyond this the National Institute for Adult and Continuing Education (NIACE) points out that only one in 10 authorities spends as much on adult education as the government allows for in its annual spending assessment. Many LEAs are planning to reduce their adult education budgets still more. The picture is especially grim for people living in areas under threat from further spending cuts and **charge-capping**.

The latest developments are set to take Colleges of Further Education out of LEA control altogether. The probable outcome is that state funding for adult courses which are not directly related to jobs will disappear altogether. Money is more likely to be spent on vocational courses (those which feed the needs of commerce and industry), **access courses** and—perhaps—**special needs**. Tap-dancing, bee-keeping, yoga and calligraphy evening classes may become a thing of the past. Eight out of 10 adults on these endangered courses are women.

For further information, contact

National Institute for Adult and Continuing Education (NIACE)
19b De Montfort Street, Leicester LE1 7GE

Northern Ireland Educational Service for Adults
Room 208, Bryson House, 28 Bedford Street, Belfast BT2 7FE

Scottish Community Education Council
West Coates House, 90 Haymarket Terrace, Edinburgh EH12 5LQ

Unit for the Development of Adult and Continuing Education in England and Wales
Christopher House, 94b London Road, Leicester LE2 0QS

Workers Educational Association
Temple House, 9 Upper Berkeley Street, London W1H 8BY

(See also **community schools and colleges, Open University**.)

advisers

Advisers were traditionally employed by **Local Education Authorities (LEAs)** to support **teachers** by advising on the content of courses, and organizing **in-service training**.

Increasingly advisers are being given an inspectorial role. This means that in addition to supporting teachers they are being asked to report on their efficiency. Many advisers feel they have lost the confidence of teachers as a result.

With the current changes affecting Local Education Authorities and **HMIs**, advisers could find themselves competing in the open market place offering an inspection or monitoring service to increasingly autonomous schools.

Advisory Centre for Education (ACE)

A charity offering free advice to parents on a wide range of educational matters.

ACE produces a regular newsletter and a range of other publications.

For further information, contact

Advisory Centre for Education (ACE) Ltd
1b Aberdeen Studios, 22–24 Highbury Grove,
London N5 2EA

advisory services

See **Local Education Authorities (LEAs)**

AEO

See **Area Education Officer**

after-school activities

Activities, usually in the form of clubs or workshops, which are run out of school hours. Some may operate during lunch breaks rather than at the end of the school day.

The range of after-school activities offered by different schools varies enormously. Sport and craft activities are the most common. Almost all are run by volunteer teachers or parents and as a result the activities on offer are likely to reflect their individual interests.

Schools are not allowed to charge for any activity that relates to a syllabus for a public exam, or the demands of the **National Curriculum**, though they may ask for voluntary contributions. The issue is less clear-cut for things like stamp-collecting, canoeing or rock-climbing. Again, the school might ask for contributions or they may choose to fund the activity from the school budget.

After-school activities are generally popular with children: a point worth bearing in mind when **choosing a school**. Transport problems can make it difficult for your child to join in if you live some distance away from the school. As well as being able to develop their interests beside others who share their enthusiasm, children are also likely to benefit from the more informal contact with **teachers**.

After-school activities might not always be so popular with today's teachers. Although teachers cannot be forced to run a club outside school hours, they often come under pressure to do so from **headteachers** and **governors** anxious to create a good impression for prospective parents.

You should ask for details of after-school activities when you are choosing a school. If your child is interested, it is a good idea to make enquiries at the beginning of term. Many clubs operate on a first-come, first-served basis.

Alternatively, if you think you have a particular skill or interest which you are willing to share, talk to the headteacher and other like-minded parents about the possibility of setting up a club. Many successful school clubs could not operate without the invaluable help of parents.

(See also **funding, home–school partnership**.)

AGM

See **Annual General Meeting**

agricultural colleges

Colleges of Further or **Higher Education** which offer courses in rural industries.

These colleges offer a wide range of studies at all levels. For more information contact your local college of agriculture.

(See also **Further Education (FE), Higher Education (HE), training**.)

AIDS (acquired immune deficiency syndrome)

AIDS is not a single disease. It is a late consequence of infection by the human immunodeficiency virus or HIV. This virus attacks the body's normal defence against illness and leaves the person with AIDS open to attack from a wide range of diseases, most of which can be fatal. There is no cure for AIDS.

The virus is spread from an infected person via semen, vaginal fluids or blood. The primary routes are through unprotected sexual intercourse, the sharing of unsterilized needles and drug-injecting equipment, and transfusions of contaminated blood. A pregnant woman carrying the infection may also pass the virus on to her child. There is no evidence that HIV can be passed by means of crockery, cutlery, toilet seats, touching, kissing or sharing swimming pools.

Research has shown that many school children are sexually active before they receive any education about AIDS—or even about sex. This, coupled with the steady increase in HIV infection among both heterosexuals and homosexuals, makes AIDS an issue for all schools.

Government campaigns have done little to dispel widespread ignorance and prejudice about HIV and AIDS among young people. Some teenagers felt the campaigns had a moralistic aim and were primarily designed to discourage them from having sex. Others concluded that HIV and AIDS only affect homosexuals, drug addicts and people over 20. Many school children still tend to see 'safe sex' in terms of avoiding pregnancy, rather than avoiding AIDS.

This gloomy picture is made worse by widespread ignorance about teenage sexuality and an unwillingness on behalf of most adults to talk openly about the subject. One piece of potentially life-saving advice that can be given to any teenage child is: use a condom. Suggesting abstinence is an approach that has been tried by generations of parents. Generations of children have taken no notice.

Local Education Authorities (LEAs) and school governing bodies need to have a policy on AIDS and its management. Without it, deciding what to do about pupils and teachers who are HIV positive will be difficult. More significantly, the appropriate health education policies are less likely to figure in the curriculum at the time they are really needed—now.

If your child has AIDS, you should think carefully before you make the fact widely known. Ideally, the headteacher should be informed but you are under no legal obligation to tell him or her. With the prevailing attitudes towards HIV and AIDS, you will need to consider the possible consequences for your child and discuss the matter with experts.

For further information, contact
The National AIDS Helpline: 0800 567123 (24 hours)

Terence Higgins Helpline: 071-242 1010 (3.00 pm–10.00 pm)

Terence Higgins Trust
52–54 Grays Inn Road, London WC1 8JU Tel: 071-831 0330

(See also **Sex 'n' Drugs 'n' Rock 'n' Roll.**)

A-level

The traditional English academic qualification taken by students at 18. The **Higher Grade** of the **Scottish Certificate of Education (SCE)** is a similar examination north of the border although it is a one-year course, less detailed, with five subjects commonly studied. A-levels provide the entrance requirements to most university and polytechnic degree courses.

Students in Sixth Forms generally take three A-levels, though **A/S levels** now provide a possible alternative. A-levels are intellectually demanding exams aimed at the top 30 per cent of the population and, of those who begin A-level courses, almost a third drop out. A quarter of those who take the exam fail. For this reason A-levels have carried much of the blame for the exceptionally poor staying-on rate in schools at 16—amongst the worst in **Europe**.

Proposed Reforms

Attempts to reform the A-level system have been going on for at least 20 years. Opinion is divided between those who regard them as the benchmark of excellence and others who believe that they are too narrow in scope, test only a small range of skills, and encourage specialization too early. Most reforms have focused on broadening the range of subjects studied by individual students, perhaps along the lines of the **Baccalaureate** studied in other countries of Europe—as well as one or two centres in Britain. A recent proposal to replace the normal three A-levels with five 'leaner and fitter' exams of broadly the same type was quickly rejected.

Another proposal being considered is to replace the current system of two years of study and a single final exam by a modular course. (See **modular courses**.) Pupils would study a series of self-contained modules that could be assembled—like bricks in a wall—to make up the qualification. There could be several advantages to this system: the outcome would not depend on an all-or-nothing exam; different modules could be combined into A-levels or more vocational **qualifications**; and people who failed to finish the full course would still get credit for the work they had done.

There is now a wide range of options available for pupils at 16, but not all are available in schools. Encourage your child to see what is on offer at local Colleges of Further Education. (See **Further Education (FE)**.) You might also suggest to your head-teacher and **governors** that they join the growing number of schools offering **BTEC** in the Sixth Form.

(See also **beyond 16, vocational education.**)

alternative education

A general term used to describe a range of options available to parents who cannot find a school in either the maintained or independent sector that satisfies them.

Under the terms of the 1944 Education Act which established the principle of free, compulsory education for all, parents have the right to educate their children 'otherwise' than at school.

If you wish to educate your child outside the mainstream school system, you must obtain permission from your **Local Education Authority (LEA)**. The LEA will want to examine your suggested alternative arrangements and make regular visits. Officials are unlikely to make it easy for you, and you must be prepared to fulfil their requirements. The LEA reserves the right to serve an **attendance order** for the child to be put back in school if the alternative provision appears inadequate. However, in practice, the LEA is unlikely to be able to spare the time or the personnel to visit regularly.

Before deciding to go it alone, it is worth considering these points:

What are your reasons for wanting to educate your child at home? Is it you or your child who is unhappy with the school? Have you spent time discussing your concerns with the **teachers**? Have you considered other schools in the area? You must be sure that your motives have your child's best interests at heart. Has he or she fully understood what it will mean in terms of day-to-day contact with both you and children of his or her own age?

How will you organize the work and monitor progress?

Do you have access to adequate and stimulating resources? Although it is not always necessary to spend a fortune on commercially produced schemes of work, educating your child at home can be expensive.

What will you do about your child's social development? In

schools children meet all sorts of people and hopefully make new friends regularly. Although educating your child yourself need not mean isolation from others, it is not easy to re-create a sense of wider community.

Educating your child at home requires a huge commitment on your part and considerable staying power, although, of course, you can always opt back in if things do not work out.

Many parents do manage to overcome all the obstacles, educate their children happily and achieve very good results. It may be helpful to get together with other parents in the area who have taken the alternative education route. Pooling resources and sharing experiences make sense.

For further information, contact

The Children's Home-Based Education Association
14 Basil Avenue, Armthorpe, Doncaster DN3 2AT

Education Otherwise
25 Common Lane, Hemmingford Abbots, Cambs PE 9AN

World-Wide Education Service
Barleymow Passage, London W4 4PH

Parents of children with serious physical or psychological handicaps may have no choice but to educate their children outside the school system. In such exceptional circumstances, LEAs are allowed to provide free home tuition. Many parents are unaware of this service. It is in any case left entirely to the discretion of the LEAs to decide under what circumstances home tuition is granted. If you feel your child needs this kind of help, you will have to fight quite hard to get it. Contact the education department of your local council.

If educating your child at home is not an option, you might like to consider some alternative types of schools. (See **choosing a school**.) This is not an exhaustive list of alternative arrangements but you will find out a lot if you talk to at least some of them. Not all of them will be available in your area.

Flexischooling

This arrangement attempts to combine the benefits of a home-based education with time spent in schools. Under this system, which is as yet difficult to arrange, children at home can spend some time at school, sharing resources and mixing with children of the same age, and some time at home.

For further information, contact

Education Now Publishing Co-operative
PO Box 186, Ticknall, Derbyshire DE7 1W7

(Their publication is called *Flexischooling: Education for Tomorrow Starting Today.*)

Free Schools

These are small, independent but non-profit-making schools, founded on the principle that children have the right to control their own learning in an atmosphere of democracy. Decisions on all aspects of school life are made by committee, with parents, children and teachers having an equal voice. In the heyday of the free school movement during the early 1970s, there were only ever 18 free schools in England. Now there is just one although several fee-paying progressive schools are still going, including the first and most famous, Summerhill, founded by A.S. Neil.

For further information, contact

The Advisory Centre for Education (ACE) Ltd
1b Aberdeen Studios, 22–24 Highbury Grove,
London N5 2EA

Montessori Schools

These are independent schools usually in the nursery sector which use teaching methods developed by an Italian called Maria Montessori. The essence of the Montessori method is that children are encouraged to learn from their natural surroundings and through their senses. **Music**, dance and movement for example may be an integral part of the day. Make sure you spend some time looking around, as differences between establishments advertising themselves as Montessori are quite marked.

For further information, contact

London Montessori Centre (LMC)
18 Balderton Street, London W1Y 1TG

Steiner Schools

These cater for children between the ages of 4 and 18. All the schools take both boys and girls and each school is broadly Christian in outlook. Boarding places are sometimes available. (See **boarding schools**.) Steiner schools do not receive any central-government **funding**, relying instead on a sliding scale of fees and private donations. Although the curriculum is based on Albert Steiner's own holistic philosophy (the need to develop the inner self), it is very carefully structured. No attempt is made to teach **reading** until children reach the age of 6 and then only after the rudiments of writing have been mastered. **Teachers** stay with the same children for eight years, but from year one pupils are taught specialist subjects such as **music** or **modern languages** by specialist teachers. During the last four years children are taught by separate subject specialists. There are no internal examinations at any stage but some pupils sit **GCSE** and **A-level**s. (See **holism**.)

For further information, contact
Steiner Schools Fellowship
Kidbrooke Park, Forest Row, East Sussex RH1 85JB

ancillary staff

A term used to cover non-teaching staff who help in the running of a school. Ancillary staff include welfare assistants, laboratory technicians, secretaries and librarians.

As a result of restrictions on local authority spending it has become harder to find the money to pay for ancillary staff. This already difficult situation has been made worse by the arrival of **Local Management of Schools (LMS)**.

LMS—which gave schools control over their own budgets— has put many **headteachers** in the difficult position of having to choose between, for example, much-needed secretarial help and teaching staff in order to balance the books. Inevitably, with **funding** linked to the number of children at the school (all of whom need **teachers**), it is the ancillary staff who are usually made redundant. As with so many of the recent developments in education, the loss of ancillary staff is also likely to hit children with **special needs** particularly hard.

The term ancillary staff is sometimes used to refer to domestic staff such as cleaners and cooks.

Annual General Meeting (AGM)

A yearly meeting which school **governors** in England and Wales are required to call, by law, in order to report to parents.

Many of these meetings are so poorly attended that the governors often outnumber interested parents. Yet this is an important occasion: particularly when you bear in mind recent educational changes and the greatly increased powers of both governors and parents. It is certainly worth making the effort to attend. You might materially be able to influence the development of your child's school.

(See also **jargon**.)

appraisal

See **teachers**

apprenticeships

Traditional routes to employment and training for school-leavers interested in becoming skilled craftspeople, such as electricians, carpenters, and hairdressers.

Under an apprenticeship scheme, young people can gain a recognized qualification, such as the **City and Guilds**, by agreeing to work for a small wage as they learn the job alongside an experienced worker. Although apprenticeships still exist in some areas, they have largely given way to **Youth Training (YT)** or vocational courses organized through Colleges of Further Education. (See **Further Education (FE)**.)

Apprenticeships have clear advantages over Youth Training schemes. A contract may extend for between two and a half and three years and may help a young person gain formal **qualifications**. Employers may also decide to pay more than the minimum allowance for Youth Training. Apprenticeships are theoretically available for anyone between the ages of 16 and 63.

(See also **training**.)

apprenticeship to reading

See **reading**

approved schools

See **community homes**

Area Education Officer (AEO)

A representative of your **Local Education Authority (LEA)** who is responsible for education in your part of the county. He or she will be your first port of call after the headteacher and the **governors** in case of complaint or enquiry.

(See also **complaints**.)

art

One of the seven foundation subjects of the **National Curriculum** which supplement the core subjects of **English, mathematics** and **science**. Art can be taken at **GCSE, A-level** and beyond. (See **art colleges**.)

The status of art as a subject in its own right is threatened by the complexities of timetabling the National Curriculum in schools. Government ministers currently favour the merging of art with other non-scientific subjects, such as **music** or **drama**, and making it an optional subject for 14–16-year-olds. Thus art could appear on a timetable as aesthetics or performing arts for 11–13-year-olds and then be dropped. Critics fear this approach might squeeze out essential elements of art and design teaching.

The expressive arts have an important part to play in a child's educational and emotional development. Fortunately, few young children need much encouragement to explore the possibilities of paint and clay. All parents need do is provide materials, opportunity and interest in sharing the results. As children get older their spontaneity and creativity can be submerged under the demands of an exacting academic schedule that encourages them to specialize at an early stage. It is at this point parents might have to look outside the school for opportunities in art, music, dance and drama.

(See also **How to help with art and music**.)

art colleges

Colleges which specialize in **art** and design courses.

Most courses begin with a foundation year. Prospective students usually need two **A-levels**, or their equivalents, and must support their application with evidence of their own work. This will include a portfolio and ideally evidence of work in a range of different media.

Art courses do not qualify for mandatory grants. Some local authorities will award them, but you may have to look elsewhere for finance.

(See also **beyond 16, grants and loans**.)

Articled Teachers Scheme

See **teachers**

arts/science divide

Traditionally, the English school system has encouraged children to specialize in either arts subjects or the sciences. The common phenomena of scientists who cannot express themselves in lay terms, or the art specialist who goes pale at the sight of a mathematical equation were the inevitable consequences.

Specialization began at 13 or 14 with the choice of subjects taken at **GCSE** (until recently, O-levels). If someone was good at **science**, then **mathematics, physics**, chemistry and biology would be the obvious choices. Someone good at **English** would concentrate on **modern languages, history, geography** and other arts subjects. In many schools timetables were arranged so that it was impossible to mix, for example, a foreign language with chemistry, or literature with physics. (See **options**.)

The problem became more acute at **A-level** where until recently it was extremely difficult to take a mixture of arts and science subjects. Some of the proposed reforms to the A-level system are designed to tackle just this point.

There were also other factors affecting this division between the arts and sciences—in particular a **hidden curriculum** which steered girls towards arts subjects and boys towards the more technical sciences.

A broad-based curriculum has benefits for both pupils and employers. A mixture of arts and sciences encourages the development of a wider range of skills. It is also likely to make individuals more adaptable and better able to cope with the demands of a rapidly changing world. The **National Curriculum** acknowledges these benefits by ensuring that all pupils take the core subjects of English, maths and science at **GCSE** and study a broad range of other subjects, including a foreign language. However, recent developments have weakened this approach by effectively abandoning the National Curriculum beyond the core subjects for 14–16-year-olds.

The appearance at the end of the 1980s, of **City Technology Colleges (CTCs)** also worked against moves to limit specialization. CTCs do not have to follow the National Curriculum and are free to concentrate on a technology-based curriculum. (See **magnet schools**.)

A/S level

A qualification which is equivalent to half a traditional **A-level**. A/S levels were introduced in an attempt to broaden the spread of most pupils' A-level courses. It was thought that pupils might be encouraged to take a mixture of arts and sciences by combining two A-levels with two A/S levels. The initial response was disappointing: few students were persuaded the new exam offered a realistic alternative to A-levels. (See **Higher Grades**.)

(See also **beyond 16, vocational education.**)

assembly

A daily gathering of part or all of the school used as an occasion for a collective act of worship.

The 1988 Education Reform Act reaffirmed a school's obligation to hold daily acts of worship 'of a broadly Christian character'. These can take place at a daily assembly of the whole school or smaller assemblies based for example on year-groups. The requirement applies to Sixth Forms and **Sixth Form Colleges**.

It is up to individual schools to decide the exact nature of assemblies. Some schools satisfy the legal requirements by telling children stories with a broadly Christian theme: perhaps, the importance of caring for those less fortunate than themselves. Other schools take a more direct approach, perhaps by reading Bible stories and singing hymns.

Assemblies are also used to give out messages and announce forthcoming events when groups of children are together in one place.

Parents are entitled to withdraw their children from assemblies on religious grounds.

(See also **religious education (RE).**)

assessment

See **National Curriculum**

Assisted Places Scheme

A scheme designed to help pupils from low-income families take advantage of private education. Under the scheme the government pays part or all of the fees for secondary pupils who win places at selected **independent schools**. The scheme does not cover the cost of boarding.

The scheme has been much criticized since its introduction in 1980. To many people it seemed a government subsidy (over £50 million in 1990) for private education at a time of great shortages in the state sector. It has also been accused of undermining the state system by creaming off the more able pupils.

The scheme has not been an unqualified success. While some children have unquestionably benefited, many places remain unfilled (4000 in 1991). More damaging for its supporters is that recent research has shown that the scheme has been appropriated by the middle classes and is not reaching the families for which it was intended.

For further information, contact

England
Department of Education and Science (DES)
Mowden Hall, Darlington DR3 9BG

Wales
Welsh Office Education Department
Phase 2, Government Buildings, Ty Glas Road, Llanishen,
Cardiff CF4 5WE

Scotland
Scottish Office Education Department (SOED)
Room 4/14, New St Andrew's House, St James Centre,
Edinburgh EH1 3SY

Attainment Targets

See **National Curriculum**

attendance order

A court order instructing the parents of truants or persistent absentees to ensure their children attend school regularly.

(See also **truancy**.)

How to help at home

Helping at home is something all parents can do whatever their educational backgrounds. You do not need to be an expert in **mathematics**, or **geography** or **science**. You do not need access to expensive equipment. More important is a willingness to get involved. This means knowing what your children are doing at school, talking to them, listening, supporting in simple practical ways. Above all it means using your interest and encouragement to help them make the connection between the lessons they learn at school and the world outside. (See **home–school partnership**.)

You will find suggestions about helping with individual subjects in the **How to** sections of this book. In addition, here are a few general points to bear in mind:

Confidence is the key to effective learning. Make sure that when you help at home, your children have lots of opportunities to succeed. Do not be tempted to push them beyond their capabilities. Work at their pace and listen to their suggestions.

Offer plenty of praise and encouragement: even if the piece of work looks a mess, try to say something positive about it first.

Although it is very difficult, try not to compare your child's abilities with others. Children all have different strategies for learning things and develop at different rates. If one of your children learned to read without the slightest hiccough, there is no guarantee that your younger child will follow suit.

The aim of helping your children at home is to develop their individual strengths and weaknesses—not to get them ahead of the pack.

Children generally learn more through practical activities—from collecting shells to designing a motorized go-cart—than paper and pencil exercises—although these have their place.

Get into the habit of asking your children open questions like 'I wonder what would happen if . . .' Encourage them to speculate rather than putting them on the spot. Play the naive accomplice. Give them room to make their own decisions.

Do not be afraid of admitting you do not know—it puts you and your child on the same side. Even if you do know it is sometimes worth keeping quiet and setting off to explore the possibilities together.

It is not the amount of time you spend with your child that counts, but rather the consistency and quality of that time. (See **quality time**, **working parents**.)

Children with Difficulties

Everything that has been said about helping so far applies to children with difficulties—only more so. Parents may wonder what they can possibly do if their children are not thriving on the specialist help that **teachers** are providing. However, again it is not necessarily specialized help these children need: it is concentrated attention and time (something it is difficult for **teachers** to provide in a class of 35).

You need to be particularly sensitive to your child's state of mind. Again confidence is the key. If children are failing repeatedly at something—perhaps an aspect of maths—put it on one side and let them try something they are good at to remind them what success tastes like. This need not be a traditional academic subject. All children are good at something: BMX-racing, swimming, **art**, socializing, telling jokes. This does not mean that you gloss over the difficulty; have another go when confidence has been boosted, or try a different approach.

You should also keep in close contact with the school and any other educational experts that are involved. If a child is having difficulties, the best policy is close co-operation. (See **special needs**.)

21

B

baby booms and bulges

Large-scale variations in pupil numbers which have repercussions throughout the school system.

The baby boom of the 1960s led to a rapid expansion of education provision—more **teachers** were recruited to cope with the numbers of children, and more schools opened. Then, during the 1970s, the birthrate dropped by a third and the trend was reversed. Since 1977 the overall number of pupils has been falling. The effect is worse in some sectors than others—the number of secondary pupils has declined by 20 per cent since the end of the 1970s.

When the bulge of 1960s baby-boomers worked its way through the system, schools were left with unfilled places. This led to school closures—particularly severe among small **village schools**. Other schools had to shrink. This meant losing members of staff as well as pupils—sometimes limiting the range of subjects pupils could study. The contraction in the education system also closed off avenues of promotion within the teaching profession. However the end of the decline in school population may be in sight as the number of primary school pupils has been rising since 1986. It will be some years before this new bulge works its way into the secondary system.

(See also **class size, school closure**.)

Baccalaureate

A qualification—roughly equivalent to **A-levels** or Scottish **Highers**—which governs entry to university in most European countries.

The exam is broad based and requires success in a whole range of subjects. A typical course might include **mathematics**, a foreign language, physics, biology, **history**, literature, economics, philosophy and religious or ethical education. This is very different from the high degree of specialization encouraged by the A-level system where students usually study only three subjects.

Many of the suggested replacements for the A-level system involve attempts to make them more wide-ranging. So far no one solution has proved acceptable to the strong vested interests in schools and universities. The long delay in reforming A-levels (over 20 years at the last count) has led to a small but significant number of schools in Britain offering the Baccalaureate as an alternative.

Different versions of the Baccalaureate are available in different countries. There is also a European Baccalaureate awarded by the European Schools movement and an International Baccalaureate which can be taken at selected institutions worldwide.

(See also **Europe**.)

banding

A system used mainly by middle and **secondary schools** for sorting children into ability groups for individual subjects. This is sometimes known as setting.

Banding or setting makes it easier for teachers to organize their material knowing that children within the group are of roughly the same standard. The possibility of leaving behind those who are struggling or of boring children who already have a clear understanding of a particular concept is therefore reduced. The major advantage for children is that they can perform on a more equal footing with other members of the group.

Problems with banding and setting occur when the system becomes too rigid. For it to work well there needs to be flexibility so that individual children who suddenly blossom or who find a particular area especially difficult can be moved into the appropriate set. In reality, of course, it is very difficult for schools to organize teaching groups in this way. Children put into a particular set or band at the beginning of a year tend to stay there. This can be very demoralizing.

Banding is preferable to whole-class **streaming** which puts children into ability groups for all subjects. The danger here is that children tend to perform according to the label attached to them.

If you are concerned that your child has been put into an inappropriate set or stream, talk to the year head or subject teacher. Be wary of pushing your child into a group which is beyond his or her capabilities.

behavioural problems

See **special needs**

beyond 16

Sixteen marks the end of compulsory schooling. Major decisions have to be taken about what to do next—whether to carry on in education or to find a job.

Britain's staying-on rate is poor compared to the rest of **Europe**. This is mainly because schools have little to offer the majority of 16-year-olds. The system is geared towards the top 30 per cent of pupils who take **A-levels**. The situation in Scotland is slightly more encouraging where students have a wider range of options. Nevertheless, there are alternatives and most of these are to be found in **Colleges of Further Education**, which offer a much broader spread of both academic and work-related courses and cater for students of all abilities.

The major options at 16 are the following:

Staying on at school either to do more **GCSEs** or to take **A-levels**. The choice of subjects at A-level will depend upon GCSE results, the size of the Sixth Form and any ideas your teenagers may have about going on to **Higher Education**. Make sure that the A-level subjects chosen match the entry requirements for possible degree courses. Some Sixth Forms in **secondary schools** are too small to offer pupils the blend of subjects that interests them. Before your 16-year-old decides to stay on in the Sixth Form, find out from the head-teacher how big the Sixth Form is, and make sure that the number of pupils on roll is sufficient to make teaching groups viable. (See **Sixth Year Studies (Scotland)**.)

Enrolling at a Sixth Form College. **Sixth Form Colleges** cater exclusively for pupils between the ages of 16 and 19. They are not available in all **Local Education Authorities (LEAs)**, but where they exist they offer a good alternative to the traditional Sixth Forms in secondary schools. As Sixth Form Colleges usually take pupils from several feeder comprehensive schools, the numbers on roll are bigger, generally around 500. This should give pupils a wider choice of subjects. Sixth Form Colleges may be a good choice for young people who are interested in continuing with academic studies but who need a more mature approach.

Joining a College of Further Education. School-leavers of all abilities will find a wide range of courses available to them in Colleges of Further Education. Besides A-levels, Colleges of Further Education offer a range of vocational **qualifications** such as **BTEC**.

Enrolling at a tertiary college. **Tertiary colleges** combine the functions of a College of Further Education and a Sixth Form College.

Finding a job. Even if your 16-year-old is lucky enough to find an employer, it is wise to think about the educational aspects of the job. Does the employer offer any kind of in-service training and provide opportunities to gain further quali- fications for example? Many employers offer their recruits **block release** or **sandwich courses** at local colleges. A few occupations still offer **apprenticeships**.

Unemployment may be the only option for many school- leavers. Youth unemployment is high and rising. Officially, there are places for all unemployed teenagers on **Youth Train- ing** schemes. But, in reality, provision is very patchy. In some areas young people find it very difficult to get on to any kind of training scheme or to claim unemployment benefits. (See **dole, training.**)

Decisions about which of these to go for largely depend on your children's achievements at school so far, opportunities in **Further Education (FE)** locally and the state of the job market. It is important to discuss all the available options with the school and with your children. Ask the school about the sort of **careers advice** available.

bicycle sheds

Prefabricated sheds used for storing bicycles and for exploring basic gender issues.

(See also **Sex 'n' Drugs 'n' Rock 'n' Roll**.)

bilingual children

Children who speak or use two languages. Children who speak or use more than two languages are described as multilingual.

In much of Britain we look on people who can speak more than one language as exotic and clever. In fact, there are many more people in the world who speak two (or more) languages than who speak one. The monolingual British are the exception rather than the rule.

Bilingual children are a growing minority in the British education system. A recent survey revealed that there were over 170 different languages spoken by children attending London schools alone. Many of these children do not have English as their first language.

Individual schools will have their own ways of addressing this situation, but in general good practice the following points will be recognized:

Poor performance in English as a second language is no indication of the child's intelligence.

Extra help for those who need it should be provided alongside teaching conducted in English, rather than on the basis of withdrawing the child for special help.

Above all, the presence of languages other than English in a school should be seen as an asset. This benefits everyone. Monolingual children are given an insight into the world language community; and for non-native speakers, respect for their mother tongue is likely to improve motivation and overall performance. (See **language differences, multicultural education.**)

The Situation in Scotland

Special grants are available from the Scottish Office Education Department to support the Gaelic language. Gaelic medium primary education can be found in schools in: the Western Isles, Highland and Strathclyde Regions, and Edinburgh. At Secondary level, courses exist at **Standard Grade** and **Higher Grade** for both native speakers and learners.

The Situation in Wales

English is the medium of instruction for 85 per cent of schools in Wales. However there are many schools where the teaching is done in Welsh. Some of these are formally designated Welsh Schools (Ysgolion Cymraeg); others are schools serving primarily Welsh-speaking communities.

The Welsh language is a compulsory part of the **National Curriculum** for all children in Wales. It is a core subject for Welsh-speaking schools, and a foundation subject for schools where English is the language of instruction.

Modifications of the National Curriculum are allowed to take account of the fact that some children in Wales do not begin formal study of English until they are 7.

(See also **UK education systems**.)

block release

A method of study where employees spend an extended period—perhaps a term—in a **College of Further** or **Higher Education** to study for work-related **qualifications** such as **BTEC** or **City and Guilds**.

(See also **day release, Further Education (FE)**.)

boarding schools

Schools which provide accommodation for pupils on a termly or weekly basis.

Most boarding schools are independent of the state system and charge fees, but there is also a limited number of schools in the state sector with boarding places. (See **state boarding schools**.)

The **Assisted Places Scheme**, which provides help with fees at selected **independent schools**, does not cover the cost of boarding.

Some boarding schools specialize in the education of children with behavioural and educational difficulties, others concentrate on dance, **drama** or **music**. (See **special schools**.)

Some parents have no choice but to send their children to boarding schools—either because they live abroad and suitable provision is not available in their country of residence, or because they are not in one place long enough to establish a stable school life. Here are some points to consider:

Have you consulted your child's opinion?

Are you prepared to leave the education of your child entirely to other people? Remember that a good deal of a child's education actually takes place at home. Parents remain an important educational influence long after the child has started school. (See **home–school partnership**.)

Is boarding for your benefit, or your child's?

Do you have complete confidence in the regime of care at your chosen school? Young children in the care of others are particularly vulnerable. You will need to take steps to visit the school, talk to pupils, parents and staff, inspect accommodation, find out about supervision outside school hours, check visiting arrangements and in general follow the advice in **choosing a school**.

Some children thrive on the independence from family life that boarding school offers; others find the break traumatic and detrimental to their academic and emotional lives.

books

After **teachers** themselves, books are still the main source of information available to pupils. Although they lack the glamour of **computers** and videos, they are comparatively cheap, easy to use and cover a far wider range of subjects than the more modern technologies. At a time when budgets are under pressure, some schools are desperately short of books. With the arrival of the **National Curriculum** many textbooks—some of them new—had to be abandoned and replaced. Few schools can claim to have enough. Sharing books is not always the answer. Pupils need to spend time with books, not simply to share them for half an hour and see them gathered up at the end of the period.

It is not just textbooks that are important. The library, too, needs to be kept up to date for readers of all ages. A variety of lively picture books is vital if schools are to stimulate young readers. Beyond this, modern teaching methods rely more on individual research by pupils. For this to work satisfactorily there has to be a wide range of books available for them to consult. (See **libraries**.)

Despite widespread stories about falling standards, most schools do a good job of teaching their pupils to read. The fact that not all of these children arrive at adulthood as readers can at least partly be blamed on the home end of the **home–school partnership**. There is a great deal you can do to encourage children to become readers—from making books part of the toybox to showing them where the 'off' button is on the **television**. You might also look at the kind of model you provide. Parents who seldom read should not be surprised to find their children following their example. For more on this, see **How to help with reading**.

For further information, contact
The Children's Book Foundation
Book House, 45 East Hill, London SW18 2QZ

brochure

See **prospectus**

BTEC

See **Business and Technician Education Council**

buildings

Britain spends far less on school buildings than most other developed countries. As a result, many children are taught in classrooms which are unsuitable, unhealthy and substandard. The problem is not restricted to Victorian inner-city schools which have remained basically unchanged since the day they were built. Many newer buildings also show signs of neglect and decay: the inevitable consequence of long-term under-funding.

Recent legislation has left schools across the country facing huge repair bills. With the arrival of **Local Management of Schools (LMS)** the responsibility for finding this money was passed on to the headteacher and **governors**. Many **head-teachers** complained that along with their new responsibility they inherited a huge backlog of repairs. **Local Education Authorities (LEAs)**—accused of a deliberate policy of neglect—pleaded poverty.

While arguments over who is to blame and who will foot the bill continue, the effects are already being felt in the classroom. Many school governors are having to choose between tackling essential school repairs, such as leaking roofs or insanitary toilet blocks, and employing enough experienced staff to teach effectively. This has in some cases led to increased pressure to opt out of Local Education Authority control altogether. (See **funding**.)

Surveys by **HMIs** have drawn attention to a second problem— the widespread unsuitability of many school buildings for the sort of teaching which is now expected. Many of the more ambitious programmes of reform—notably the demands of restructured **GCSE** courses and the **National Curriculum**—were imposed upon schools without the extra money needed for improvements to classrooms to develop these courses.

As parents it may be difficult to see what you can do about the state of the school buildings in your area, but remember that under the system known as **open enrolment**, you do not have to send your child to the school which has been allocated to you by the LEA. It is your right to choose a school which you consider suitable for your child. Look carefully at the state of the school buildings and ask the headteacher about any plans for improvement. It is probably also worth asking if the school has inherited a large repair bill.

Do not automatically discount schools which are not carefully landscaped and boast bright airy classrooms. It is true children are more likely to thrive in these sorts of surroundings—but they are not by themselves enough to make a good school. A caring atmosphere, carefully organized schemes of work, and good home–school links are in the end worth more than custom-built **science** blocks and fresh paint.

(See also **choosing a school**.)

bullying

Physical or psychological violence directed against an individual.

Bullying can take many forms: from name-calling to systematic physical abuse. Amongst girls, bullying tends to involve social exclusion, boys are more likely to use physical violence. The true scale of bullying in Britain goes largely unrecognized. It was not until 1991, for example, that the **Department of Education and Science (DES)** launched its first study into the problem. Fear of reprisals and the belief that telling tales is wrong mean that children are often reluctant to report incidents. Many adults—both **teachers** and parents—also condone bullying by arguing this aspect of playground culture is actually part of growing up and learning to take life's knocks. This view seriously underestimates the effects of an experience which can turn school into a nightmare for some children. Bullying can lead not just to misery but to serious psychological damage. It has resulted in suicide and—on at least one occasion—murder.

Headteachers may be reluctant to admit that there is bullying in their schools, especially as the pressure to compete for pupils increases. You should not be palmed off by comments like 'We don't have that problem here.' Every school should have a policy on bullying. If there is no strategy for dealing with incidents, the problem is far less likely to be recognized and tackled if and when it does occur. If the headteacher is unimpressed by this argument, remember that you have representatives on the board of **governors**. Talk to them about a school policy on bullying.

It is not always easy to tell if children are being bullied—particularly if they are unwilling to talk. Nevertheless, it is something to be considered if you notice changes in behaviour, an unwillingness to go to school, or a general falling-off in performance.

If you do discover something is wrong, talk to your child's teacher first or, in **secondary schools**, the member of staff responsible for **pastoral care**. With the sympathetic support and co-operation of children, headteachers, parents and staff there is every chance the problem can be solved.

Information and advice on dealing with bullying can be obtained from Kidscape, World Trade Centre, Europe House, 3rd Floor, London E1 9AA.

A useful booklet, 'Bullying—A Positive Response', is available from Delwyn Tattum, Faculty of Education, Cardiff Institute of Higher Education, Cyncoed Road, Cardiff CF2 6XD.

(See also **hidden curriculum**.)

bursar

Someone with financial expertise employed by a school or college to look after money matters.

Until recently bursars were only found in **independent schools** and some colleges and universities. The arrival of **Local Management of Schools (LMS)** in 1988 is likely to make them a more common feature of the educational scene. The effect of LMS was to give **headteachers** control over their own budgets and make them responsible for balancing the books. Many who lacked any kind of financial training found this prospect daunting.

At first glance a bursar looks like the obvious answer. The catch of course is that the school has to finance the bursar. Faced with the relative costs of buying in financial expertise and hiring another teacher, only the larger schools are likely to have a serious choice.

bursary

One of the means by which individuals can receive help with **funding** for courses.

(See also **grants and loans, sponsorship**.)

Bursary Scheme

This is one of a series of schemes designed to improve teacher recruitment in **shortage subjects**. Under this scheme, **teachers** training in **mathematics**, technology, chemistry and physics receive around £2000 extra a year. Despite costs of around £11 million incurred between 1986 and 1990 to run the scheme, there is still an acute shortage of teachers in these and other subjects.

Business and Technician Education Council (BTEC)

An organization which develops and promotes work-related educational courses. BTEC **qualifications** offer an alternative route to employment and **Higher Education (HE)**, roughly parallel to traditional **GCSE** and **A-level** courses. They are offered in most **Colleges of Further and Higher Education** in England and Wales and are starting to appear in schools.

BTEC courses cover a wide range of vocational subjects, such as agriculture, business, caring, construction, design, engineering and hotel and catering. More subjects are being added all the time. Qualifications are offered at three main levels:

BTEC First (roughly equivalent to four or more GCSEs);

BTEC national (equivalent to a-levels and accepted as a standard entrance qualification for related courses at university);

BTEC Higher National (approaching pass-degree standard).

Each qualification is offered at Certificate or Diploma A-level. Both are of the same standard but Diploma courses offer a wider range of subjects. Certificate courses are usually studied part time, Diploma courses full time.

Most BTEC courses are made up of different units or modules. (See **modular courses**.) These usually include a core of compulsory subjects plus a series of options to be selected by individual students. Each unit is separately assessed and graded pass, merit or distinction. Methods of study include project work, assignments, and periods of work experience. BTEC qualifications are more popular with some employers than traditional academic courses because of their practical emphasis. For the same reason they have proved attractive to students who have dropped out of conventional academic courses.

BTEC is working closely with the **National Council for Vocational Qualifications (NCVQ)** to make sure its qualifications fit within the NVQ framework. They have also established links with vocational education systems in **Europe** to try to ensure BTEC qualifications are recognized abroad.

For further information, contact
BTEC
Central House, Upper Woburn Place, London WC1 OHH

In Scotland the equivalent qualification is the **National Certificate**, offered by the **Scottish Vocational Education Council (SCOTVEC)**.

C

calculators

Simple electronic calculators capable of adding, subtracting, multiplying and dividing can be found in most classrooms. They are cheap and readily available—quick, accurate and easy to use.

Parents are often concerned at the use of calculators in schools. They worry the machines will stop children doing mental arithmetic, prevent them from learning their tables, and leave them helpless in the face of flat batteries. These fears are understandable—particularly among a generation brought up on paper and pencil methods of calculation—but they overlook the real advantages of putting calculators in pupils' hands:

Pupils like them. Calculators stimulate a great deal of experiment and exploration—even among very small children. It is hard to generate this sort of enthusiasm with pencil and paper.

To use a calculator effectively you have to understand how numbers work. Calculators help mathematical understanding rather than limit it. They can be used to reinforce the number patterns of multiplication tables.

They allow pupils to deal with much larger numbers than would have been possible with pencil and paper. This is particularly useful in project work where the overall aims can easily get lost as pupils struggle with unwieldy calculations.

They allow children to concentrate more on what the figures mean than on the process of calculation.

Calculators can provide a short-cut to the more interesting areas of **mathematics**.

There is no evidence that increased use of calculators reduces the standard of children's arithmetic. In the real world no one needs to spend time working out the mechanics of long division or learning to master complicated ways of multiplying large numbers. Calculators are here to stay—there is no special virtue in trying to do without them.

(See also **teaching methods.**)

capitation

See **funding**

careers advice

Advice which should be offered by **secondary schools** to help their pupils decide what they want to do **beyond 16.**

It is important that careers advice starts early, ideally around the age of 14 when pupils have to choose the subjects they wish to pursue up to school leaving age. Careers advice should not simply be a question of fitting individuals to the needs of the labour market. Good advice looks at the all-round potential and interests of individual children. Advice on **Further** and **Higher Education** as well as vocational courses should also be included.

Restrictions on educational spending have hit careers services very hard in some **Local Education Authorities (LEAs).**

Careers advice has been under the supervision of the LEAs since the mid-1970s, but it is possible they will soon lose this role to private enterprise.

Some suggestions for parents

Ask the headteacher of your child's school about the sort of careers advice he or she has on offer. Find out if there is a particular member of staff responsible for careers education.

Ask for information about vocational courses and training schemes.

Contact the careers service through your Local Education Authority offices.

For further information, contact

Careers Advisory Service
Education Guardian, 119 Farringdon Road, London EC1R 3ER

(See also **options.**)

caretakers

Caretakers—janitors in Scotland—are responsible for the day-to-day maintenance and cleaning of school premises.

The ideal caretaker for most teaching staff is someone who is entirely invisible, yet who can be relied on to keep the school in pristine condition and materialize with a bucket of sawdust if things turn messy. This image of caretakers as menial workers can sour relationships with staff. Caretakers are key members of the school team. Most are also managers—often in charge of a group of poorly-paid, part-time workers who have little or no job-security.

Conflict between caretakers on one side and **teachers** and pupils on the other is not uncommon—it is, after all, the caretaker who has to clear the graffiti from the toilet walls and repair the damage to the hall floor following the all clog-dancing version of *Fiddler on the Roof*. **Headteachers** and **governors** can minimize this conflict by making sure caretakers are not taken for granted. It would be helpful, for example, to encourage caretakers to attend relevant staff meetings to enable them to keep abreast of developments in the school and contribute to discussions of issues that affect them.

(See also **competitive tendering**.)

catchment area

The geographical area from which a school normally draws its pupils.

(See also **choosing a school, open enrolment**.)

CDT

See **craft, design and technology**

CEO

See **Chief Education Officer**

Certificate of Sixth Year Studies (CSYS)

Certificate available to Scottish secondary pupils who take their **Higher Grades** at the end of the fifth year and who wish to continue their studies into the sixth year.

(See also **Sixth Year Studies (Scotland)**.)

chancellor

The honorary head of a university. A chancellor, often a well-known figure such as a member of the royal family, performs ritual or ceremonial duties like the conferring of degrees.

The day-to-day running of a university is the responsibility of the vice-chancellor who is in overall control of academic content and co-ordination of university courses.

charge-capping

A device used by central government to impose a limit on the spending of local authorities.

Charge-capping was introduced by the Conservative government to soften the blow of its politically unpopular poll tax or community charge. By restricting the money local councils were allowed to spend they hoped to reduce the burden on individual taxpayers.

The immediate effect of charge-capping is to force local authorities to make cuts in their overall spending. As education accounts for at least 50 per cent of most local authority budgets, it is inevitable that schools, colleges and **Local Education Authorities (LEAs)** will feel the pinch. Soft targets like **adult education**, **music**-teaching, discretionary grants, and nursery provision are particularly vulnerable.

Chief Education Officer (CEO)

Head of the local authority education service. In some areas the CEO is known as the Director of Education.

The CEO is a permanent employee of the council and reports to the **Education Committee**.

(See also **Local Education Authorities (LEAs)**.)

child abuse

The term child abuse covers many different forms of ill-treatment towards children, from emotional neglect to sexual assault and physical injury. Abuse occurs in children of all ages, to both boys and girls in all classes of society and frequently within the home.

Children who are known to have suffered abuse or who are thought to be in imminent danger are placed on 'at-risk' registers. These registers are the responsibility of social services departments. The number of children (many of them under four years of age) placed on at-risk registers is increasing sharply. Almost half of England and Wales has no local centre for the treatment and protection of abused children.

Teachers are often the first adults outside the home to suspect that a child is being abused. They are in daily close contact with children and quickly become aware of behavioural or emotional changes. They may pick up on strange social behaviour—perhaps an unusual awareness of sex or an obvious mistrust of physical contact for example. They may also notice persistent bruising or injury to a child's body in **PE** lessons. This is a difficult situation which needs to be handled with great sensitivity. Effective liaison with social services departments—perhaps through the intermediary of the **Education Welfare Officer (EWO)**—is vital. Unfortunately, in many areas the partnership between the education authorities and social services does not work as well as it should.

Teachers, especially in the primary sector, are generally strict about arrangements for collecting children at the end of the day. So although you might find it irritating to discover that the school might not allow your child to leave the premises with your friend because you had to work late, remember that they have your child's safety in mind. Make sure you inform the school if you have to arrange for your child to be collected by somebody else, or if you need to take them out of school at lunch times to visit the dentist or doctor.

Increased public awareness of child abuse has had at least one unfortunate side-effect on teachers. Many are now reluctant to make physical contact with their pupils for fear of being misinterpreted. Teachers of even very young children may now think twice before giving a distraught 6-year-old a reassuring cuddle.

The situation in **independent schools** is less reassuring. Reports in the early 1990s revealed an increasing number of pupils in **boarding** and **special schools** who had been subjected to unnecessarily harsh disciplinary regimes and physical abuse. (See **children in care**.)

For further information, contact

Childline
The Royal Mail Building, 50 Stud Street, London N1 OQJ

Childline offers free counselling to children (tel: 0800 1111, open 24 hours).

National Society for the Prevention of Cruelty to Children (NSPCC)
67 Saffron Hill, London EC1 8RS

childcare

See **pre-school provision**

child-centred

See **teaching methods**

Childline

See **child abuse**

childminders

People who look after children on a daily or sometimes a weekly basis, for a fee, in their own homes.

Childminders do not offer a formal educational service. What good ones do best is provide continuity of care in a small homely setting. Continuity is essential for a young child's sense of well-being.

Childminders, especially in rural areas, often barely earn enough to cover the cost of the orange juice and biscuits.

Places with registered childminders increased by 30 per cent between 1984 and 1988. This trend is likely to continue as more mothers re-enter the job market and nursery places are at a premium.

Childminders must register with the local social services department so that inspections can be made to assess the safety and suitability of their premises. Because the demand for day care far outstrips supply, check that your childminder is registered. Under present legislation it is difficult to monitor standards. (See **pre-school provision**.)

For more information, contact
The Day Care Trust
Wesley House, 4 Wild Court, London WC2P 5AU

children in care

Children whose immediate basic welfare is in the hands of the local authority rather than their natural parents or guardians.

Reasons for taking a child into care include **child abuse**, neglect or that a child is beyond the care and control of parents or guardians. Responsibility for the welfare of children at risk rests with social services departments, which, in most cases, arrange residential or foster care. (See **community homes**.)

Educational provision for children in care is problematic. Because they are the joint responsibility of education and social services departments, red tape and poor liaison frequently hamper progress. Young people in care tend to be moved from place to place frequently—maybe from one residential home to another or between foster parents. It is not unusual for a 13-year-old to have had as many as 10 different foster placements.

It is hardly surprising that an estimated 50 per cent of such children have serious problems at school. This further adds to the feelings of frustration, failure and inadequacy. While it is, of course, essential that a child's physical safety be uppermost in everybody's minds, there is a growing awareness that educational considerations have been consistently undervalued.

It is through education that children who have been seriously disadvantaged socially may be able to improve their chances. Hopefully, increased public awareness of the problems involved will lead to a change in attitude and closer co-operation between educational departments and the social services.

If you think you may be interested in fostering children, contact:

National Foster Care Association
Francis House, Francis Street, London SWIP 1DE

The welfare of children considered to be beyond the control of their parents or guardians is governed by the Children and Young Person's Act, 1969. This Act has been ambitiously reformed by the Children Act which finally became law in October 1991.

(See also **children's rights, young offenders**.)

children's rights

Under the terms of the European Convention on Human Rights, all countries, including Britain, must ensure that all school children have basic rights and freedoms. These basic rights concern things like physical protection, an adequate diet and opportunities for learning.

The issue of children's rights extends beyond basic legal protection, and concerns the right to be involved with decision making, to express an opinion and to be listened to as an individual.

Not everyone agrees that children should have these rights. In some quarters, the view that children should be seen and not heard is still alive and kicking. The plaintive cry from generations of children has been, 'It's not fair.' In certain countries adults are beginning to agree and have sought to improve the balance. In 1990, 60 countries adopted the United Nations Charter on the Rights of the Child. This covers everything from nutrition to prostitution. The charter favours the granting of increased powers to children—for example, the right to be heard in legal proceedings.

Although Britain was one of the signatories to the United Nations Agreement, the convention has yet to be adopted in this country. For this to happen, several laws concerning imprisonment, physical punishment, employment and education will have to be changed. Some of these are covered in the Children Act which became law in 1991, but there is still much work to be done in this area.

Within education, English law gives almost all rights to the parents rather than the child. The 1986 Education Act abolished the right of the under 16s to be school **governors**. Pupils over 16 are allowed to look at their own school records, but so too are their parents.

In the area of special educational needs, there is no provision for the children themselves to be involved in decision-making. In England none of the rights contained in the 1981 Education Act, which fundamentally changed the concept of **special needs**, can be exercised by the children themselves. Scottish law, on the other hand, transfers some parental rights to children over the age of 16 who are able to express an opinion.

There are good reasons why adults need to look at the rights of their children. The way people choose to run their family is a personal thing and child-rearing will always require a degree of compromise and negotiation. Anything you can do to make your child feel valued will work wonders for his or her **confidence**—a crucial element in all learning.

Schools burdened by a them-and-us philosophy generally have more problems, especially when it comes to discipline. Schools which actively seek the co-operation and opinions of the children—perhaps through playground projects or **school**

How to help with the under-fives

Before children start school, parents teach their children things all the time. It is usually parents who teach them how to eat, talk, dress themselves, share, socialize, and follow instructions. Learning at this stage is shared quite naturally between parent and child. It is generally agreed that many of life's fundamental lessons are learned in these early years. As the prospect of full-time school approaches, parents begin to wonder if there are other things they should be doing to help their children prepare for school. Anxiety may creep in— perhaps your four-and-a-half-year-old cannot read a word, write his or her name accurately or count up to 10. The question parents invariably ask at this stage is: What do **teachers** expect children to be able to do before they start school?

Most people think in terms of academic skills, **reading**, writing, **spelling**, number, but it may be more useful to look at other factors:

Confidence is the key to all effective learning later on and something which all parents can foster—or damage—long before school starts.

Tolerance of others: children who have some experience of being with other children before they start school full time will have realized that everybody is different and may not always comply to their demands—lessons that will be reinforced constantly at school.

Independence: young children who have been shown that they do not need adults to take charge of every situation and make all the decisions for them are more able to rise to the challenge of finding things out for themselves in the classroom.

The ability to take some responsibility for themselves: giving even very young children a chance to look after something or organize themselves helps them to deal with the demands of school.

The ability to hold a conversation with adults and other children—conversational skills are highly prized in today's schools. (See **teaching methods**.)

Beyond these factors, if children can also write their own name with some degree of accuracy, recognize numbers up to 10, identify basic shapes (eg square, triangle, circle) and know their colours, this will be helpful, but it is not essential.

The message must be: it is fine to help your children with the rudiments of writing, reading, number if there is no pressure and if the child is keen. Successful learning rarely happens by force.

Here are some of the ways you can encourage these key points at home:

Young children learn through **play**.

They learn by doing, through imitating others. Involve them in as many everyday activities, such as cooking, shopping, travelling, digging the garden, cleaning, as you can manage. Much incidental learning happens this way. Many useful mathematical skills, for example, can be learned from rolling pastry or helping to put the shopping away (shape, colour, weight, etc).

Talking and listening. Talk to your children a lot about anything, and listen in return. Discuss with them the things you can see and hear. As well as developing their language skills, you will be showing them that what they have to say is valuable.

Encourage lots of physical activities: things like playing with a ball, climbing, running, hopping are obviously essential for healthy growth, but they also help children's co-ordination and control, something they will need all the time at school.

Gradually encourage children to spend time away from you to foster their feelings of independence and confidence. (See **pre-school provision**.)

Resist the temptation to overplan your child's daily activities. It is important that children have time to themselves to invent their own games and explore their own imaginative world.

You can find out more about the approach to take, when helping your child at home once school starts, by following the hints in the **How to** sections of this book.

councils—tend to be the happiest. This is something to bear in mind when **choosing a school**.

For further information, contact

Children's Legal Centre
20 Compton Terrace, London N1 2UN

(See also **school councils**.)

choir schools

Independent preparatory schools which specialize in choral training for children between the ages of 7 or 8 up to 13.

Competition for places is fierce and your child will have to be unusually talented and deeply committed to succeed.

As yet the only choir schools admitting girls are in Edinburgh and Salisbury.

For further information, contact

Choir Schools Association
c/o Westminster Choir School, Ambrosden Avenue,
London SW1P 1QH

choosing a school

Since 1981 parents have had the right to choose a school for their child other than the one allocated to them by the **Local Education Authority (LEA)**.

This arrangement, known as **open enrolment**, is not quite the free for all its name implies. LEAs still organize their educational provision on the assumption that most children will go to their local school. If you wish to beat the system and send your child to another school, you must first get their permission.

The LEA will usually agree if three conditions are met: a place is available at the school you have selected; you are prepared to transport your child to and from school at your own expense; the **Area Education Officer (AEO)** gives his or her consent. This last condition is usually a formality if the first two are met.

If a particular school is in great demand, priority is given to children who live in its **catchment area**.

While greater choice has clear benefits, there can be drawbacks to sending your child to a school which is some distance from home. Transport can present major problems. What seemed like an easy run in the car at the outset can easily pall for drivers and passengers alike when it has to be done twice a day for five years. Children are also likely to find themselves living a long way from their new friends—something which can make socializing and taking part in **after-school activities** a logistical nightmare.

What to Look for

Just why you will choose one school rather than another will depend very much on your own personal preferences. Some parents will look for evidence of a traditional approach with uniforms and desks in straight lines, others will be looking for something more informal. Whatever your individual preferences you will clearly have to consider things such as size, location, the state of the school **buildings**, class sizes and examination or **assessment** results. In addition, two features stand out as being especially important in any good institution: the leadership qualities of the headteacher, and the strength of the relationship between home and school. (See **headteachers, home–school partnership**.)

Listen to other parents who have children at the school by all means. Read the **prospectus** carefully. However, do not allow either of these things to override impressions gained from spending time in the school and watching it in operation.

Choosing a Primary School (5–11)

Write to or telephone the headteachers of some schools within a few miles of your home, asking for an appointment to visit the school. It is probably best not to take your child along at this early stage. Once your choice is made, you can arrange to visit the school together before term starts. Schools which have worked to develop a good relationship between school and home encourage this early contact to lessen the trauma of the first day of school.

Initial impressions of a school and staff can speak volumes in **primary schools**, but there are certain key things to look for. Is the entrance hall welcoming and stimulating? Has the work on display been done by the children themselves? Does the school appear well equipped with **books**, games equipment and **computers**? Ideally, there should be opportunities for creative **play** in all the classrooms, especially in infant classes. How are classes organized, according to age or ability? (See **teaching methods**.)

As you visit various schools it is advisable to ask the headteacher or deputy the following basic questions.

Has the arrival of the **National Curriculum** presented the school with any difficulties?

How many pupils are there on the school roll, and are the numbers rising or falling?

What provision is made for children with special educational needs?

Does the school encourage parental involvement? Are there any workshops or meetings to show parents how best to support their child's school work at home?

Is there a school policy on **bullying**?

Has the school any plans to opt out of LEA control?

(See **special needs**.)

Choosing a Secondary School (11–18)

The key issues are the quality of the headteacher and the co-operation between home and school. But at this stage parents are naturally concerned with their children's chances in public examinations such as the **GCSE**.

To the questions in 'Choosing a Primary School', you can add the following:

Are children taught in mixed-ability classes or are they streamed? (See **streaming**.)

Is there a Sixth Form? What proportion of pupils stay on beyond the minimum school-leaving age (ie 16 years)?

Does the school offer any vocational courses such as **BTEC** in addition to GCSE and **A-levels**?

Does an **exchange scheme** operate for language pupils?

What clubs or after-school activities operate within the school?

Are there members of staff responsible for **pastoral care**, **careers advice**, and **health education**?

Does the school have links with local industry and commerce? How many pupils go on **work experience**?

(See also **selection**.)

Church and denominational schools

Schools whose general ethos and approach to education is determined by a particular set of religious beliefs.

These schools are of two kinds:

state schools (usually Church of England or Roman Catholic);

independent schools (often representing various minority groups such as Muslims, Quakers or Evangelists).

State Church schools are either **voluntary-controlled** or **voluntary-aided schools**. Voluntary-controlled schools are entirely funded by the **Local Education Authority (LEA)** and follow the same policy on **religious education (RE)** as other schools in the area. Representatives of the Church sit on the board of **governors**. Voluntary-aided schools are funded partly by LEAs (85 per cent) and partly by the Churches (15 per cent). These schools take their lead in religious matters from a group of **trustees** and so retain greater control over the religious climate in the classroom.

The **independent schools** are privately funded (they receive no money from the LEAs). Some independent schools, notably those run by Evangelists and Muslims, would like to become voluntary aided. If they succeed they will be entitled to 85 per cent of their capital costs from the LEA, while still retaining control over their policy on religious education.

Not all parents who choose denominational schools for their children do so on religious grounds. Many are attracted to these schools because they are seen to have resisted changes taking place elsewhere and managed to retain a traditional rather than a progressive approach to education.

citizenship

See **National Curriculum**

City and Guilds

Qualifications of the City and Guilds of London Institute. These are work-related **qualifications** which cover the whole range from basic skills to professional level.

For further information, contact

City and Guilds of London Institute
76 Portland Place, London W1N 4AA

(See also **BTEC, Further Education (FE), vocational education**.)

City Technology Colleges (CTCs)

Secondary schools (11–18) which have a bias towards **science** and technology designed to be funded jointly by the government and private sponsors such as businesses, charities and trusts. They are independent of **Local Education Authorities (LEAs)** but do not charge fees. In Scotland CTCs are known as **Technology Academies**.

City Technology Colleges were launched in 1986 amidst a blaze of publicity by Kenneth Baker, then Education Secretary. A network of 20 CTCs was to be established by the end of the 1980s. All of them were to be located in inner-city areas as part of the government's grand plan to breathe new life into deprived urban areas. The government was to pay for the day-to-day running, while businesses were expected to meet the costs of buildings and equipment. Ownership of CTCs would then be given to the sponsors.

Intended as a flagship for the government's educational reforms, and a certain vote-catcher, the CTC initiative soon ran into troubled waters. The business community did not share the government's enthusiasm for the scheme; indeed, despite political pressure, many refused to have anything to do with it. The vast sums of money from private enterprise envisaged by the politicians did not materialize. CTCs were seen as divisive from the start, and the business world was wary of lining up behind unpopular initiatives which might sour public relations. Beyond this, it was felt that the taxpayer rather than the shareholder should pay for educational services.

The LEAs did not like them either and refused to co-operate in many cases. The financial burden fell increasingly on the government who found themselves paying the lion's share. This in turn led to further criticisms that a disproportionate amount of money was being spent on relatively few children. Parents, the business world and educationalists felt that the money would have been much better spent elsewhere: on essential repairs to school **buildings**; boosting resources in mainstream schools struggling to meet the requirements of the **National Curriculum** and on urgently needed nursery places.

The prognosis is uncertain. By May 1991, 15 CTCs had been opened, only two of them in inner cities—the rest had to relocate to the suburbs early on. Various revamped models have been discussed, including new partnerships between LEAs and sponsors and adjustments to the legislation concerning **Opting-**

out. But the scheme, once a showpiece, is likely to lie dormant for some time.

classroom assistants

Classroom assistants—sometimes called welfare assistants—work beside class **teachers**, usually in **primary schools**. In Scotland classroom assistants are known as auxiliaries.

Classroom assistants may be employed to do a specific job such as helping a child with a disability, or they may carry out a range of activities throughout the school—preparing materials, helping in the library or working with small groups of children under the overall supervision of the classroom teacher.

Restrictions on educational spending threaten the future of classroom assistants—many schools cannot afford to employ them, even though rates of pay are generally low.

Increasingly, schools are turning to parents for classroom help in areas such as craft activities or reading with the children. Most teachers see contact with parents in the classroom as valuable in itself, as well as welcoming the extra pair of hands. If you are interested in helping, you should talk to your child's teacher—especially if you have skills (anything from candle-making to tightrope-walking) or an area of professional expertise (if you are a dentist or a vet or a shopkeeper) which you would be willing to come in and talk about.

Some schools keep a list of areas where they would like help. If yours does not, why not suggest one?

(See also **home–school partnership**.)

classroom organization

See **teaching methods**

class size

If you are **choosing a school**, it is important to find out how big the classes are. In many schools teacher shortages and insufficient funds mean that classes are overcrowded and **teachers** hard pushed to extend the potential of all their pupils.

The National Union of Teachers has been campaigning since 1982 for a national agreement on class size. They recommend that there should be a maximum of 23 children in infant reception classes, 13 in **special needs** groups, 18 in practical groups such as laboratory work, 24 in classes containing mixed age groups and 17 in primary and secondary classes. In practice many schools contain classes much higher than these recommendations.

When you discuss class size with the headteacher, you are likely to be given a **pupil–teacher ratio** such as 27:1. This means that officially there is one member of staff for every 27 pupils. This can be a bit misleading. Classes are often bigger than ratios would suggest. This is because ratios usually include all members of staff whether or not they have a full timetable commitment. **Headteachers**, for example, very often teach for only part of the time. In larger **secondary schools** they may not have time to teach at all. Other members of staff are only employed on a part-time or temporary basis. But all members of the teaching staff may be included in the stated staff–pupil ratio.

Although there are examples of excellent teaching in large classes (30 plus), your child will obviously receive more individual attention where the numbers are smaller. The teachers are also likely to stay in one school for longer.

The 1988 Education Reform Act made school **governors** responsible for staffing levels. Parents now have real rights and powers on governing bodies. It is important to make your views known about class size. If you say nothing about there being 37 children in your child's class, it will be assumed that you are happy.

(See also **funding**.)

Clause 28

The popular name for Section 28 of the 1988 Local Government Act which forbids local authorities from promoting homosexuality.

Clause 28 has caused a great deal of uncertainty in educational circles in both the heterosexual and the gay communities. Most of the practical problems have been caused by the vagueness of the clause's wording. Nervous local authorities, unable to decide what actually constitutes the promotion of homosexuality, have played safe. This has meant the end of funding for a variety of gay societies, theatre groups and helplines. **Books** with homosexual references have been removed from **libraries**. The clause also led to the extreme case of Kent County

Council, banning Benjamin Britten's opera, *Death in Venice*, from a school's festival because it has a homosexual theme.

Clause 28 has also done a great deal of damage to homosexual/heterosexual relations by enshrining discrimination against homosexuals in law.

clubs

See **after-school activities**

coaching

See **private coaching**

co-educational schools

Schools in which boys and girls work alongside each other in the same institution. Most state schools are now co-educational.

While it is generally thought to be preferable for boys and girls to be educated in the same classroom, there might be advantages in **single-sex schools** for some pupils—especially girls.

Colleges of Further Education

See **Further Education (FE)**

Colleges of Higher Education

See **Higher Education (HE)**

Common Entrance Examination

The qualifying examination for independent **secondary schools** taken at the age of 13.

Although **independent schools** are not obliged to use the examination to assess prospective pupils, Common Entrance is taken by virtually all independent boys' schools and more than a third of girls' schools.

Most children sitting Common Entrance will already be in the independent school system and are offered advice through their preparatory school. Parents thinking of moving from the state to the private sector as their children reach secondary school age can obtain advice from the following address.

Independent Schools Information Service (ISIS)
56 Buckingham Gate, London SW1E 6AH

(See also **preparatory schools**.)

community homes

Community homes are secure **boarding schools** for **young offenders**. Before the passing of the 1969 Children and Young Person's Act, community homes were known as approved schools.

Admission to community homes is controlled by the social services. Following a policy change, fewer young offenders are now given custodial sentences. As a result, the number of community homes has fallen significantly.

Over the years, major weaknesses in the educational provision offered by community homes have been highlighted. The curriculum tends to be narrow while pupil and teacher expectations remain low. Children with special educational needs fare worst. Teachers in community homes commonly feel isolated from their colleagues in mainstream schools and their career prospects are limited. Friction and confusion between social workers and education departments are not unusual. There has also been considerable concern over some of the harsher disciplinary regimes operating in some residential homes.

Numerous studies have demonstrated that a majority of young people discharged from community homes continue to commit offences following release. Clearly it is time for a fundamental reappraisal of the policies covering the care and rehabilitation of young offenders.

(See also **children in care, special needs**.)

community schools and colleges

Institutions which provide traditional schooling alongside facilities which can be used by the wider community.

In most community schools adults and children can be found working and learning on the same site, pursuing activities as varied as **GCSE mathematics**, Spanish, **art**, computing and jewellery-making.

Community schools open for longer hours during term time, and usually remain open during school holidays. Some community schools are purpose built, perhaps incorporating a sports complex, library or theatre. Others, mostly large **secondary schools**, have evolved over time and in response to local need.

Small **primary schools**, especially in rural areas, have traditionally been the focal point for community activities. With all schools in England and Wales set to manage their own finances by the mid-1990s, **headteachers** will be encouraged to maximize the use of existing school **buildings** and resources. This might in time lead to more institutions developing along community lines.

(See also **adult education, Youth Training (YT)**.)

community service

An opportunity for pupils to undertake work in the local community either as part of their school course or as part of schemes, such as the **Duke of Edinburgh's Award**. This might involve helping elderly people or working to improve the local environment.

The demands of the **National Curriculum** timetables are making it difficult to find time for community service. Community service is also used as an alternative to a custodial sentence for **young offenders**.

Compact

A scheme pioneered in London which aims to form close ties between local businesses and individual schools.

Under the scheme employers undertake to give priority in job offers to pupils in the Compact who achieve certain educational targets. These include completion of their coursework, achieving an 85 per cent attendance record, 90 per cent punctuality, attending two weeks' **work experience** and completing a community project. This information is summarized in a **record of achievement** given to pupils on completion of their studies.

On the surface it simply makes explicit the educational aims that already exist in the school. This bargain between employers and schools cannot guarantee jobs. Nevertheless, initial results have been encouraging. Reports by **HMIs** have shown that the schemes have had a significant impact on the schools taking part—improving staying-on rates as well as attendance and some academic performance.

The scheme has the support of Prince Charles and is likely to be extended in the future.

(See also **education and the market place.**)

competition

Competition has traditionally been used in schools to encourage children to improve their performance. Some schools, notably in the private sector, have competition as a stated educational aim, others encourage it in less obvious ways.

Competition pervades the whole curriculum. Children are often put into house teams and encouraged to earn points for academic work that count towards house league tables. Sport is organized along similar competitive lines with the emphasis on playing to win rather than on personal improvement or simple enjoyment.

Some children thrive in this competitive atmosphere, others do not. Introduced to failure early in life, they have the message reinforced at every turn. For this reason many educationalists feel that there are better ways of encouraging personal and academic development than pitting individual children against each other in a competitive atmosphere.

Serious moves have been made in some schools to find alternatives. These usually involve rewarding personal development rather than outright victory in an academic or sporting context. Awards schemes are not abandoned altogether. Instead, they focus attention on improvements in individual performance at all levels rather than concentrate exclusively on high achievers. This gives every child a chance to share in the honours. Under this system even a child with learning difficulties who is a complete stranger to the academic limelight might receive an award for 'The Most Improved Pupil'. A similar approach can be taken to sport and games with individual children striving to better their own performance rather than to be top of the sporting heap.

In recent years competition has entered the educational arena on a broader level. Changes introduced in the 1988 Education Reform Act have left schools operating in the harsh world of the market place in open competition for pupils and resources. In this sort of atmosphere it is hard to see how the competitive ethos can fail to be reinforced in the classroom.

(See also **education and the market place, holism.**)

competitive tendering

The practice of inviting private companies to compete for ancillary services traditionally provided by the **Local Education Authority (LEA)**.

The squeeze on educational spending is making competitive tendering more popular. Services such as catering and cleaning are increasingly being offered to the private sector as LEAs and individual schools try to make the most of limited resources.

Advocates of competitive tendering argue that the element of competition will increase efficiency and give schools more value for money. There is, however, a danger that firms will be encouraged to submit unrealistic tenders in order to win contracts. These might be attractive to schools anxious to save money but in the long run would result in a poor-quality service.

(See also **funding, school meals**.)

complaints

Parents who wish to pursue a complaint against their school or the local authority should first try to resolve matters through informal discussion with **teachers, headteachers** and school **governors**. If this proves unsatisfactory, there are formal complaints procedures which can be followed.

By law, **Local Education Authorities (LEAs)** have to make arrangements to deal with complaints about the **National Curriculum** and religious worship. Most education authorities also have arrangements for matters which fall outside these areas.

Formal complaints should be made in writing first to the headteacher, then to the school governors, and then to the LEA. If parents are still not satisfied with the outcome, they can appeal to the **Secretary of State for Education**—but they cannot do this until they have exhausted local procedures.

The local ombudsman (whose proper title is the Commissioner for Local Administration) can investigate LEAs but cannot get involved in the internal affairs of a school.

The best advice for parents pursuing a complaint is to be polite but firm. It rarely helps to storm in and trample on everyone's sensibilities. However, a degree of persistence might well be necessary to overcome the inevitable inertia of most bureaucratic machines.

For further information, contact
Advisory Centre for Education (ACE) Ltd
1b Aberdeen Studios, 22–24 Highbury Grove,
London N5 2EA

Children's Legal Centre
20 Compton Terrace, London N1 2UN

comprehensive schools

State **secondary schools** which take pupils of all abilities. Comprehensive schools have now almost entirely replaced the old **grammar** and **secondary modern schools**. Comprehensive schools were introduced during the late 1960s and early 1970s as one response to the shortcomings and inequalities of the **eleven plus** system.

Not all **teachers**, politicians or parents took the comprehensive ideal—of equal educational opportunity for all—fully on board. A few **Local Education Authorities (LEAs)** in England retained selection procedures and hung on to their grammar schools. Northern Ireland still operates the grammar school selection system. In Scotland all state secondary schools are comprehensive. Consequently, comprehensive schools vary enormously from place to place. They go by different names (high schools, upper schools) and organize themselves along different lines. Some arrange their pupils into ability groups from the beginning—usually through some form of testing procedure—others arrange children into different ability groups for individual subjects; yet others teach children in mixed-ability classes. (See **streaming**.) This makes it all very confusing for parents.

Concern about comprehensive schools focuses on two issues: first, that they are too big—parents worry that their children will become anonymous in such large sprawling schools; and, second, that academic **standards** may not be as high as they were under the old system. These fears were partly fuelled by bad planning and lack of investment at the beginning. The newly organized schools often had to make do with existing **buildings** or operate from split sites. The continued existence of schools which actively seek more academically able pupils has confused things still further.

Although it has become fashionable in certain quarters to claim that standards are falling, there is as yet no impartial evidence to prove it. Certainly none that specifically targets comprehensive schools.

Comprehensive schools remain vulnerable to changes of government policy. They are under pressure from the newly created **grant-maintained schools**, made possible through **Opting-out** policies, and the likelihood of the gradual reintroduction of selection procedures.

When you are looking at a secondary school for your child, remember that the size of a school does not determine its quality. Many of the larger comprehensives have worked hard to organize their pupils into smaller, more personal groups, to allocate year tutors and members of staff responsible for **pastoral care** and achieve excellent results.

(See also **choosing a school, selection**.)

computer-aided learning (CAL)

See **information technology (IT)**

computers

Today's children are the first to have grown up with computers as part of their educational world. Although the computerized classroom is still in its infancy—there are not nearly enough machines to go round, or teachers who know how to make the most of them—all pupils will use microcomputers during the course of their schooling. This is not just in scientific or technical subjects—computers have applications across the whole curriculum. (See **information technology (IT)**.)

The computer revolution can be very intimidating for parents who want to help their children. Many who buy a computer for the home feel handicapped by their own lack of knowledge. In fact things usually are not nearly as frightening as they appear from the outside. You do not have to know how a computer works in order to use it to write a letter, keep your accounts or play a variety of games—any more than you have to know how a fridge works before using it to cool a bottle of wine. What you do need to know is how to make individual programs work, and this is usually relatively straightforward. The message here must be—roll up your sleeves and have a go.

Many home computers are used almost entirely for games. This might appear to be a waste, but in order to play the games children have to draw on a wide variety of skills. Hand/eye co-ordination, reading, problem-solving, and sequencing are all involved in most arcade-type games. It might be wise to add a word-processing program and the odd educational package (which often looks just like another game) in order to counteract the ZAP! factor that children find so attractive. Information on suitable programs can usually be obtained from your child's class teacher or from magazines available from newsagents.

The other way of helping your child is to support your **Parent–Teacher Association** in fund-raising activities. In the current economic climate schools are finding it increasingly difficult to buy and maintain their own machines. As a result, many of the computers in today's schools have actually been paid for by parents. (See **funding**.)

confidence

Confidence is one of the most important factors in successful learning. Children who go to school feeling able to tackle a task, address a problem and take some responsibility for their own actions have a head start. Where there is no confidence the fear of failure is never very far away and all learning becomes a trial.

Given the general agreement on its importance, it is surprising how many common educational practices actually make acquiring confidence difficult for children. **Competition**, **testing** and **selection**, sarcastic remarks from **teachers** and marking methods that leave work covered in red ink—all these can damage both children's self-esteem and belief in their academic abilities.

The best schools and the best teachers recognize this and develop approaches and schemes of work that avoid these pitfalls.

Parents can do a great deal at home to build their children's confidence. It starts with listening to your child—really listening—even though you may have heard it all before and you have to be out by 7.30 am. Try to avoid the traditional 'oh-really-dear-that's-nice' approach when your children are talking about something that matters to them. They are seldom taken in by it. Get involved with the conversation and your child will be left with the feeling that what he or she has to say is valued—this is the key to confidence. Try to set aside some time every day, or as often as you can reasonably manage, when you and your children do things together—let them take the lead for a while. (See **quality time**.)

As far as school work is concerned, try to accentuate the positive. Even if the piece of work your child produces looks a mess, is covered with red ink, and the remains of yesterday's snack, try to say something good about it first. Resist the temptation to compare your child's work with others'. Offer constructive criticism by all means, but do not put your child under too much pressure. This is especially important if school work is proving difficult, and as older children face the prospect of their first public examinations. If your child is seriously worried about his or her work, go and talk to the teachers, leaving it to fester will only make matters worse.

(See also **home–school partnership**.)

consortia

Groups of schools banding together to pool resources. Consortia are also known in some areas as clusters.

This option is particularly attractive for small schools struggling to make the most of limited resources. By forming a consortium with other schools in the area they can share **teachers** and equipment. The consortium would also enable them to draw on a wider range of expertise than would be available to individual schools—something that would be very useful in implementing the **National Curriculum**, for example.

In some areas larger schools are forming consortia to share major purchases that would not be available to individual establishments: for example, there are schools in Letchworth sharing access to a mainframe computer which, with its ancillary equipment, cost £2 million. The money was raised from industry and benefits a wide range of different schools—both private and state.

In Scotland consortia of schools and **Colleges of Further Education** are becoming increasingly popular. These allow students to study a mixture of vocational and academic courses. (See **Sixth Year Studies (Scotland)**.)

construction toys

Construction toys are kits from which children can build and make things. As an added extra, kits such as Duplo®, Lego® or Mobilo® also help children to understand many basic educational concepts. Construction toys, such as technical Lego®, are used in schools as a way into **design and technology**.

From playing with construction toys, children find out about the way shapes fit together; about balance and weight; they think about how to solve problems and learn how things work. These are the same skills that **teachers** encourage at school.

There is a bewildering array of construction toys on the market. Some are better than others and some are very expensive. If you are thinking of investing in some, spend time looking around first. It is important to buy the ones which are within your child's capabilities—there is nothing but frustration to be gained from giving your 4-year-old a complicated toy full of little nuts and bolts. Simple interlocking blocks are better at this stage. It is worth taking advice from the nursery or infant school near you or from a playgroup assistant. **Toy libraries** are an excellent way of providing your child with construction toys if money is tight.

Construction toys have traditionally been the domain of boys. Be firm with those friends and relatives who buy your sons Lego® and your daughters a Sindy® doll: such stereotypes seriously disadvantage both sexes.

(See also **play, sexism, structural apparatus**.)

continuous assessment

A method of assessing performance by monitoring pupils' work throughout the duration of their course. Continuous assessment supplements or entirely replaces the traditional final exam.

Continuous assessment has clear educational benefits. To succeed under this system, pupils have to demonstate an extended commitment. It is no longer possible to adopt the traditionally relaxed approach to your coursework and hope to make up for it by frantic cramming in the days before the exam. This form of assessment also limits the possibility that the result will be distorted by factors such as illness, exam nerves, or by students simply having an off day. As a consequence many courses, including **GCSEs** and degrees, now include an element of continuous assessment—although there is some disagreement among politicians about how important this element should be. Continuous assessment is also a fundamental part of the **National Curriculum**.

Continuously assessed courses bring with them a corresponding increase in administration. Up-to-date records have to be kept on individual pupils in each subject. This brings an additional work-load for **teachers** used to teaching the course and letting the **examining boards** take care of the formal assessment.

Some people feel that continuous assessment, with its increased emphasis on coursework, unfairly discriminates against children from disadvantaged homes. Enlightened schools recognize this and have set up homework clubs which operated during the lunch break or after school.

(See also **exams**.)

corporal punishment

A form of **punishment** which involves the physical beating of a pupil.

Corporal punishment was abolished in state schools in 1987. In **independent schools** it can still be used—except on children whose fees are paid by the state.

(See also **discipline**.)

correspondence courses

See **open learning**

counselling

See **pastoral care**

craft, design and technology (CDT)

A subject which has taken over and expanded on the traditional **art** and craft lessons in schools. These used to be limited to woodwork and metalwork but now the subject has been widened to include a range of other materials and to include new skills such as problem-solving and computer-aided design.

CDT as a subject will appear on many school timetables. It forms a major part of the **design and technology** component of the **National Curriculum** (together with art and design, business education, home economics and **information technology**).

The skills necessary for CDT can be developed at home from the earliest years. All craft activities will encourage children to explore the way things are constructed and how they work. (See **construction toys, junk-modelling**.) This hands-on approach does a great deal more than develop craft skills—it

How to help with reading

Remember that we all learn things in different ways and at different rates. Some children walk at 10 months while others are only just staggering around at two. The same applies to **reading**. Be patient. Whatever the level of your child's reading, work with the school: make sure you know how they run their reading programme and what is expected of you at home. You do not need to be an expert to practise the activities below. You will probably find you can invent your own reading games—listen to your children's suggestions.

You can do nothing wrong, provided you do not damage your child's **confidence**.

Read to your child every day—even if it is only for a few minutes. As well as communicating the enjoyment that can be had from **books**, you will be reinforcing essential skills: for example, the important fact that you move through a book (and through a page) from left to right, that the squiggles on the page have a meaning, and that we get other clues from the title and the pictures.

When you share a book with your child, remember that there is no such thing as a book which is too easy.

This applies to the pre-school child and remains true long after the reading habit has been established. After all, not everybody relaxes with Tolstoy, sometimes a comic works best.

As your children begin to show an interest in books and reading, talk about some of the words. Point to the print as you read and encourage them to join in. Use the pictures as clues. Encourage them to predict what may happen next.

Look more closely at the words and letters themselves. Look at other words that begin with the same letter and put a sound to them—for example, s for Sam, sock and sausages.

Label objects in the house: oven, television, fridge, etc. Play games—try swopping the labels round and getting your child to put them right.

Buy magnetic letters for the fridge door and invent your own games, for example, sorting letters into tall or round shapes.

Write a short note and pin it on the bedroom door so your child can read it first thing in the morning.

Once at school, most children will progress quite well in the programme being run by the school. The best thing you can do to help now is carry on the good work you have started. Support and encourage your children to read the books brought home from school. Try not to compare your child's progress with others, racing through a reading scheme does not necessarily prove that a child can read well.

Remember reading does not just happen in books. Use the words around you in the home and in the street. See how many letter s's you can see on a trip to the shops (*S*TOP, For *S*ale, Fi*s*h *S*hop, etc).

Encourage your children to look up the times of television programmes in a listings magazine or newspaper. Help them make a list that can be read later.

Join a library. Try to make choosing books a regular activity.

Remember, children learn by making mistakes. Encouragement will get them to their goal faster than criticism.

If your child seems to be having problems, these and similar types of activities will be more beneficial and less stressful than pushing through formal exercises.

(See also **home–school partnership, How to help with spelling, How to help with writing, special needs, television.**)

is an excellent way for children to meet the basic concepts of **science** and **mathematics**.

(See also **How to help at home**.)

crammer

A slang expression for a private institution offering intensive coaching to help pupils pass exams.

Crammers are a feature of today's increasingly competitive education system. They exist at all educational levels–even catering for the young pre-school child. Most offer tuition geared to particular exams, such as **GCSE**, **A-levels**, Oxford or Cambridge University Entrance, and the **Common Entrance Examination** used by many **independent schools**.

Some of these institutions claim a high degree of success. Pupils can undoubtedly benefit from some of the courses offered by these institutions but there are drawbacks parents should bear in mind before signing up:

If the courses are in addition to a full school timetable, pupils are likely to be tired and unreceptive.

Forcing pupils through a particular exam might simply put them in educational environments where they will be out of their depth.

The rapid growth of this sector has led to the appearance of institutions whose services are of a very poor quality.

In the competitive society of the 1990s crammers will unquestionably thrive. However, if you feel your child is in need of extra help, it is usually better to take the matter up with his or her school rather than attempt to buy in extra tuition.

(See also **private coaching**.)

crèche

A crèche provides basic childcare for young children while their parents are working. Some crèches are run as commercial concerns while others may be provided by employers or educational establishments.

Crèches are known increasingly as **workplace nurseries**. The government offers tax incentives to companies who provide these facilities. Parents are no longer taxed on crèche fees.

Along with other childcare facilities for the pre-school-age child, there are rarely enough crèche places in any one area to go around. Quality of care varies so it is a good idea to spend some time investigating the ones which might best suit the temperament of your child. (See **pre-school provision**.)

CSYS

See **Certificate of Sixth Year Studies**

CTCs

See **City Technology Colleges**

curriculum

A programme setting out everything children will study at school. The curriculum includes subject areas, information and skills. People argue that there is a second **hidden curriculum** which can have a strong influence on school life.

(See also **National Curriculum**.)

D

day nurseries

These are run by local social services departments to provide basic care for the under-fives while their parents are working or otherwise engaged.

Day nurseries generally stay open long hours during the week to cater for parents who work late, and do not close during the school holidays. Places are generally scarce and rarely match demand. Most have to operate a waiting list, and priority may be given to children from disadvantaged families.

Day nurseries are under pressure to expand their social-welfare role. More children with **special needs** are being referred earlier to nursery in order to begin the lengthy statementing procedures.

(See also **pre-school provision, statement.**)

day release

A method of studying where employees attend Colleges of Further Education for one day a week to study for work-related qualifications, such as **BTEC** or **City and Guilds**.

(See **block release, Further Education (FE).**)

deferred entry

The postponement of entry to a **Higher Education** course for one year. There are two ways of going about this. The first is simply to take a break when school finishes and do something different. Alternatively, you can apply for a place first at your chosen college or university, get accepted and then ask them to defer your entry for a year.

Higher Education institutions generally recognize the value of a break away from studying and the chance to gain wider experience, but you may have to convince them that you intend to do something worth while.

This is an option worth considering during the final year of

A-levels. Take advice from the member of staff responsible for careers. You should also check the policy on deferred entry with the admissions secretary at the Higher Education establishment concerned.

degree courses

See **Higher Education (HE)**

DENI

See **Department of Education Northern Ireland**

Department of Education and Science (DES)

The government department responsible for education in England.

The DES is headed by the **Secretary of State for Education and Science**. The traditional role of the DES has been to advise **Local Education Authorities (LEAs)** who were the real controlling power in schools. The DES cannot influence directly what is taught in the classroom or interfere with the day-to-day running of schools.

Current educational reforms are changing all this by eroding the powers of LEAs. For example, the new **grant-maintained schools** are funded directly from the DES. **Local Management of Schools (LMS)** has devolved many of the financial responsibilities from LEAs to schools themselves. These and other changes leave the DES poised to take a more active role in an increasingly centralized system.

For further information, contact

Department of Education and Science (DES)
Sanctuary Buildings, Great Smith Street, London SE1 7PH

Department of Education Northern Ireland (DENI)

The government department responsible for education in Northern Ireland.

For further information, contact

Department of Education Northern Ireland (DENI)
Rathgael House, Balloo Road, Bangor, Co. Down BT19 2PR

(See also **UK education systems**.)

Department of Trade and Industry (DTI)

The Department of Trade and Industry (DTI) has been actively involved in promoting links between industry and education. For example, it was behind initiatives to secure industry placements for **teachers** and pupils and provided **funding** to help introduce **design and technology** into schools.

Many of the DTI's responsibilities for fostering industry–school links have now been assumed by the **Training and Enterprise Councils**.

(See also **education in the market place**.)

DES

See **Department of Education and Science**

design and technology

Design and technology is a subject that asks pupils to apply knowledge and skills to solve practical problems. This can involve anything from designing and marketing a new mousetrap, to compiling a travel guide, or writing computer software.

Design and technology is one of the seven foundation subjects of the **National Curriculum**. It is the only one of the National Curriculum subjects which had to be designed from scratch.

The National Curriculum covers five traditional disciplines:

art and design;
business education;
craft, design and technology (CDT);
home economics;
information technology (IT).

The technology curriculum is the clearest indication of the government's desire to give education a more practical bias in order to prepare pupils for our technologically demanding society. It has been given 'enhanced status' among the National Curriculum foundation subjects.

Some schools are using the subject to introduce mini-enterprise schemes where pupils go through all the stages of designing, producing, and marketing a product. These are a stimulating and realistic way of introducing pupils to the demands of the commercial world, but they have been criticized in some quarters for introducing the profit motive into the classroom.

Parents should not be intimidated by the technological aspects of this subject. Encouraging young children to use **construction toys**, and enjoy **junk-modelling** will do a great deal to develop the skills necessary for this part of the curriculum. As your children get older, encourage them to build on these skills and apply them to practical situations; making a tool box; computerizing your shopping list, etc.

(See also **How to help at home, How to help with older children.**)

designated courses

Courses for which a mandatory grant is available—that is, if you qualify and are offered a place, the **Local Education Authority (LEA)** has to provide a grant.

The **Department of Education and Science (DES)** keeps a list of all courses which are eligible for mandatory grants. Other courses, such as **art** and **drama**, are funded at the LEA's discretion. If you are turned down for a discretionary grant, it is usually worth appealing against the decision. If this fails, you will have to look for other sources of finance.

(See also **grants and loans.**)

detention

A form of **punishment** in which a child has to do extra work outside normal school hours. In **secondary schools** this might involve staying behind at the end of the school day; in **primary schools** it is more likely to mean missing playtime or part of the lunch break.

Schools should give sufficient notice if they propose to detain a child at the end of the school day so that parents are aware of what is happening and the appropriate transport arrangements can be made.

If your child is frequently punished (in this or any other way), you should take steps to find out if there is some underlying problem that needs to be addressed.

(See also **discipline.**)

direct method

A method of foreign-language teaching which avoids all use of the learner's mother tongue. French lessons would be taught entirely in French, German lessons in German.

Most schools now use a form of the direct method. With its greater emphasis on practical mastery of the language, pupils are likely to find themselves having to speak French from the very first lesson. This represents a considerable change from language classes of just a few years ago when most of the lesson would be conducted in English with a few (mostly written) French exercises thrown in.

(See also **language schools, modern languages**.)

discipline

Usually thought of as a regime of control adopted by a school or college. In fact discipline is far more than a system of rules and prescribed punishments; it is part of the whole ethos of a school, which determines the way it looks and feels. Any parent who takes the time to visit a number of schools will find a whole range of different approaches, from ordered, uniformed, desk-bound institutions with gowned masters and mistresses to those with a far more informal atmosphere, where pupils and staff wear what they like and call each other by their first names.

It is easy to interpret these differences in style as a lack of discipline—particularly for parents who experienced a strict uniform code and regimented classrooms in their own school days.

The 1986 Education Act makes it clear that **headteachers** are responsible for making and enforcing school rules, acting along lines laid down by the **governors**. The governors in turn have to prepare a 'written statement of general principles' and to offer guidance on individual disciplinary cases when this is required.

Parents will make their own choice of school based on personal preference but here are some points to think about:

Does the school have a strict policy on uniform or merely guidelines for appropriate dress?

Does the school have a policy on **bullying**?

What punishments are available to the staff?

If the school is independent, is **corporal punishment** still used?

Most children respond better to encouragement and reward

rather than **punishment**. What positive steps does the school take in this direction?

(See also **hidden curriculum**.)

discovery learning

See **teaching methods**

distance learning

A form of home study which allows students to follow courses by correspondence, sometimes supported by broadcasts on radio and television.

(See also **open learning, Open University**.)

dole

The slang name for benefits available to the unemployed. The dole is a feature of young people's lives in many parts of the country.

Benefits were withdrawn from 16–17-year-olds in 1988 and officially there are now places for all unemployed teenagers on **Youth Training (YT)** schemes. But in practice, provision is patchy and in some parts of the country there is a shortage of suitable courses on training schemes and benefits are extremely difficult to obtain. This has left many young people on the streets without any visible means of support.

(See also **beyond 16, twenty-one-hour rule**.)

drama

A subject which can be studied in its own right, and a tool that can be used in other disciplines.

Most people still think of drama as a branch of English studies or a recreational activity that ends up as the school play. In fact it is far more than this. It is increasingly being used as a means of expanding and exploring a whole range of other subjects as different as **history** and **health education**.

Drama exists as a separate **GCSE** subject but is not one of the core or foundation subjects of the **National Curriculum**. It can be pursued beyond **A-level** as an academic discipline in polytechnics and universities, where it usually takes the form of a theatre studies or theatre arts course. These courses combine practical drama with academic work. **Drama schools** provide an alternative for those primarily interested in going on to the stage.

(See also **Higher Education (HE)**.)

drama schools

Institutions which provide professional training for the theatre.

Most drama schools will not consider students under the age of 18. Usually no formal **qualifications** are required but students with a broad educational background are at an advantage. It takes talent and perseverance to get into drama school. Entry is by audition and interview. The number of places is limited and competition is fierce—particularly as schools like the Royal Academy of Dramatic Art (RADA) audition in New York as well as London. Courses are demanding and require considerable dedication and a high degree of physical fitness. To complete a gloomy picture, even graduating successfully cannot guarantee work in the professional theatre.

Funding is a major headache for students. Drama and dance do not qualify for mandatory grants. This means that grants are awarded at the discretion of **LEAs**. If a student is turned down for a discretionary grant, it is usually worth appealing against the decision. There are a number of bursaries and scholarships available. Due to the long hours involved in a drama course, most institutions forbid their students to take part-time jobs to help pay their way.

Most drama schools run courses in stage management as well as practical courses in acting. Competition for these places is almost as fierce as for acting courses.

Some university and polytechnic **humanities** departments offer an alternative to drama schools in the form of theatre studies or theatre arts courses. These usually have a more academic bias than courses at drama school but still provide a realistic option for students who want to pursue an interest in the theatre.

(See also **Higher Education (HE)**.)

DTI

See **Department of Trade and Industry**

Duke of Edinburgh's Award

An award aimed at developing young people's character and social awareness by encouraging them to undertake a series of challenges and adventures.

Young people between the ages of 14 and 25 can achieve awards at three levels—bronze, silver and gold. Each level has four sections: community service, expeditions and explorations, skills and physical recreation.

In Britain alone the scheme has up to 80 000 entrants each year. Of these, 6000 young people receive their gold award—usually at a ceremony in St James's Palace.

The scheme can be operated through any organization involved with young people, such as Scouts, Guides and schools—though some people argue that too close an identification with school is not necessarily a good thing. The **headteachers** of many **independent schools** are very keen on the awards and organize expeditions and activities as part of the curriculum. This is less common in state schools.

Employers will usually take the award into consideration as evidence of interests outside school and an ability to sustain commitment over an extended period.

Local schools or youth organizations should be able to provide information about the scheme. Beyond this, each local authority has at least one staff member at the Town or County Hall with special responsibility for the award. (See **Local Education Authorities (LEAs)**.)

dyslexia

A term used to describe a range of reading and writing disorders affecting—in some estimates—up to 10 per cent of the population.

The precise nature (even the very existence of) dyslexia is the subject of a great deal of controversy. What is undeniable is that there are a significant number of children whose levels of **reading**, writing and **spelling** are well below those expected for children of their age and intelligence.

The failure to master written language can have a devastating effect on children. It is not just their English that suffers—children need to be able to read and write in every area of the curriculum. It is hard to deal with the instructions on a maths work-card if you cannot make out what the words say. Repeated failure is demoralizing, destroys confidence, and can remove all motivation to learn. These problems are compounded when parents or **teachers** put them down to mere laziness or stupidity.

Features

Children described as dyslexic display some or all of these features:

reading progress which is significantly delayed—by as much as two to three years compared to their actual age;

serious problems with writing—dyslexic children tend to make bizarre and erratic spelling mistakes and see words or individual letters back-to-front, and have problems sorting them into any meaningful order;

confusion over left and right—many dyslexic children cannot decide which hand to write with or know how to track words across a page;

difficulty with following instructions—especially if a sequence is involved ('Maggie said can you peel the potatoes, make a salad, feed the cat and put the casserole in at 4.30 pm');

physical clumsiness;

lack of fluency in speech and a tendency to stumble over long words;

parallel difficulty with number.

It is important to note that many of these features are part of the normal learning process. Do not assume your child is dyslexic simply because he or she produces pieces of written work full of spelling mistakes, occasionally gets his or her b's and d's the wrong way round, and is not progressing through the reading scheme as fast as his or her friends. All these are common hiccoughs in the learning process and usually sort themselves out with time. Only if the problem is persistent and beginning to affect other areas of the curriculum and your child's self-image, should you worry.

You should also be wary of the medical overtones that creep in when people talk about dyslexia. It is not a disease. Dyslexia does not 'cause' reading and writing difficulties in the way a sprained ankle causes a limp. The word is only a label for problems that already exist. So you should be wary of commercial organizations or individuals charging high prices to identify the condition. Developing a strategy for dealing with your child's range of problems is more important than spending time and money deciding whether or not it is appropriate to describe them as dyslexia.

How to Help

It is vital to develop a strategy that includes parents, teachers and any specialists who might be involved. Close co-operation will improve the effectiveness of everyone's contribution and make life much easier for the child. (See **home–school partnership**.)

The most useful work parents can do at home does not involve any specialized techniques. What you need are the kinds of support activities that you will find in **How to help at home** together with time, patience and a willingness to respond at your child's pace to his or her concerns. (See **quality time**.)

Most important of all is developing **confidence**. The best way forward is not necessarily through reading and writing exercises, important though these are. Think of things your child can do well and encourage those. Give him or her a taste of success to counteract the feelings of failure that will have become all too familiar. Be positive in your approach—find points to praise rather than criticize.

Encourage your child to express him- or herself in ways other than reading and writing. Let him or her experiment with **music**, **art**, handicrafts, dance, **sport** and anything else that motivates him. Remember that typewriters, computer keyboards and tape recorders are useful for children struggling with the mechanics of handwriting. (See **How to help with spelling**, **How to help with writing**.)

Whatever you do at home, try to take the pressure off. Do not let your anxiety about progress (or lack of it) communicate itself to your child. Comparing children with others in their age-group will not help.

For further information, contact

British Dyslexia Association
98 London Road, Reading, Berks RG1 5AU

(See also **special needs**.)

E

educating your child at home

See **alternative education**

educational psychologist

A professional psychologist specializing in children with educational problems. These problems can range from severe handicaps to intermittent anti-social behaviour and specific learning difficulties.

You are unlikely to come across an educational psychologist unless you have a child who has **special needs**. If you or your child's school (or all of you together) consider that there is a significant long-term problem, a referral to an educational psychologist may be made. (See **statement**.)

The job of the educational psychologist is to work out, through various kinds of testing and assessment procedures, consultations with **teachers**, parents and child, the exact nature of the problem. It may be decided that it would be valuable to have the opinion of other experts such as a **speech therapist** or an **occupational therapist**.

This can be a very lengthy business. Many **Local Education Authorities (LEAs)** are seriously under-funded for special needs provision, and there are simply not enough educational psychologists to meet the demand. There has been controversy about educational psychologists being told by education authorities to tailor their statements to suit the resources available. (See **funding**.)

Parents have frequently been frustrated and confused by the length of time it takes for an appointment to be made and help to get under way. The message for parents here is to be polite but persistent.

Unless all those concerned are sensitive to the feelings of the child, being tested and discussed by strangers can be a traumatic and self-defeating exercise. However, handled properly, the advice of an educational psychologist can be very valuable for child, teacher and parents.

You do not have to pay for the services of an educational psychologist, but some see children privately and charge a fee. If you can afford it and you are worried about the length of time it all seems to be taking, this may be worth considering.

If you see an educational psychologist privately, it is sensible to keep the school fully informed to reduce the risk of confusion and possible bad feeling. Nothing is gained by keeping secret any reports you receive. The best way of helping is for everyone to be co-operative and consistent.

For further information, contact
Association of Educational Psychologists
3 Sunderland Road, Durham DH1 2LH

education and the market place

In recent years there have been significant moves to make education more relevant to the demands of employers. This development is associated with the Thatcher years but its beginnings go back to 1976 and a Labour Prime Minister—James Callaghan. In a speech at Ruskin College, Oxford, Callaghan called for a great debate on the nature of education and in particular focused attention on the importance of matching education to the needs of industry. As a result, the period since 1976 has seen the erosion of the principle that had governed educational thinking since the end of World War II: the idea that education had its own intrinsic merit and was not merely a mechanism for producing a trained workforce.

The influence of industry can be seen in many areas in today's educational scene—in the weight given to **science** and **technology** in the **National Curriculum**, in schemes by the **Department of Trade and Industry** to give **teachers** and pupils **work experience**, in the **Technical and Vocational Educational Initiative (TVEI)** and in the rapid development of vocational **qualifications**, such as **BTEC**.

The changes are not limited to the content of the curriculum. Perhaps more significantly, the harsh realities of the market place have made dramatic inroads into the structure and organization of our education system. A number of major initiatives during the 1980s changed the educational map. The introduction of **Local Management of Schools (LMS)**, **open enrolment**,

Opting-out, and the **assessment** procedures of the National Curriculum seem likely to leave schools operating as small businesses in open competition for pupils and resources. Central government assumed these measures would force schools to raise standards or—in the language of the market place—go to the wall. (See **magnet schools, sink schools**.)

There are inherent dangers in exposing schools to the boom or bust world of the market place. No market system can take account of the needs of individual children—particularly those who are essentially non-academic. Less able pupils and those with recognized **special needs** will become increasingly unattractive to successful schools. (See **funding**.)

Competition between individual schools is also likely to make it more difficult to co-ordinate educational provision at a local level. The crux of the matter is money. Allowing market forces to determine provision cannot compensate for the lack of adequate funding and consistent long-term planning.

(See also **holism**.)

Education Committee

A committee of elected councillors responsible for the education service.

The **Chief Education Officer (CEO)** (or Director of Education) reports to this committee.

(See also **Local Education Authorities (LEAs)**.)

education otherwise

See **alternative education**

Education Support Grant (ESG)

A sum of money set aside by central government for specific school projects which the **Secretary of State for Education** considers especially important. It is up to **Local Education Authorities (LEAs)** to bid for this money.

ESGs help to explain why some schools appear better equipped than others. Schools have to compete for this extra **funding**. The role of the headteacher is crucial here. If, for example, a school wished to improve its technology teaching, the headteacher could apply for an ESG to help cover the cost of additional equipment.

Education Welfare Officer (EWO)

A professional employed by a local authority to support children and parents in social and educational matters.

EWOs are primarily concerned with 5–16-year-olds, though they can be called on to help with children from pre-school age to Sixth Formers.

The role of the EWO differs from county to county. Most will have responsibility for a group of schools which they visit on a regular basis. A case-load for a typical EWO might include dealing with children with social and behavioural problems, acting as a link between school and family in cases of suspension or exclusion, offering support in cases of family break-up and working with persistent truants. Children are referred to EWOs by **teachers**, other agencies and even parents. In some areas senior EWOs are first in line for referrals in cases of suspected **child abuse**.

EWOs will also advise on grants available from **Local Education Authorities (LEAs)** and local charities.

EFL

See **English as a Foreign Language**

eleven plus

An examination taken by children at the end of the primary-school years (around 11) in areas which retain the grammar-school system. (See **grammar schools**.) The eleven plus was rendered largely obsolete by the introduction of **comprehensive schools** during the 1970s. The examination usually consists of a test of performance in **English**, arithmetic and verbal reasoning (IQ). Since it is no longer a national examination, there are no official statistics for the numbers of children still sitting the eleven plus. But only a handful of **Local Education Authorities (LEAs)** in England now operate the system. It is extinct in Scotland, but still used in **Northern Ireland**. (See **UK education systems**.)

The eleven plus examination was rooted in the school of thought, popular until the 1960s, that intelligence could be measured as a fixed quotient from a very early age. It was argued that children could be tested at 11 and would fall into two broad categories: either academically able (above average intelligence) or less academic (average intelligence or below).

Those who did well in the exam were offered a place at the local grammar school. Those who failed went to **secondary modern schools** or their equivalent.

Criticisms of the eleven plus focused on the reliability of the tests themselves and the uneven distribution of grammar-school places.

Research shows that learning happens at different rates and in a great variety of ways. Many children who have struggled with number or spelling at 10, for example, suddenly blossom as they mature. The eleven plus did not allow for these variations.

Some areas offered more grammar-school places than others and therefore where you lived could also affect the whole **selection** process. The eleven plus became more and more difficult to defend.

Recent developments, notably the birth of **grant-maintained schools**, the assessment and testing procedures contained within the **National Curriculum** and proposals to publish league tables of test results, may herald the reintroduction of selection procedures by the back door.

employment of children

Laws relating to the employment of children of compulsory school age are complicated. It is the responsibility of employers, rather than parents or guardians, to comply with the following regulations:

Children under the age of 13 cannot legally be employed.

Anyone employing children between 13 and 16 should apply for a work permit from the **Local Education Authority (LEA)**. In practice, it is very difficult to enforce this regulation. Many children are exploited as a result.

Children are not allowed leave of absence from school to take jobs, except under special circumstances.

Children cannot take part in any performance which is not licensed by the local authority.

The 1989 Employment Act removed most of the restrictions on the employment of 16–18-year-olds. They can now work the same hours as adults. This includes night shifts and Sunday work.

In general, the experience of a Saturday job, which also gives a child some degree of financial independence, can be a good thing. Jobs which have to be done before or after school should be looked at more carefully. Paper rounds, for example, are usually too early, and an evening job is likely to conflict with homework. School is a demanding experience for most children and their performance will not be helped if they are over-tired or too busy to do school work properly.

English

English—often referred to simply as language in **primary schools**—is one of the three core subjects of the **National Curriculum**, along with **mathematics** and **science**. This means that all children in state schools are expected to study English throughout the compulsory school years up to **GCSE**. Beyond GCSE, English literature and English language can be studied both at **A-level** and at degree level.

English is the vehicle through which all aspects of the curriculum are delivered. A good command of the language is essential if pupils are to progress in any subject. Not surprisingly English-teaching has attracted a good deal of criticism from those who are convinced educational **standards** are falling.

Part of the problem is that since most of today's parents were at school, ideas about the nature of English have changed. It is now a much broader subject: speaking and listening have been added to the traditional concerns of reading and writing. Much greater emphasis is placed on a child's all round ability to communicate and interpret the vast range of messages carried by the different media. **Computers**, tape recorders, **television** and video are an integral part of the English classroom. Much of this is a far cry from traditional English-teaching, with its emphasis on correct **spelling**, parts of speech and formal essays. Traditionalists—often government ministers—are fighting a stern rearguard action. They have recently rejected a multi-million pound report into language in the National Curriculum because it failed to recommend the kind of formal grammar-teaching they want to see reinstated. (See **grammar.**)

There has been much debate about the effect of National Curriculum requirements on English at GCSE level. The amount of time allocated to English has been reduced from the 15 per cent originally envisaged at the planning stages to 10 per cent in many schools. This is largely as a result of curriculum overload; schools are finding that there are simply not enough hours in the day to cover all the requirements. Attempts to introduce a dual GCSE, in English (a combination of language and literature) have been squashed. This has caused some anxiety about the future of English literature as an option for GCSE.

(See also **How to help with reading, How to help with spelling, How to help with writing.**)

English as a Foreign Language (EFL)

The English language as taught to overseas students.

The teaching of English as a foreign language is a major industry both in this country and abroad. In many countries English is seen as the key to success in academic, commercial and professional life. As a result, large numbers of overseas students travel to Britain each year to enrol for courses.

Methods vary, but, because the classes are drawn from many countries, a form of the **direct method** is usually used, in which the teaching process is conducted entirely in English.

Most teaching takes place in private **language schools** which tend to be concentrated in the south of England in tourist and cultural centres such as London, Oxford and Cambridge.

EFL has a poorer cousin in ESL (English as a Second Language) or ESOL (English for Speakers of Other Languages). Here students tend to be members of ethnic minorities resident in Britain, whose mother tongue is not English. Teaching takes place in schools and **Colleges of Further Education** alongside mainstream subjects. These institutions often cannot match the resources and expertise of private **language schools**.

(See also **bilingual children.**)

environmental education

A subject which looks at man's influence on the environment.

With the growing awareness of the damage we are doing to our world from the ozone layer to the sea-bed, it was hoped that the **National Curriculum** would give prominence to environmental education. This has not happened. Instead of appearing as a subject in its own right, environmental education features only as a cross-curricular theme.

Environmental education plays a more prominent role in the Scottish equivalent of the **National Curriculum**. (See **Scotland: 5–14 Development Programme.**)

Many people expected **geography** to be the obvious candidate for delivering this aspect of the curriculum. Geographers, however, found themselves presiding over a trimmed-down version of their subject from which contentious issues—such as many environmental concerns—had been removed.

(See also **How to help with green children**.)

equal opportunities

Equal opportunities legislation is designed to make sure no sector of society is discriminated against in terms of education and employment. The term is most often applied to discrimination against women.

There are many ways in which your children, especially your daughters can have their educational and social opportunities limited through discrimination. Some of these—notably society's attitude towards girls and the sciences—may not be obvious and they will almost certainly not be admitted by **headteachers**. They are nevertheless real. (See **sexism**.)

The existence of equal opportunities legislation has not ended discrimination but it does provide a legal framework where it can be tackled.

If you feel you or your children are being discriminated against, you can get help from:

> The Equal Opportunities Commission
> Overseas House, Quay Street, Manchester M3 3HN

(See also **racial discrimination, special needs**.)

ESG

See **Education Support Grant**

Europe

With the removal of the last trade barriers at the end of 1992 residents of the 12 European nations now have rights within the education system of member states. Families living abroad are guaranteed equal treatment with nationals with regard to education, apprenticeship and vocational training. This extends to grants and **funding** as well as access to appropriate courses.

If you are thinking of moving to Continental Europe, you will clearly be concerned about educational provision for your children. For some, **boarding schools** in this country will be the solution. While this might be the right move for some children, the benefits of foreign travel and contact with another culture should not be underestimated. However, if you are likely to have a nomadic life (perhaps following the demands of your own career), you need to be especially careful. Children will need some time to settle into their new life and frequent moves can be unsettling and harmful to their educational and emotional development.

Which School?

The national education system of individual countries might not be the first choice for British residents moving into Continental Europe. Older children—even those who can manage the language—might find it difficult to adjust to new **teaching methods** and examinations. The following are the main alternatives: (not all are available throughout Europe).

British Schools

Schools catering for expatriate children, run along UK lines and working within the UK examination system of **GCSEs** and **A-levels**.

> *For further information, contact*
> European Council of International Schools
> 21b Lavant Street, Petersfield, Hants GU32 3EL

European Schools

These are schools set up to put the European ideal into practice. Pupils from different nations study side by side for the European **Baccalaureate**—a widely recognized university entrance qualification. A number of different languages are used throughout the school, both for teaching and administration.

> *For further information, contact*
> International Schools Association
> CIC Case 20, 1211 Geneva 20, Switzerland

International Schools

These schools (operating in different countries throughout the world) offer the International Baccalaureate.

Schools in Member States

Beyond the small number of international schools each European country has its own distinctive education system. If you are considering working abroad, you should contact the representative of the individual country in Britain and try to gather as much information as you can. A visit would be wise, to see for yourself what schools are like. There can be no foolproof way of assessing the system before you arrive, but here are some points you should consider:

The language problem: if your children do not speak the language, is there special provision available to help them?

Beware labels like 'private' and 'public' when applied to schools: they mean different things in different countries. The private sector might also fulfil a very different role to the one it has in this country. In France, for example, private schools are geared to helping students who drop out of the highly competitive and academically demanding state system.

What **pre-school provision** is available?

What provision is there for children with **special needs**?

Does the system vary greatly in quality between country and town?

How long is the school day? When does it start and finish? When are the major holidays?

Teaching methods might vary considerably. In many European countries teaching is more formal than in the United Kingdom, with pupils expected to listen while the teacher delivers the lesson.

What **qualifications** are available? Are they transferable if you choose to move on at a later date?

European Convention on Human Rights
See **children's rights, Europe**

evening classes
See **adult education, community schools and colleges**

EWO
See **Education Welfare Officer**

examining boards
There are five examining boards in England and Wales and

How to help with writing

The best way of helping your children with writing is to show them that there are good reasons for learning how to do it. Help your children to see that writing is one of life's most useful skills and helps us in a huge range of activities— leaving messages, making up stories, writing to friends, filling in membership forms, making labels, keeping diaries and many more.

It may be worth pausing for a moment to consider what it is we expect children to do when we ask them to write: they must devise the content; think which words to use and how to get them in the right order; work out which order the letters should go in to make up the words; then they have to worry about forming these individual letters so that other people can recognize them and use punctuation so that the whole thing makes sense. This is a daunting prospect for many adults—for beginners it is often overwhelming.

The following by no means exhausts the possibilities for helping at home but it should give you a start. Keep the emphasis on the practical.

When your children first show an interest in writing for themselves provide as many writing tools as you can afford and which inexperienced hands can cope with. Jumbo-sized crayons, fat paint brushes even sticks and fingers are generally easier to manage than fine pencils and felt tips at this stage.

Help your child collect an assortment of pebbles, pasta, shells or anything else you can think of and use them to make letter pictures. Keep the letters on a large scale at first.

Have a go at picture-writing: instead of writing words, use pictures to get some of the message across (draw an eye, a deer, etc). Point out picture-writing on shops, buses or advertising hoardings as you walk around together.

Play games with letters and help your child feel the different letter shapes—'drawing' the shapes on his or her back or pacing around an outline helps to fix them in the young child's mind.

Encourage children to make their own books. In the early stages try cutting out pictures of animals or cars and making a book out of them. It helps if you write under each picture a few words which are repeated on each page, such as: 'this is Joseph's red car, this is Joseph's blue car'. If children seem keen, encourage them to write their own words. They might want to trace over yours first until they have the confidence to write themselves.

If you are making a conscious effort to help with writing, it is worth finding out how it is taught in your local school. When you write something for your child, try to be consistent in the way you form the letters, and do not mix up capital and lower-case letters. (See **handwriting**.)

As your children gain in confidence, encourage them to take down telephone messages and help with the shopping list.

Encourage your children to keep a diary—perhaps of a holiday or during the build up to Christmas or a birthday party.

As their schedules become more complicated with swimming lessons, clubs, visits to friends get them to write their own timetables and put them somewhere at their eye-level so that they have to take some responsibility for organizing themselves.

Once your children are at school full time, do not stop helping with writing at home. (For more on other aspects of language see **How to help with reading, How to help with spelling.**)

(See also **handwriting, How to help with older children.**)

one in Scotland. These boards are primarily responsible for academic courses—**GCSE**, **A-levels**, and their Scottish equivalents.

Vocational courses are assessed by a wide range of different bodies which increasingly are coming under the auspices of the **National Council for Vocational Qualifications (NCVQ)**.

The number of examining boards has been reduced in recent years in an attempt to create a more coherent picture and help ensure exams from different boards are of a similar standard.

(See also **exams**.)

exams

Exams are changing. The traditional end-of-term written exam still survives but in many areas it is being supplemented by a new approach to testing, based on assignments, project work and **continuous assessment**. In some cases final exams have disappeared altogether.

The advantages of these new ways of assessment are increasingly being recognized—both by students and **teachers**. They discourage cramming. They test a wider range of skills than an all-or-nothing written exam. And above all they do not require students to justify two years' work in the space of three hours.

Vocational courses as BTEC rely heavily on this multi-pronged approach. Among more academic courses the old-style O-levels have been replaced by GCSE, which uses a range of assessment methods. A-levels are being reformed and might develop in the same way, though there are powerful vested interests in the universities, who would like to see them remain as they are. Moreover, the enthusiasm at the start of the 1990s amongst some politicians for the return of traditional written tests may put the future of these new-style exams in jeopardy.

For more specific exams see entries on **A-level**, **BTEC** and **GCSE**.

(See also **modular courses**.)

exchange scheme

A scheme in which language students stay with a family abroad in order to improve their command of a foreign language. The scheme usually involves a reciprocal arrangement where a young person from the overseas family returns to this country to practise his or her English.

Exchange schemes give pupils an invaluable chance to experience a foreign language in its cultural setting—as well as providing social opportunities to meet their contemporaries overseas. If the scheme is not already operating at your school it might be worth suggesting it to the head of **modern languages**.

expulsion and suspension

The permanent or temporary exclusion from school of a pupil for disciplinary reasons.

The rules governing exclusions are complicated. They are laid down in the 1986 Education Act and differ between various types of schools. **Local Education Authorities (LEAs)** have their own guidelines on the subject.

Essentially, the headteacher initiates suspensions and expulsions acting along lines agreed by the **governors**. In their turn, it is the governors who must decide if an excluded pupil is to be reinstated. The law makes it clear that it 'assumes' the great majority of exclusions will be temporary and short.

Parents of a pupil who is excluded permanently— expelled—have access to a formal appeals procedure. (See **complaints**.)

Suspension from school for any reason is usually a move of last resort, an admission that normal disciplinary procedures have proved inadequate. In this situation it is essential for parents to keep all channels of communication open. In cases where relations between school and home have broken down, either side can call on the **Education Welfare Officer (EWO)** to act as go-between.

Equally important for you as parents is to talk to your child. In particular you should take steps to establish if the wrong-doing which led to the exclusion is merely misbehaviour or if there is a serious underlying problem that needs to be addressed.

(See also **discipline, punishment**.)

extended day

Schools that operate an extended day stay open after lessons are over to allow pupils to do homework or take part in **after-school activities**.

Some schools operate homework clubs or offer other facilities to help children of working parents.

With the advent of **Local Management of Schools (LMS)** it is becoming increasingly common for schools to offer their premises for hire after-school hours.

(See also **funding, school day**.)

extra-mural studies

These are courses offered by extra-mural studies departments in universities to members of the public. Options may include **evening classes**, summer schools and day schools. Some of these courses may lead to non-degree **qualifications** such as diplomas.

If you are interested in one of these courses, you should contact the local **Higher Education** establishment for details.

F

fees

See **funding, grants and loans**

field study trips

See **school trips and visits**

first schools

Part of the primary-school provision in some areas. First schools cater for children from the age of 5 up to the age of transfer to middle schools—usually 8 or 9. (See **primary schools**.)

flash cards

See **reading**

flexischooling

See **alternative education**

football

Football has an importance among youngsters in Britain unmatched by any other **sport**. Other games such as rugby, cricket and tennis have their enthusiastic supporters but there is no comparable sport which large numbers of children—or at least large numbers of boys—play formally or informally every day of their lives. Being part of the football culture is a serious and emotional business for boys in **playgrounds** all over the country.

For many adolescent youngsters football becomes an obsession. The enjoyment they get from playing is self-evident but there are health risks associated with too much football that are increasingly being recognized. It is gifted youngsters who are most at risk. Networks of local leagues and clubs can lead to adolescents playing too many competitive games. It has been estimated that some youngsters are playing as many as 140–150 games a year on pitches designed for adults. Growing youngsters are particularly vulnerable to certain kinds of injury—particularly stress and overuse injuries. The problem is serious enough to have forced a growing number of promising youngsters to abandon the game.

It has been argued that the problem is made worse by the British style of play. Training is geared to work-rate and positional play rather than to developing all-round fitness.

Parents who try to limit the football played by an enthusiastic youngster will not be popular but the risks to young bones associated with intensive playing ought to make them guard against being over-zealous in their support.

(See also **physical education (PE)**.)

foster parents

See **children in care**

free activities

A period in **primary schools** when pupils are allowed to choose from a series of activities after a period of more directed work.

You may feel that this time is bit of a soft option for the teacher and a chance for your 6-year-old to indulge in a free-for-all. This is not usually the case. Free activities are usually structured by the teacher but not in ways which are immediately obvious to the participants. After a long morning of project, number and language work, for example, pupils may be allowed to choose how to spend their time—maybe in the home corner creating a restaurant (reading from menus, weighing, trying out ideas) or constructing structures with Lego®.

The best way of finding out what happens during free activities is go along to the school and see for yourself. Perhaps you could also offer some assistance—**teachers** of young children are usually grateful for an extra pair of hands.

(See also **after-school activities**, **home–school partnership**, **play**.)

free schools

See **alternative education**

funding

At first glance, the way the government chooses to finance schools might seem of little interest to parents—especially when there are more pressing issues to think about, like testing and the **National Curriculum**. However, these financial issues cannot be ignored. Changes in the system for funding have been at the heart of the government's education reforms. Many schools—and many parents—will already be feeling the effects.

Traditionally, schools were controlled by the **Local Education Authority (LEA)**. The LEA provided expert advice, monitored **standards** and—most importantly of all—held the purse strings. If schools wanted a new teacher, they asked the LEA. If schools wanted to improve their **special needs** provision, or to buy a computer or paint the outside of the building, it was the LEA they turned to. Not all **headteachers** were happy with this arrangement: some found all the red tape time-consuming and frustrating; others disagreed with the political line taken by their own LEA. The government decided it was time for a change.

Local Management of Schools (LMS)

The government's answer was LMS—Local Management of Schools. In essence the scheme was very simple. Instead of the LEA providing for schools out of a large central kitty, individual schools were to be given control over their own budget and run like small businesses. The change was not just financial. The headteacher and the school **governors** were given an important managerial role. Under LMS many of the decisions that used to be taken by the LEA were now to be taken by the school management team.

While some headteachers were understandably alarmed—particularly in view of the flood of paperwork already being generated by the new National Curriculum—others liked the idea. It meant that they would be able to agree their own staffing levels—within their allocated budget—and decide how best to use the resources available to them. A timetable for implementation was set: by the end of 1993 all **secondary schools** and large primaries were to be managing their own budgets. Small primaries and some schools in inner London were to follow in 1994. Unfortunately, even for many heads enthusiastic about the scheme, what looked like a good idea in theory turned out to be distinctly uncomfortable in practice.

Formula Funding

The problems lay in the way the funding for individual schools was decided. LEAs were told by the government they had to devise a formula which could be used to produce an appropriate budget for individual schools. This formula took into account local factors as well as the traditional capitation allowance based on the number of pupils at each school. When this complicated formula was applied, many headteachers suddenly found themselves having to make cuts to balance the books. As the realities of formula funding began to bite, some felt they had been over optimistic in their welcome for LMS.

What it all Means

Some schools have thrived on the financial independence of LMS, others have undoubtedly suffered. Most problems can be traced to lack of money and the difficulties of adjusting to formula funding. For example, the formula worked out the allowance for staff by calculating the average cost of a teacher. The trouble was that this ignored the fact that a real live teacher (instead of the theoretical average one) is on a pay scale which has regular increments. This means that as teachers get more experienced—and more valuable educationally—they become less attractive to headteachers and governors trying to save money. In some cases the pressure to replace experienced teachers with cheaper probationary staff has been impossible to resist. LMS and formula funding are thus having an immediate effect in the classroom, particularly in vulnerable areas such as provision for children with special educational needs. (See **probationary teachers, special needs**.)

A further problem facing headteachers was the lack of any tradition of large-scale financial management within the school. By definition, most heads are trained as teachers, not as financial experts. Some money was made available for training but few headteachers received the help they needed and many still find the prospect of managing a large budget daunting.

In some areas LMS has increased the pressure for opting out of local authority control. When LEAs allocate money for school budgets they hold back a proportion to cover their own costs and provide support services such as educational welfare and the advisory services. By opting out and achieving grant-maintained status, schools can actually get their hands on this money.

(See also **Opting-out**.)

Further Education (FE)

Further Education refers to a wide range of pre-degree courses, available to students from the age of 16. Courses lead to both academic and vocational **qualifications**, such as **GCSE, A-levels, BTEC, City and Guilds** (or their equivalents). These courses, which may be full or part time, are offered through Colleges of Further Education.

Historically, most Colleges of Further Education were technical institutions dealing primarily with courses in work-related areas such as engineering, catering and the clothing industry.

Colleges of Further Education provide a good alternative to school for many students who are interested in continuing their education but who feel they need a more independent and mature approach to learning. The colleges tend to be large with around 1000 students, which results in a wider spread of courses. Opportunities in Colleges of Further Education are not limited to those students with high academic qualifications. Most colleges offer **access courses** or a chance to improve basic skills. These courses have started many students on the ladder to **Higher Education (HE)**. (See **beyond 16**.)

Colleges of Further Education have responded well to government demands that education has to compete in the open market and most of them have developed strong links with industry and commerce. There are plans to remove Colleges of Further Education from the control of **Local Education Authorities (LEAs)**. This would put the finance and control of Further Education colleges into the hands of government-appointed councils. These councils are likely to be business lead and there are fears that educationalists may be underrepresented on governing bodies.

For more information on courses in your area, contact your local college and ask for a prospectus.

(See also **education and the market place**.)

G

General Certificate of Secondary Education (GCSE)

An academic qualification taken by pupils at 16. The GCSE replaced the old dual system of O-levels and CSEs (Certificate of Secondary Education) with a single combined qualification. In Scotland the equivalent is the **Standard Grade** of the **Scottish Certificate of Education (SCE)**.

GCSEs are available in a wide range of subjects and provide the basic measure of a pupil's academic achievement at the end of the compulsory school years. Unlike the two-tier O-level/CSE system, the GCSE was designed for pupils of all abilities.

The arrival of the GCSE heralded a change in the way pupils worked. O-levels traditionally involved two years' study and a final exam. With GCSE the significance of the final exam was reduced, and in some cases dropped altogether. **Continuous assessment** and assignment work were introduced, accounting for the bulk of the marks. Greater emphasis was given to practical and oral work. **Modular courses** gave manageable short-term goals to pupils in place of the long haul of the traditional O-level course. Perhaps most significantly students were encouraged to work more independently—it was no longer sufficient to absorb information like a sponge and reproduce it in the exam room.

The new courses were generally well received by pupils and **teachers**, who saw clear benefits in the new ways of working. However, in 1991 the Conservative government began to challenge some of the principles on which the GCSE was based. In particular they decided to reaffirm the importance of the final exam by imposing new limits on coursework. At the same time they began to suggest that GCSE might not after all be a suitable exam for everyone. It was argued that the less academically able could not cope with either the course work or the exam. It seems likely that these pupils will be offered other types of courses—perhaps vocationally based—which could lead to the return of a two-tier system.

This is all very confusing for parents, and is likely to become more so when the **National Curriculum** levels of attainment replace the familiar GCSE grading system (A, B, C, etc) in the mid-1990s. Clearly, there is nothing parents can do to change the exam itself, but there is one recent development they need to be aware of. While GCSEs are designed to suit every level of ability, some courses are already using what is called differentiated assessment. More are likely to follow. Under this system, different work is set for pupils of varying abilities. More able pupils studying, for example, **mathematics** might be given the most demanding work for which they could be awarded the highest grades. Less able pupils tackle a work-load more suited to their abilities, but only leading to lower grades. This practice is open to the criticism that it denies some pupils access to higher grades almost before they have begun.

Parents should ask about differentiated assessment during their regular discussions with teachers and make sure they fully understand its implications. They should keep an eye on the **streaming** arrangements within the school, making sure, for example, that it is possible for pupils to move between different streams if their work improves. This is especially important for parents of girls who are studying technical and scientific subjects.

(See also **A-level, options, sexism.**)

General Teaching Council

A statutory body responsible for maintaining a register of **teachers** in Scotland.

There have been calls for a broadly similar institution to be established in the rest of the United Kingdom which might act as a regulatory body for the teaching profession. It might function much as the General Medical Council does for the National Health Service, monitoring **standards**, overseeing **training**, and conditions of service.

geography

Geography is one of the seven foundation subjects of the **National Curriculum**. It can be studied at **GCSE** level, **A-level** and as a degree subject at university.

In primary school, geography is unlikely to be taught as a separate subject. For most children it will begin with a look at their immediate surroundings—perhaps the playing field outside the classroom—before moving on to take in the larger world around them. This work will probably be based on projects such as 'Our Town', 'The Seashore' or 'The Weather'— projects which draw on other areas of the curriculum as well as geography. (See **teaching methods**.)

In secondary school there will probably be a segment of the timetable reserved for geography. What is taught under this heading has been the subject of a good deal of debate.

Traditionally geography looked at a wide range of different issues—everything from the formation of continents, to the economy of individual countries, to the way we treat the environment. With the arrival of the National Curriculum all this changed. To the dismay of **teachers** and geographers alike,the curriculum was stripped first of the earth-sciences component (which found its way into the **science** curriculum), and then of the major issues that used to be grouped under the heading of political and social geography. What was left was a curriculum based on the sorts of facts that could be looked up in a good atlas—countries, capital cities, rivers, main exports. Pupils were steered away from the difficult and interesting questions which, in many people's eyes, made geography such a worthwhile subject.

This meant children could consider the physical damage caused by the Gulf War, but not about the conditions that produced it. They could talk about land use, but not compare the arguments for and against building large superstores in the green belt. They could talk about logging as part of a country's economy but not about the problems of mass deforestation.

Geographers felt their subject was being squeezed from all sides. This was made worse by proposals to link a slimmed-down geography curriculum with **history** in a combined **humanities** course. This has aroused strong opposition.

(See also **environmental education, How to help with geography and history**.)

gifted children

A term used to describe children who display exceptional ability.

The 1981 Education Act identified children of exceptional ability as having special educational needs, and therefore entitled to extra provision. This extra provision has not been forthcoming.

To some extent this is due to differences of opinion about what a gifted child actually is. From time to time the media highlights the achievements of a child genius—taking a degree in mathematics at 12 or performing Grieg's Piano Concerto in A Minor at 7. Educationalists, meanwhile, may refer to children whose abilities are way ahead of others of the same age as gifted. In the end definitions do not help very much.

Parents are naturally flattered (and occasionally terrified) if their children appear to be exceptionally talented. **Teachers** may find such children stimulating and rewarding, although some feel threatened by giftedness. However, the gifted child can have problems. These arise from two main sources: high expectations and boredom.

Being labelled as gifted raises the level of other people's expectations. Gifted children may find themselves under great pressure to achieve. Adults tend to assume that children who are always so good at everything will be happy to display those talents to others. Often the fear of failure and the constant striving towards perfection commonly felt by the gifted child are overlooked. This may become a barrier to healthy development in later years.

Conversely, where the needs of the gifted child in terms of stimulation are not met this can lead to acute boredom and lack of motivation.

Although gifted children can be a delight to teach, they can also become something of a headache for teachers struggling to educate 30 children of all abilities in overcrowded classrooms. Unfortunately the tendency is to give those children who always finish their work first and get it all right more of the same. This is very demoralizing and can lead the child to switch off. In this way the gifted child may come to be seen as lazy.

Parents of gifted children need to be sensitive to these potential problems. There is much that you can do to help. The most useful tip is to take the pressure off. Facilitate lots of opportunities for your child to test his or her ideas and to develop projects of his or her own. Try to keep your own high expectations out of it and give him or her a chance to fail in a secure setting. Remember that the gifted child is not necessarily the confident child.

If you feel that your child has abilities and needs that are not being stimulated at school, go and talk to the teaching staff about ways that you can all get involved. (See **home–school partnership**.)

For further information, contact

The National Association for Gifted Children
Park Campus, Boughton Green Road, Northampton NN2 7AL

girls and the sciences

See **GCSE, hidden curriculum, sexism**

Girls' Schools Association (GSA)

A body representing girls' schools in the independent sector.

(See also **Headmasters' Conference, independent schools**.)

governors

Governors—along with **headteachers**—are responsible for managing most schools and colleges in England and Wales. In Scotland school boards provide a local focus for school management but they do not have the extensive powers and responsibilities of their counterparts south of the border.

Traditionally, governors have performed a largely ceremonial function: appearing at Christmas concerts or opening summer 'fayres'. The assumption was that headteachers ran schools and major financial considerations could be left in the hands of the **Local Education Authorities (LEAs)**. All this changed with the 1988 Reform Act, which devolved new and powerful duties to school governors. Parents (outnumbering **teachers** by at least 2:1 on most governing bodies) now have the power to influence directly the process of their children's education for the first time.

In the great proliferation of research which has been spawned since 1988, there is much to suggest that the newly constituted governing bodies are not working as well as they should.

Faced immediately with the prospect of implementing the **National Curriculum**—something few teachers, let alone parents, understood at the time—and the complexity of handling school budgets, many school governors were soon out of their depth. Consequently, resignation rates amongst school governors are high, while attendance at **Annual General Meetings** is so low in some areas that governors often outnumber parents. Many parents still do not know who their representatives are, or what governors do. Parent governors themselves are often intimidated by the educational 'experts' and the enormity of the task itself.

Who sits on Governing Bodies?

The number of available places on a governing body depends upon the size and type of school. Those with fewer than 100 pupils have two parent governors; and in schools of more than 600 there are five. Different rules apply to **voluntary-aided** and **voluntary-controlled schools**.

There are representatives from the Local Education Authority (LEA); elected teacher representatives and parents. Recently there have been moves to ban teachers from sitting as parent governors in an effort to prevent professional educators dominating the governing body. Representatives from the local community are invited to join as co-opted members. These are often chosen from local businesses. The headteacher can choose whether or not to become a governor. Teacher governors automatically relinquish their place on the governing body when they leave the school. Parent governors are allowed to complete their four-year term even if their children leave the school in the meantime.

Governors are responsible for:

Implementing the National Curriculum, including **religious education (RE)**.

Managing the school budget. (See **funding**.)

The appointment and dismissal of staff, and an increasing involvement with teacher appraisal. (See **teachers**.)

Discipline—including the exclusion of children considered troublesome.

Governors must produce a document setting out their policy on **sex education**.

Identifying children with special educational needs and making some provision for them. (See **special needs**.)

Equal opportunities policies.

Publishing information for parents and calling an Annual General Meeting (AGM).

Hints for Parent Governors

As with any other organization, a school depends upon the quality of its leaders and managers. Confusion and disharmony amongst the governing body inevitably filters through to the staff and the children they teach.

If you are interested in becoming a governor, you should ask at the school for details of nomination and voting procedures. Elections for governors are held every four years. However, many governing bodies have unfilled vacancies and it might not be necessary to wait until the next round.

Make sure that you are really well informed about what goes on in the school. Ask the headteacher to arrange visits for you during term time. The information you need cannot be gleaned from educational documents alone, especially if they are peppered with **jargon**.

Ask the headteacher to focus in on one area of the curriculum per visit. Talk to the subject leader, and consider ways of reporting back at the next meeting.

Familiarize yourself with the names of the staff and their positions within the school. Be sensitive to the circumstances under which they work: they need your support as well as your constructive criticisms.

Talk to the cleaning and welfare staff—they know best about the condition of the **buildings** and what needs to be spent on them.

Enrol on a training course. Contact the National Association of Governors and Managers (NAGM). There should be money available from the LEA for governor training.

Ask for relevant paper work well in advance of meetings and do not be afraid to ask for important issues to be explained in ordinary language.

Make yourself known to the parents whom you represent and encourage them to voice their concerns.

(See also **home–school partnership**.)

grammar

Once upon a time all children began their English education with lessons in grammar. They learned how to identify the parts of speech (verbs, nouns, adjectives, etc) and how to break sentences into their component parts. Then, for a while, grammar became a dirty word. A whole generation of children grew up without having to trouble about the difference between defining and non-defining relative clauses or the peculiar habits of the gerund.

People who were convinced standards of literacy were falling were quick to point to the decline in grammar-teaching as a prime cause. A series of reports commissioned to look into the matter failed to confirm this view. Instead they concluded that the traditional approach to grammar was not a very helpful way of improving an individual's performance.

The **National Curriculum** steers a careful course between these two views. It, sensibly, treats the grammar debate itself as part of the curriculum. It resists the calls for a return to sentence analysis for its own sake, yet at the same time recognizes the helpfulness of a specialized vocabulary (verbs, nouns, gerunds) derived from traditional grammar that will make it easier for pupils to talk about language and the way it works.

(See also **How to help with spelling**, **How to help with writing**, **standard English**.)

grammar schools

Grammar schools provide a mainly academic education for pupils aged between 11 and 19 who have been selected on the basis of ability.

These schools have now almost entirely been replaced by comprehensive schools in England, Scotland and Wales. Northern Ireland has retained its grammar-school system.

(See also **comprehensive schools, selection**.)

grant-maintained schools

Schools which have opted out of **Local Education Authority (LEA)** control and are financed directly by central government. (Grant-maintained schools should not be confused with **independent schools**, which are private schools with fee-paying pupils.) In Scotland, grant-maintained schools are called self-governing schools.

Grant-maintained schools were the creation of the 1988 Education Reform Act. As part of their major overhaul of the education system the government wanted to break the LEA's monopoly on the control of state schools. The idea was to give more independence to school managing bodies—the head-teacher and the **governors**. The decision to apply for grant-maintained status rests with the parents. (For the procedure, see **Opting-out**).

All grant-maintained schools must follow the **National Curriculum**.

The creation of grant-maintained schools was just one aspect of the Conservative government's programme of reforms. Exactly what lies behind their thinking is the subject of much debate— particularly when schools achieved freedom to manage their own budgets under Local Management of Schools (LMS). (See **funding**.)

There are fears that the arrival of this new category of schools could be a way of introducing selection by the back door. Schools which have opted for grant-maintained status are free to apply for a change of character. A successful comprehensive might for example choose to revert to a grammar school. It could then introduce its own selection procedures perhaps based on results of National Curriculum assessments. This is a particularly bleak scenario for the less able and children with **special needs**.

(See also **magnet schools**.)

grants and loans

Allowances awarded to students, usually in Higher Education institutions (colleges, polytechnics and universities) to cover the cost of fees and sometimes maintenance.

In England and Wales **Local Education Authorities (LEAs)** are legally obliged to provide grants for students on most full-time advanced courses leading to a recognized qualification: a first degree, or a teacher training course, for example. These are known as mandatory grants. The amount of money awarded is generally decided by means-testing parents—the more parents earn, the less students receive in grants. Different rules apply for **mature students**, or students who have been living independently for three years. Grants for non-degree courses, agriculture, drama, art or hotel management, for example, are left to the discretion of the LEA. These are known as discretionary grants.

From 1 September 1990 the value of mandatory grants was frozen by the government, and a system of top-up loans was introduced. Under this system, students are entitled to borrow up to £420 per annum (1991) to supplement their grants. The proportion of the grant raised by the loan will be increased progressively until it equals the entire value of the grant. The amount of capital available to finance the loans scheme is set to rise in line with inflation. Students are expected to repay these loans after completing their courses if their subsequent earnings rise above 85 per cent of the national average.

The loans scheme has not been well received. Costs to the government are high. Educational establishments have pointed to the difficulties of administering the scheme; loans have been delayed in many cases. It is especially unpopular with students who were hit at the same time by the community charge and loss of housing and welfare benefits. The whole system of grants and loans is under review.

Many students face years of financial hardship and are forced to find alternative means of supplementing an already meagre income: finding part-time jobs, borrowing from parents or looking to private companies for **sponsorship**.

In Scotland the grant-awarding body is the **Scottish Office Education Department (SOED)**.

If you run into difficulties over funding for courses, talk first to your LEA to check the official position. The **National Union of Students (NUS)** may also be able to offer advice. *The Directory of Grant-Making Trusts* (available in reference libraries) lists foundations and charitable trusts that may finance students if LEA funds are not available.

(See also **designated courses, funding, special needs**.)

GSA

See **Girls' Schools Association**

guidance

See **pastoral care**

H

handwriting

British school children, unlike many of their European counter-parts, have often had to learn to write twice during their school career—once when they learn to print and once when they learn how to join up (cursive writing). This is the result of a decision made in the 1920s by **HMIs** who thought children would be confused if they had to read one type of script in books (unjoined letters) and write another (joined up).

Many children make the change-over to cursive writing without any great difficulty—usually around the age of seven. However, the switch can present problems for some, especially if they have started to learn cursive writing in one way and then are moved to a school which uses a different system. Many children of secondary age still resort to fast printing in examinations and tests.

Some schools are no longer teaching printing—particularly as there is some evidence to suggest that learning cursive script from the outset not only avoids confusion but helps with spell-ing too. Joining letters in a flowing uninterrupted movement helps to fix the letter sequence of individual words in the child's mind.

Schools often use a commercial writing scheme to teach hand-writing, some have a scheme of their own developed by the **teachers**. There are many different handwriting schemes around, all with their own particular style. Choice of scheme may depend as much on finance as quality.

It is worth finding out how your child's school teaches hand-writing and if they use a particular scheme. Knowing what the teachers expect helps to avoid confusion when you help at home.

Parents worry a great deal about the neatness of their children's handwriting. It is worth remembering that while legibility is important, there are times when neatness should take second place. If your child is struggling with composing a piece of writing (thinking of the words he or she is going to use and arranging them in sentences), you will only make life more difficult if you insist on perfectly formed letters at the same time. It is far better to allow him or her to do what a professional writer would do: create a rough draft and then tidy it up later by making a final, neat, copy.

(See also **How to help with spelling, How to help with writing.**)

Headmasters' Conference (HMC)

An organization representing the most prestigious **independent schools**. Most of the pupils in HMC schools are boys. The **Girls' Schools Association** is the equivalent organization for independent schools for girls.

headteachers

Headteachers, along with school **governors**, are responsible for the day-to-day running of a school. In smaller schools, mostly at primary level, many headteachers also teach for part or all of the day.

The headteacher holds the key position in any school. He or she (and there are many more male headteachers than female, especially at secondary level) sets the tone and ethos of a school and is arguably the single most important factor in its success.

Recent reforms have made life difficult for headteachers. In a very short space of time they have had to cope with sweeping changes in the educational system. They have been responsible for implementing major curricular reforms, notably the **GCSE** and the **National Curriculum** with all its paraphernalia of testing and assessment. They have had to come to terms with the new powers of school governors, and the implications of greater parental choice. They have often been in charge of a demoralized and undervalued teaching force. Competition for pupils and resources has become a fact of life. On top of all this, they have had to deal with the arrival of **Local Management of Schools (LMS).**

LMS, more than anything else, is changing the role of headteachers. Under LMS, they were given many of the powers and responsibilities that used to be the preserve of the **Local Education Authority (LEA)**. These included control over their own budget. With little expertise or training, headteachers suddenly found themselves turned into chief executives of small—and sometimes not-so-small—businesses.

Some headteachers welcomed this development with its promise of a greater administrative independence, but for the majority the reality was harsh. Required by law to balance the books, they discovered that limitations on government spending and the vagaries of formula funding meant that budgets would no longer stretch. This forced them to take some very unpleasant decisions which weighed the cost of teachers against the cost of repairs, or **special needs** provision against secretarial help. Stress levels were high; more than a few heads gave up the struggle and opted for early retirement.

Inevitably, the upheavals of recent reforms are leading to the emergence of a new breed of headteacher. No school is likely to thrive in the market-led educational world of the 1990s unless it can call on management, marketing and finance skills. In this climate there is a real danger that these business skills will come to seem more important than educational expertise.

When **choosing a school** for your child, the headteacher is likely to be your first point of contact. A good deal of information can be gained from this initial interview. Make sure you ask how the recent changes have affected the school. Beyond these practical matters, ask yourself the obvious question, 'Is this the sort of person to whom I can confidently entrust my child?'

(See also **funding, teachers**.)

health education

That part of the curriculum which deals with a child's physical, and emotional well-being. In schools it is unlikely to appear as a separate subject but as a theme, included in various lessons such as **science** or home economics.

In 1991 the government substantially increased spending on preventative health. This was largely the result of increased public concern about **AIDS** and drug abuse. Much of this money was spent on **in-service training** for **teachers**.

National Curriculum guidelines suggest that children between the ages of 5 and 16 should receive some instruction on the following:

Use and misuse of drugs and substances such as alcohol, tobacco and medicines.

Sex education.

The importance of family life as a social institution.

Safety on the roads and at home.

The importance of exercise in promoting good health.

Personal hygiene.

Environmental aspects of health.

Psychological aspects of good health.

It is up to individual schools to decide how and when to introduce these various aspects of health education into the timetable. In the primary age range, teachers may cover personal hygiene in a project on food. In **secondary schools** sex education may be dealt with in biology classes.

(See also **physical education (PE)**.)

Her Majesty's Inspectorate (HMI)

HMIs are charged with inspecting schools and reporting on their quality. In addition they produce reports and discussion documents on aspects of the curriculum, teacher training, and other general educational issues. Inspectors employed by **Local Education Authorities (LEAs)** perform a similar function at local level. (See **advisers**.)

HMIs—usually former **teachers**—operate from within the **Department of Education and Science (DES)** but retain a degree of independence.

Recently plans have been announced to change the way HMIs operate. They are effectively to be privatized. In future schools may have to buy in their services. HMIs may find themselves competing with a similar service offered by Local Education Authorities.

hidden curriculum

The official school curriculum sets out what children should learn. The hidden curriculum refers to all those parts of school life that are unstated in the formal curriculum: for example, attitudes towards race, gender, teacher expectations, dress codes and discipline. These issues can exert a pressure which, some argue, is at least as strong as the stated curriculum.

Sometimes these attitudes are invisible to everyone concerned—even the children involved. For example, although no school would admit that it discourages girls from taking scientific and technical subjects, there may be deeply ingrained

How to help with spelling

Parents who remember the rigour of the weekly **spelling** test and the frustrations of grappling with slippery grammatical rules, often feel cheated when their children bring home pieces of written work showing little evidence of the teacher's red pen. Recent edicts that examiners must impose stiffer penalties for poor spelling in examinations would seem to underline these concerns.

Teachers do still teach children how to spell but not always in obvious ways. Do not worry if your child's teacher does not seem to be correcting all the spelling mistakes. Sometimes it is important to concentrate on other things—like getting the story moving rather than bringing a beginner to a halt over the complex technicalities.

As with all other aspects of learning, children develop their own strategies for dealing with spelling. Some children learn to spell visually—they remember the shape of whole words—others rely more on patterns and sounds by breaking up individual words into manageable chunks. Most will use a combination of these as we do as adults (think how many times we say: 'Is that how you spell rhubarb/liaison/committee? It doesn't look right.').

Before you try to help your child with spelling at home it is worth laying to rest two popular myths. First, spelling is not directly related to intelligence or all-round academic ability; some clever people can also spell brilliantly, others are hopeless at it. Second, encouraging your child to read more, while clearly a good aim to have, will not automatically improve his or her spelling.

As with writing and **reading**, some of the mystery disappears from spelling with familiarity—playing word games, and leaving messages will help.

You can help you child with spelling in the following ways:

Play lots of games like Scrabble®, Boggle®, hangman, charades so that children can see how letters fit together

to make words. There are some good, commercially produced games which help with spelling; word dominoes,
sound lotto word jigsaws amongst others. Be wary of
material that promises to 'Get your child through **SATS**'.

Help your child to make word banks: write down on pieces
of card families of words which have either the same
sounds or letter groups: night, right, bright, playing,
looking, doing . . . You can use these word banks for making
up your own games or building stories or simply as a
reference.

Label everyday objects around the house so that your
children become familiar with the shape of words like
'cupboard', 'saucepans', 'fridge' or 'door'. Try moving the
labels around and asking your children if they can spot the
deliberate mistake.

Help your child with crosswords and wordsearches. Try
getting them to make up their own.

As your children progress, encourage them to look more
closely at their mistakes and to correct their own work.
Help with the weekly spelling test, if the school gives one,
by getting your child to write the words down as well as
chanting them out.

The look-cover-write-check tactic of learning spellings is a
useful one which you could encourage at home. Children
first look carefully at the word, they then cover it up and
try to write it down from memory. They check their word
against the original and have another go if they have made
a mistake.

Help your children use a dictionary to look words up for
themselves. Start with picture dictionaries with younger
children and move on to more comprehensive ones later.
Play dictionary games: How many words can you find in
the letters which make up 'observation'? Are they all in the
dictionary?

(See also **How to help with writing**.)

attitudes which are steering boys towards technical subjects and girls towards the arts.

Other aspects of the hidden curriculum such as **bullying**, sexual harassment and racism are only too obvious to the people concerned. But very few **headteachers** are prepared to admit they have these problems in their schools.

All schools have a hidden curriculum, but the impact it has on the well-being of the institution varies. If the structure and attitudes of a school are healthy, the hidden curriculum can aid learning—for example, where **teachers** actively encourage racial tolerance, where pupils' opinions are respected, where bullying is tackled through co-operation and pupils are valued as individuals. Problems arise when pupils perceive that there is a gulf between what is stated officially and what actually goes on from day to day and a 'Them' and 'Us' philosophy prevails.

Because these aspects of school life are, by definition, hidden, there seems on the face of it little that parents can do. It is very difficult to work out the impact of these attitudes on a particular school. You can find out most by talking to your children about all those parts of the school day that have nothing obviously to do with academic work—are they consulted about major changes, is there a chance for them to have their interests represented? You can tell a lot from spending some time in the school just looking and talking to staff and pupils.

(See also **children's rights, racial discrimination, sexism**.)

Higher Education (HE)

Higher Education (HE) takes students—usually from the age of 18—to degree level and beyond.

HE courses are run at universities, polytechnics, and Colleges of Higher Education. Of these, universities are the oldest and most prestigious. Universities can award their own degrees and, besides their teaching commitment, have a major role to play as research centres. Polytechnics evolved from technical institutions and were often formed from the merger of two or more **Colleges of Further Education**. Colleges of Higher Education have traditionally specialized in the training of **teachers**, but now offer a wider range of degree courses.

Government reforms are eroding the differences between these institutions. Polytechnics, for example, can now award their own degrees and are to be given the same financial status as universities.

Despite their different historical backgrounds, these institutions have one thing in common: they all allow students access to the top rungs of the educational ladder. The key qualification here is the first degree. Most degree courses run for three years full time. Four-year courses are more common in Scotland.

HE institutions offer a bewildering range of subjects at degree level, covering everything from accountancy to zoology. Most courses will require two or three **A-levels** or their equivalent. **Mature students** are often welcomed on HE courses and institutions are sometimes prepared to waive formal entrance requirements for individuals who can demonstrate relevant experience.

Once you have chosen your course and been accepted, your troubles are not over. For most students finance is a major headache. If you have chosen a **designated course** and have the appropriate **qualifications**, mandatory grants will be available. For other courses alternative sources of finance might have to be found. (See **grants and loans**.)

Beyond the first degree, Higher Education offers further postgraduate qualifications. These include Masters degrees, which might be taught or based partly on research, and pure research degrees such as Master of Philosophy (MPhil) and Doctor of Philosophy (PhD).

In common with other areas of education HE is suffering from a shortage of money. Although, compared to most of our competitor countries, Britain's Higher Education population is pitifully low, numbers are increasing. **Funding** has not kept pace. Many institutions complain of poor quality buildings, inadequate student accommodation, and a deteriorating ratio of students to staff. The cash shortage has caused universities to look to the private sector in order to raise money. Some departments are forming partnerships with industry or offering consultancy services to the outside world. While entering the commercial arena might make good economic sense, it leaves academics with less time to pursue research. As a result we are losing some of our most able and highly qualified people to institutions in the United States. This is likely to have a serious knock-on effect on industry.

Further pressure will be put on the system if the government succeeds in improving the staying-on rate at 16, and persuading more students to apply for Higher Education. The development of modular vocational qualifications, such as **BTEC**, is also likely to encourage more students to consider degree courses. (See **modular courses**.)

Applications for HE courses are through **UCCA** (for universities), **PCAS** (for polytechnics) and direct to the institutions (for colleges of HE). Information on courses and entrance requirements can be found in individual prospectuses available from the establishment concerned or in: *Polytechnic Courses Handbook*; *University Entrance*; *The Student Book*—all available from public **libraries**.

(See also **Further Education (FE)**.)

Higher Grade (Highers)

The Higher Grade of the **Scottish Certificate of Education (SCE)** is taken at the age of 17 or 18. The exam is roughly equivalent to English **A-levels** in that it serves as the entry **qualifications** for the professions and all forms of **Higher Education (HE)**.

It is common for pupils to take as many as five Highers. This allows Scottish Sixth Formers to study a broader range of subjects than their English counterparts. Pupils who achieve credit level at **Standard Grade** (taken at 16) will normally take Highers after a year's further study. Pupils with general-level passes at Standard Grade might need to take two years over their Higher course.

(See also **Sixth Year Studies (Scotland)**.)

Highers

See **Higher Grade**

high schools

A widely used name for **secondary schools**. Before the introduction of **comprehensive schools** high schools referred to **grammar schools** for girls.

history

History is one of the seven foundation subjects of the **National Curriculum**. It can be studied at **GCSE**, **A-level**, and as a degree subject.

In **primary schools** history is unlikely to be taught as a separate subject. Projects as varied as 'My Family', 'The Romans', 'The

Clothes We Wear' can all be used to introduce pupils to thinking about the past. (See **teaching methods**.)

In **secondary schools** there will probably be a segment of the timetable given over to history. As with other subjects, the arrival of the National Curriculum led to a great deal of debate about what should actually be taught in these lessons.

At the heart of this debate was the question of whether history should be seen as a collection of facts about the past (kings, queens and the dates of famous battles) or if it should try to develop pupils' critical skills and show how an understanding of the past can help us interpret the present.

Broadly, supporters of the first view thought it would be reasonable for pupils to look at a newspaper report of the Boer War to find out what happened—but not to attempt to evaluate the historical evidence by asking questions like 'How do I know this is true?'

The other major area of contention concerned modern history. A new **Secretary of State for Education** decided that history should not deal with anything that happened in the last 20 years. These more recent events, he suggested, could be addressed in current affairs.

Opponents of this view pointed out that current affairs would not find a place on many schools' timetables and that as a result there would be no room to discuss events like the Gulf War in their historical context.

History under the National Curriculum has suffered a similar fate to **geography**. It has recently been suggested that students will have to choose between the two subjects at 14 or perhaps take a combined history/geography course.

(See also **How to help with geography and history**.)

HMC

See **Headmasters' Conference**

HMI

See **Her Majesty's Inspectorate**

holism

Holism is a philosophy based on the notion that all aspects of life are interconnected, and therefore what we do with any one aspect will always have an effect on the whole.

Since earliest times education has been seen as the development of an individual's intellectual, emotional and spiritual well-being. This traditional holistic approach is increasingly under threat from moves to make education more in tune with the demands of commerce and industry. Parents and **teachers** are increasingly concerned that along with these developments the all-round needs of the individual are being forgotten.

Concern has also been expressed that the **National Curriculum**, with its emphasis on 'facts' and work-appropriate skills, threatens the development of aesthetic subjects such as **art**, **music**, literature, and **drama**. These areas may be less obviously useful to employees, but they are vital to the healthy development of an individual.

While in society at large there is a significant resurgence of interest in holistic approaches to life (for example, alternative medicine, spirituality, and green issues), educational legislation seems to be swimming against the tide.

Attempts have been made by certain schools to incorporate spiritual aspects into education. If you are interested in finding out more about holism and education, start by contacting:

Schumacher College
The Old Postern, Dartington, Totnes, Devon TQ9 6EA

(See also **education and the market place**.)

home–school partnership

Links between home and school which help make parents and **teachers** partners in the educational process.

The partnership benefits parents by helping them to understand what is going on at school and showing how they can help at home. It benefits teachers by enabling them to share the parents' detailed knowledge of their child. Perhaps more significantly a sound home–school partnership helps break down the feeling, familiar to many children, that learning is something which happens between fixed hours within the walls of an institution, and is somehow unconnected with the world outside.

In any partnership there are obligations and responsibilities on both sides. Many parents are only too ready to recognize these responsibilities in the school and yet abandon their own when they hand their child over to its teacher. Part of the problem is not knowing what they can do.

What Parents Can Do

In two words: get involved. There are three main ways you can do this. First, by helping at home, sharing in and supporting the learning that is going on at school. (See **How to help at home**.) Second, you can involve yourself at school in an informal capacity: helping in the classroom, offering professional expertise (perhaps in talking about your job), getting to know the parents of your child's friends and creating opportunities for socializing outside school, attending meetings and workshops, or joining in events organized by the **Parent–Teacher Association**. Third, you can help in a more formal capacity by standing as school governor and involving yourself in the running of the school. (See **governors**.)

What Schools Can Do

Schools in their turn can develop the home–school partnership by keeping all parents properly informed about developments at the school and consulting them where necessary. This might involve running home reading schemes, workshops to explain how a particular subject, such as **reading** or **mathematics**, is taught and how parents can help, and open evenings where parents can meet teachers on a regular basis and discuss their child's progress. It also helps if they have a genuine open-door policy so that parents are always welcome in the classroom. These are all points to bear in mind when you are **choosing a school**.

(See also **after-school activities**, **Portage scheme**.)

home visits

See **Portage scheme, special needs**

homework

Work which has been set by the school for completion at home.

Homework is a frequent bone of contention between parents and **teachers**. Misunderstandings can usually be avoided if the school has a clear homework policy and parents are prepared to get involved. Homework diaries which leave room for parents' comments can work well.

As parents you probably want to know: how much homework should children have? Is it good for them? How much difference does it make to school work? Is it fair on the children whose home life is difficult? How much help should we give?

In infant and first schools, homework usually consists of reading practice. It is important that you understand exactly what it is you are expected to do. Schools which have acknowledged that parents have a crucial role to play in the teaching of reading, send home reading records and advice along with the reading book. (See **home–school partnership**.)

In general, children of primary- and middle-school age are not expected to do much formal homework. Teachers may send home pieces of work to finish, and usually expect parents to help with, for example, spellings and learning tables. (See **How to help with maths**, **How to help with spelling**.)

Most **secondary schools** expect about an hour a night rising to two hours as pupils prepare for public examinations. Some schools organize homework clubs at lunch times and after school to help children whose circumstances make homework difficult.

However, research has shown that the type of homework set may be more important than a child's home circumstances. Imaginative schools set children individual studies, which can be more easily carried out at home than at school—interviewing grandparents about the war, for example. Suitable homework in moderation does help raise **standards** but your children might need persuading.

Some suggestions for parents

Talk to your children about what they are doing, offer praise as well as helpful suggestions about presentation and working methods.

Helping is not cheating, but doing homework for your child will not help in the long run. Talk to the teacher if you have to help a lot.

Set a fixed time for homework and if possible be on hand to help.

Find a suitable place for homework to be done. This need not be a book-lined study; the kitchen table is fine so long as someone is not baking a cake at the same time. Returning books with jam on the cover does not create a very good impression.

It is worth bearing in mind that when your secondary-school child brings work home, this may not just be preparation for the **GCSE**, it might be the GCSE itself. (See **continuous assessment**.)

Do not pressurize your child too much—forcing the issue is unlikely to help. If your child is really anti-homework talk to him or her (and to the teacher if necessary), there may be something worrying him or her. It might even be the fault of the tasks themselves.

In some schools, basic **books** and resources are too scarce to allow children to take them home on a regular basis. If this is the case in your child's school, talk to the headteacher or your parent governor about why resources are in such short supply.

(See also **How to help at home**.)

hospital education

Educational help provided within a hospital for both long-stay patients and those who are temporarily incapacitated. This might be provided by visiting **teachers** or—in larger hospitals— in fully integrated schools.

There is no statutory obligation for **Local Education Authorities (LEAs)** to provide hospital education. This makes the service particularly vulnerable at a time when LEA budgets are under severe strain. Some hospital schools under threat of closure are beginning to look towards **Opting-out** in a last-ditch attempt to stay afloat.

The teaching covers the whole ability range—from encouraging children to learn to play and master basic social skills, to the full paraphernalia of the **National Curriculum**, and **GCSEs**.

In the current financial climate it is not possible to guarantee that teachers will be available. If you have a child who is recovering in hospital from a protracted illness or injury, you may have to organize educational provision yourself. Talk to your own school in the first instance—they will often be willing to set work or advise on suitable activities. Any friends you have with teaching experience will also be a valuable source of advice.

(See also **special needs**.)

house points

See **competition**

humanities

Where it appears on most timetables, humanities will probably be an amalgam of traditional arts subjects such as languages, literature, **history** and **geography**.

Humanities courses represent a serious attempt to integrate a range of disciplines. This approach allows pupils to cross the traditional subject boundaries and bring together the study, for example, of the art, language, history and geography of a particular culture.

There have also been suggestions that the history and geography components of the **National Curriculum** could be combined to form a separate subject called humanities.

Since humanities is not a precise term, if you see it mentioned on timetables or in prospectuses you should ask exactly what the subject entails.

(See **How to help with geography and history**.)

hyperactivity

A condition associated with symptoms such as excessive crying or screaming, prolonged sleeplessness, an acute inability to concentrate or to remain in one place for any length of time, aggressive behaviour or speech difficulties.

Genuine hyperactivity is a distressing condition. However, the term has passed into common speech where it is loosely used to describe any child who seems to have a lot of energy. This confusion with natural exuberance is not very helpful—particularly as it can encourage **teachers** and parents to ascribe hyperactivity to individuals who do not happen to fit their image of the quiet, well-behaved child.

Medical research has made a strong link between hyperactivity and diet. Food additives such as sweeteners and colourants are thought to be especially harmful to children who display symptoms of hyperactivity.

You should be wary of labelling your child as hyperactive simply because he or she is reluctant to sit still. If you are worried that the condition is more serious than this, talk to your doctor or health clinic, and to the teachers at school.

For further information, contact

Hyperactive Children's Support Group
71 Whyke Lane, Chichester, Sussex PO19 2LD

(See also **special needs**.)

I

independent schools

Private schools with fee-paying pupils. Independent schools are not financed by central government or **Local Education Authorities (LEAs)**. Most are endowed as charitable trusts—others are run as a business and have to make a profit to survive. Independent schools are also known—confusingly—as public schools or private schools. (More confusingly still, in Scotland a public school is a state school and not an independent school at all.)

The Independent Sector

The independent sector in England and Wales is small compared to other industrialized countries. It is also more socially and academically exclusive. Only 7 per cent of the school population attends independent schools (4 per cent in Scotland) but this tiny percentage is hugely influential. Over half the students attending the universities of Oxford and Cambridge have been to independent schools. When you look at the top professions the figures are even more startling—over 90 per cent of directors of major life insurance companies, over 80 per cent of High Court judges, and over 85 per cent of chairmen of merchant banks are the product of independent schools.

The term independent schools covers a wide variety of different institutions. At the top end of the scale are the élite schools of the independent sector (often still called public schools) such as Eton, Harrow, and Charterhouse. The glittering reputation of these institutions benefits a whole range of lesser schools. This is sometimes misleading. Independent status is not an automatic guarantee of academic excellence.

Alongside these long-established private institutions are some former **grammar schools** which resisted the Labour government's attempts to turn them into **comprehensive schools**.

The independent sector also includes a small number of schools serving religious groupings, such as the Muslims, Quakers and Evangelists, as well as progressive and experimental institutions, such as Steiner schools. (See **alternative education**.)

Why Choose an Independent School?

Apart for reasons of family tradition, most people choose an independent school because they are seen as offering:

social prestige;

a reputation for academic excellence;

a privileged route to the top professions;

protection from the hurly-burly world of state schools.

Some independent schools can provide all these—at a price— but this is by no means true of them all. As with the state system, there are good and bad schools.

Parents looking to the independent sector to provide a particular kind of religious or progressive approach to education are clearly guided by other priorities.

How are Independent Schools Different?

Independent schools offer broadly the same curriculum and **qualifications** as state schools. Provision runs from pre-school to university-entrance level. However, there are some differences:

they do not have to follow the **National Curriculum** (though they may choose to do so);

they tend to be run on more traditional lines—for example, many are **single-sex schools** which retain the principles of selective education;

some take boarders;

they tend to have smaller class sizes;

they can employ **teachers** without recognized teaching qualifications.

Traditionally, independent schools have not been inspected by **Her Majesty's Inspectorate**. With the new arrangements for inspection of all schools they are likely to find themselves buying in inspection and monitoring services on the open market.

How much does it Cost?

Fees in public schools vary enormously from a few hundred pounds a term to several thousands. In 1980 the **Assisted Places**

Scheme was set up to encourage children from less well-off families to take advantage of the independent sector. Money is available (on a sliding scale) to cover fees in selected schools. The scheme does not cover boarding fees.

Choosing an Independent School

Great care must be taken in choosing an independent school. Schools have to register with the **Department of Education and Science (DES)** and meet certain minimum standards in **buildings** and teaching. Schools participating in the Assisted Places Scheme must have a high record of academic achievement. Beyond this, much the same considerations apply to choosing an independent school as to any other. (See **choosing a school**.) It is important to visit the school during term time and see it in operation, to ask about **teaching methods** and academic performance, and to find out about such things as provision for those children with **special needs**.

Information about independent schools can be obtained from:

Independent Schools Information Service (ISIS)
56 Buckingham Gate, London SW1E 6AG

(ISIS also produces an annual publication called *Choosing Your Independent School*.)

The Future

During the 1970s—in the face of hostility from the Labour government—it seemed possible that the public schools would disappear altogether. However, things have changed dramatically in the last 20 years. Today's political climate clearly favours the power of the market place and, despite a decline in the overall school population, the number of pupils in independent schools is growing. The long-term outlook is unclear but it seems likely that the independent sector will have an increasingly important role to play in the 1990s.

(See also **boarding schools**, **Common Entrance Examination**.)

infant schools

Cater for children between the ages of 5 and 7.

(See also **primary schools**.)

information technology (IT)

IT as a subject looks at the application of new technologies—particularly computer technology—to the handling of information.

In the classroom the computer is no longer just a tool for mathematicians or scientists; it has applications across the whole curriculum—from language learning, to **history, music, geography** and even **sport**. The **National Curriculum** sees the development of an IT capability as necessary for all pupils.

The government has made it clear it regards IT training for everyone as essential if Britain is to have a modern and efficient workforce. However, there is still some way to go before this becomes a reality. A 1990 report revealed that most primary teachers were woefully short of training in the use of **computers**. They knew how to operate the machines and run some standard programs but no more. In particular they had little experience of integrating the computer into normal classroom practice.

Even if more training could be made available for **teachers**, the problem would not be solved. Computers are expensive. If pupils are to learn to use them as everyday tools, they need much wider access to the machines than is possible in the current financial climate. Many of the machines in schools today—particularly **primary schools**—are actually provided by parents through the **Parent–Teacher Association**. Servicing costs are an additional burden. It has been estimated, for example, that the annual cost of servicing the computers in a medium-sized comprehensive school is the same as a teacher's salary.

To expect a computer on every desk in the immediate future is clearly unrealistic. However, a recent experiment in Scotland has shown the way that things might develop. Here primary-school children were issued with a small computer the size of a loose-leaf folder. They were encouraged to use this as they might a notebook and pen. Initial results were promising. First indications suggested that children were able to write more quickly with the keyboard than with pen and paper, they produced more work, and were able to edit what they had written more constructively. Some lessons were conducted without the computers to make sure more traditional writing skills were not lost. There appeared to be no falling off in the standard of **handwriting**. (See **funding**.)

in-service training (INSET)

See **teachers, Training Days**

inspection of private schools

Under normal circumstances private schools are not inspected by **HMIs (Her Majesty's Inspectorate)**. All that is required of these schools is that they meet certain minimum requirements in terms of their buildings and teaching in order to register with the **Department of Education and Science (DES)**. This means that great care must be taken in choosing a private school—they are not the automatic passport to educational excellence some people assume. Just as in the state sector there are good and bad schools. Schools participating in the **Assisted Places Scheme** (where the government pays part or all of the fees of selected pupils) must have a record of high-academic achievement. (See **choosing a school**.)

Following recent changes to the way HMIs operate, **independent schools** may soon be able to buy in monitoring and inspection services on the open market.

The boarding element of independent **boarding schools** is soon to be inspected by **Local Education Authorities (LEAs)** under the provision of the new Children Act which became law in 1991. This inspection will examine the care and welfare of children within the school but not teaching **standards**. (See **children's rights**.)

inspectors

See **advisers**, **Her Majesty's Inspectorate (HMI)**

integrated day

A method for organizing classes so that there are no fixed slots for individual subjects.

Teachers who plan their work around an integrated day do so because they believe that a child's learning is not naturally divided up into individual compartments called **history**, **geography**, **mathematics** or **art**.

Using the integrated approach, one activity or project will cover aspects of maths, language, **science**, design, rather than cutting them up into named segments. Pupils work in small groups or individually at their own pace, rather than as a whole class. The teacher moves from group to group, extending the work covered or supporting those children who are struggling. This method demands a high level of organizational skill on the part of the teacher.

(See also **teaching methods**.)

intelligence tests

Structured tests purporting to put a fixed value on a person's intelligence. The results of intelligence tests are usually expressed as a quotient using 100 as the average: 'Diccon has an IQ of 125' (ie he is of above average intelligence).

IQ tests are often used by schools who select their pupils according to academic potential. Controversy about the reliability and impartiality of such tests lead many to believe that IQ tests were of limited value. Most **teachers** now regard them as only one of many indicators of an individual's abilities.

Be wary of the much-publicized connection between a child's vitamin intake and intelligence—many scientists are sceptical about the research.

international schools

See **Europe**

IT

See **information technology**

How to help with maths

Parents are often intimidated by the prospect of helping their children with **mathematics**. They fear so much has changed since they were at school that trying to help might do more harm than good. Previously maths most often meant arithmetic and, while this was something that could be practised, the message in the end was that you were either good at it or you were not. Maths is about far more than the ability to calculate. What parents can do best is to help their children to see that mathematics is about making sense of the world, and that we use it for solving practical problems and managing everyday activities. As with all other aspects of helping at home, the way forward is through real-life situations as opposed to endless arithmetical exercises.

As with reading and talking, your child is never too young to be introduced to maths:

Slip mathematical vocabulary into everyday conversation from an early age: That bag is heavy, why don't you carry the lighter one?, Are you bigger than grandma? Do the same with wider, taller, shorter, longer and so on.

Spend some time playing at the sink, digging in the garden playing in the sand pit with your child. Ask the kinds of questions that require some practical investigations: Which pot is heaviest? Can you get all that water in the small, wide jar?

Encourage lots of activities that encourage young children to sort objects into groups or sets: while you clean the kitchen cupboards, ask your child to sort out all the tins, all the bags, all those items with a red label, all the square shapes. Sort buttons, old Christmas cards, coins, into groups: those with the same number of holes, the same value, large or small objects.

Include your child on shopping trips, discuss the prices: Which jam is the cheapest? How heavy are these potatoes? As your children get older, help them to work out change, handle coins, calculate how many bags of crisps you can get for a pound.

Let your child help you with the cooking from time to time: rolling pastry, weighing ingredients, timing how long the mince pies take to cook—these are all useful mathematical exercises.

Help your child to count out segments of fruit or squares of chocolate, show them how to divide a cake so that everyone in the family can have some.

Use pieces of string or wool to make basic shapes: help your children to guess which piece of string is the longest/shortest. Make pictures using only squares and triangles.

As your children get older help them to make their own board games: talk about building in danger zones, lucky squares, obstacles to make the games harder or last longer. Encourage them to try out their inventions on younger members of the family.

Some commercially produced games are good for helping children to develop mathematical understanding. Play variations of the traditional domino game: instead of joining those with the same value, try just making the dots add up to six or eight. Play simple card games. The BBC publishes an excellent book of practical activities called *Help your Child with Maths*, which is simple to follow and uses everyday objects.

Playing games with a simple calculator is good for reinforcing number patterns and children generally love them. How many ways can they find of making 10 or 20 or 100, for example?

Children find the concept of time especially difficult. Start by asking them to guess how long things might take or seeing how many shiny objects they can find in three minutes. Find out what happens to your pulse after you have been hopping for two minutes? Help your children to work out journey times: to and from school, in the car, on trains and buses.

Help children to make real things: from simple wooden boxes to go-carts. Encourage them to plan their work first and think about the materials they will need, how much they might cost, are they safe? Is it necessary to measure accurately?

(See also **How to help with science**.)

J

janitors

See **caretakers**

jargon

Technical language that finds its way into everyday conversation where it can make the simplest things difficult to understand.

Jargon is a major problem for today's parents. Education has become a world of **SATS**, **Profile Components**, **Key Stages**, **NVQs**—the list grows longer by the day. This flood of technical language is more than a minor irritant. It can easily make nonsense of the government's aim to give parents more power in the running of schools—after all, it is not easy to make a useful contribution if you do not understand what is going on.

The professionals—**teachers**, **headteachers** and **governors**—have a hard time with jargon too. They have to come to grips with it in order to survive. The trouble is that once this has happened, they often find it difficult to talk in any other terms. This leaves parents who are looking for the answer to simple questions at a disadvantage. Parents who are looking for the answer to difficult questions are worse off still.

This book tries to explain some of the most common terms you will come across as a parent, but it cannot explain them all. The only way to deal with jargon is to ask for clarification and go on asking until you get a satisfactory answer. If you can do this in public (at a parents' evening, for example), so much the better. You can be sure that if there is something you do not understand, there will be other people in the same position. And remember, if the experts cannot explain easily, the fault is theirs, not yours.

job centre

Centres which provide information on local career and job opportunities.

(See also **dole**, **training**.)

junior mixed infant schools (JMIS)

See **primary schools**

junior schools

See **primary schools**

junk-modelling

An activity in which younger pupils use discarded odds and ends to make models.

Junk-modelling is children's introduction to the world of technology. To parents' eyes, the robots and houses made from toilet rolls, cereal packets and string might seem crude, but in order to make them, children have had to solve a whole range of technical problems. They have had to conceive an overall design, decide on suitable materials, work out how to make their model stand up, how to make articulated joints work, how to strengthen and reinforce. These are skills which will be of major importance across the whole curriculum.

It is important not to let prejudices about the 'junk' aspect of junk-modelling get the better of us. Parents who greet their children's creations with 'That's going straight in the bin' have not only failed to understand what is going on, they have probably undone weeks of work with a single ill-considered remark.

Junk-modelling is an activity which can easily be carried out at home. All you need is a bag or box to collect oddments, scissors, glue and paints. It might not seem much, but you should remember that children are not handicapped by our lack of imagination.

(See also **craft, design, technology (CDT); How to help at home.**)

K L

Key Stages

See **National Curriculum**

language differences

Different languages and varieties of English found throughout Britain.

Standard English—the form of the language used in the educational world—is not the language used at home by large numbers of pupils. Many pupils speak a version of English that is quite different. This might be Caribbean English, American English or a regional dialect. The home language of many pupils is not English at all, but Gudjerati, Punjabi, Polish, Welsh, Gaelic or any one of the many different languages that go to make up our multi-racial society.

The attitude of the school towards these different languages and different language varieties is important. While the **National Curriculum** insists on assessment being carried out in standard English, this does not mean that language differences have to be seen as problems. The best schools will treat the presence as a positive resource that can be used to increase all pupils' understanding of the richness of Britain's linguistic heritage. Respect for their own linguistic background is also likely to improve pupils' self-esteem and have a positive effect on progress in other areas of the curriculum.

(See also **bilingualism, multi-cultural education.**)

language laboratory

A room where language students can work with tape-recorded material in individual booths.

Most equipment will allow students to record and play back their responses to the lessons contained on the laboratory software. The lessons are monitored by a teacher from a console at the front of the class.

Language laboratories were hailed as a major breakthrough when they first appeared and became a status symbol in many institutions. However, it quickly became clear that they were not popular with the majority of students. This was put down to the artificiality of the practice situation and the poor quality of the recorded lessons.

Despite their limitations, language laboratories do provide opportunities for individual study that can complement other forms of teaching. In future, laboratories which combine the use of **computers** with the traditional tape-recorded exercises are likely to become increasingly popular.

(See also **direct method, English as a Foreign Language (EFL)**.)

language schools

Institutions which concentrate entirely on the teaching of languages.

Most language schools are privately owned and teach **English as a Foreign Language** to overseas students. They tend to be found mainly in the south of England in tourist and cultural centres, such as London, Oxford and Cambridge.

They range from major centres which offer a high standard of facilities and expertise (which sometimes extends to training **teachers**) to small-scale schools with limited resources. **Standards** vary but most reputable schools are members of the Association of Recognized English Language Schools (ARELS).

Language schools offer courses in general English, as well as English for Special Purposes (such as business, medicine, etc) and English for Academic Purposes.

There is a variety of exams available for overseas students administered by the University of Cambridge, ARELS, and other examining bodies.

In addition to these English schools there are other organizations, such as the Berlitz schools, which offer packaged courses in other languages.

For further information, contact

Association of Recognized English Language Schools (ARELS)
Ewert Place, Summertown, Oxford OXJ 7BZ

(See also **direct method**.)

learning difficulties

See **special needs**

LEAs

See **Local Education Authorities**

libraries

Centres for the lending and borrowing of **books**—though today's libraries are increasingly including other media such as magazines, records, videotapes, and computer software.

Libraries have always been central in the educational process. With the growing importance of project-based learning—where pupils are encouraged to do their own research—their role is taking on an even greater importance.

Unfortunately this change in **teaching methods** has coincided with a growing threat to library services both in schools and in the local community. The problem, as always, is money. Library services present an easy target for authorities and schools when funds are tight. Almost every local authority in the country is closing branch libraries, reducing spending on books and making staff redundant. The situation is particularly severe in authorities suffering **charge-capping**. In schools, the chief culprit is LMS (Local Management of Schools), which has had the effect of squeezing school budgets. (See **funding**.)

Also suffering—and for the same reasons—is the school libraries service which provides support for **teachers** and rotates book stock so that even the smallest primary school can have a changing range of books to stimulate young readers.

As parents the best you can do (apart from supporting your local library) is to encourage your parent **governors** to keep the school library well stocked and to take full advantage of the school library service if your authority offers one.

(See also **books**.)

licensed teachers

See **teachers**

link courses

Courses (particularly technical and work-related courses)

taught partly at school and partly at Colleges of Further Education. (See **Further Education (FE)**.)

literacy and numeracy

The basic skills of **reading**, writing and **spelling** (literacy) and **mathematics** (numeracy).

(See also **adult education**.)

LMS

See **funding**

loans

See **grants and loans**

Local Education Authorities (LEAs)

LEAs are a branch of local government based at the Town or County Hall. There are 116 LEAs in England and Wales. In Scotland, education is the responsibility of the nine regional councils and three island councils which are known as Education Authorities. In Northern Ireland, the Education and Library Boards perform the same function.

LEAs have traditionally been responsible for the service provided by local schools. Until recently their main areas of responsibility have been:

Planning: LEAs must ensure there are sufficient school places available for local children. They must take decisions about the number and size of schools

Monitoring: LEAs inspect schools and offer an advisory service to make sure educational **standards** are maintained.

Services: LEAs provide educational and welfare services, library and music services, school meals and transport. They must also make sure provision is made for children with **special needs**.

Financial: LEAs hold the purse strings. They allocate school budgets and pay **teachers**' salaries.

Much of this is now changing. Since the mid-1980s, central government policy seems geared to reducing the power and responsibility of LEAs in favour of more centralized control. The reasons for this have very little to do with education. They are seen as part of the overall plan to reform local government on the one hand, and to find ways of reducing the community charge on the other.

Two recent educational reforms in particular have reduced the influence of LEAs and, some have argued, might lead to their eventual disappearance. These are **Local Management of Schools (LMS)** and the arrival on the educational scene of **grant-maintained schools**.

Under LMS many of the functions of the LEA are devolved to individual schools. Schools are effectively turned into small businesses with the headteacher and board of **governors** responsible for their own budgets and for decisions about staffing levels and such things as the proportion of their funds to be spent on **books**. The LEAs hand over the money retaining a percentage (up to 15 per cent) to cover areas like welfare and advisory services. (See **funding**.)

Grant-maintained schools are schools which have opted out of local control altogether. These schools are not responsible to LEAs and are funded directly from central government. What this means in practice is that they can get their hands on the proportion of funds that LEAs have traditionally held back. Whether they will be better off as a result is an open question. They might have to use this extra money to buy back the services that used to be provided by the LEA.

By the end of 1991 comparatively few schools had opted out. In time more schools might take the grant-maintained route, though even this might not mean the end of LEAs. There would still need to be a local level of control to co-ordinate planning and monitor standards.

A further nail in the LEA coffin came in August 1991 when a government white paper outlined proposals (likely to be adopted by either major political party) to remove **Further Education (FE)** from LEA control. This is to include Sixth Form and **tertiary colleges** and takes away the legal right of LEA representatives to sit on the governing body of all such institutions. This right is to be taken over by the **Training and Enterprise Councils**, which are mostly made up from the business world. The most likely outcome of all this will probably see LEAs in future offering professional services in the market place to increasingly autonomous schools.

(See also **Department of Education and Science (DES), education and the market place**.)

Local Management of Schools (LMS)

See **funding**

lollipop people

Lollipop people are responsible for the road safety of pupils at major road junctions close to schools. **Local Education Authorities (LEAs)** are responsible for the provision of lollipop people and must decide, in consultation with the **police**, where they are to be sited. In times of need **teachers** may also do the job, but for insurance purposes, they must wear the white coat and carry the pole.

Lollipop people develop their own particular style of policing. Junior lollipop persons smile at cars and hope they will be shamed into stopping. More senior operatives have developed the moral authority to bring a beet lorry to a standstill with a single penetrating stare.

In the present financial climate the future of lollipop people, who have doubtless saved the lives of many a marauding school child, looks uncertain.

London weighting

An allowance added to **teachers'** salaries and some grants to compensate for the extra cost of living or working in London.

The additional payment is more a gesture than a serious attempt to offset the expense of life in the capital. London weighting on a teacher's salary, for example, is not enough to make any real impression on the problems faced by teachers trying to buy their own home—one of the prime causes of teacher shortages in London.

look and say

See **reading**

M

magnet schools

A popular (although not quite respectable) term for schools which have opted out of **Local Education Authority** control and offer particular subject specialisms.

The concept has been imported from the United States of America, where magnet schools have existed for some years. There they tend to specialize in vocational courses (linked to the needs of commerce and industry), or a particular academic subject such as **mathematics**.

Magnet schools are a likely development for British education in the future. They are spin-offs from legislation, notably the 1988 Education Reform Act, which made fundamental changes to educational **funding**. The newly created **grant-maintained schools**, which receive their money directly from the government rather than LEAs, will be allowed to change their status—perhaps from a small comprehensive to a school concentrating on sciences, for example. There is nothing to stop schools selecting their pupils if they wish, especially if there is a waiting list.

This has led to fears that only the most able children will be attractive to certain schools. **Headteachers** are already under pressure to publish their **National Curriculum** test results. This poses the worrying question about what happens to all the rest, those children whose test results are poor or who have **special needs**, left in schools with dwindling resources. (See **sink schools**.) Those in favour of magnet schools see in them a chance to improve **standards** in a market-led system. Only time will tell.

(See also **selection**.)

maintained schools

The technical name for state schools.

Maintained schools do not charge fees. They are wholly or

partially funded by the **Local Education Authority** or—in the case of schools which have opted out—central government.

(See also **independent schools**.)

marketing

See **school marketing**

mathematics

Mathematics is one of the three core subjects of the **National Curriculum**, along with **English** and **science**. All children are expected to study mathematics between the ages of 5 and 16.

GCSE mathematics is one of the yardsticks by which educational progress is measured. It is a basic entry requirement for most **Higher Education** courses and is also demanded by many prospective employers.

There has been a great deal of publicity about alleged falling **standards** in the mathematical ability of today's children. Parents are understandably worried. The situation is made worse by the changes that seem to have overtaken maths since they were themselves at school. Their children talk of sets and bonding and seem to spend a great deal of time manipulating wooden blocks. Hovering in the background is the spectre of 'new maths'.

There is a crisis in mathematics education as there is in much of the rest of the system. However, the crisis is not simply about new-fangled **teaching methods**. The root causes are more to do with severe shortages of teachers in the subject (see **shortage subjects**); the pressures on timetabling (see **National Curriculum**); a seriously demoralized teaching force (see **teachers**); and the attitudes of society itself to mathematics (see **arts/science divide, sexism**).

How Mathematics is Taught in Today's Classrooms

There are two major differences between the way maths used to be taught and the way it is practised in most schools today. First, and most significantly, has been the shift away from the rote learning so familiar to parents. Much greater emphasis is now placed on understanding the concepts and relations that lie at the heart of mathematics than on merely memorizing, for example, tables. Children are encouraged to ask questions, devise their own strategies for solving problems, and apply their mathematical knowledge to other areas of the curriculum and to real situations. In this way mathematics can become much more practical and meaningful. This is the approach adopted by enlightened **primary schools**. It is also reflected in the National Curriculum, and the new style GCSE.

The other major change in maths-teaching is the use of technology, such as **calculators** and **computers**, as part of everyday learning. Some people see these changes as heralding a decline in basic arithmetical skills. This attitude ignores the mathematical advances of children at a deeper level.

(See also **How to help with maths, teaching methods**.)

maths schemes

Structured programmes which are designed to take children through a series of mathematical concepts in predetermined stages.

Most schools use commercially produced maths schemes, although some prefer to produce their own. There are many different schemes on the market, catering for pupils of all ages. Many parents and **teachers** like the idea of maths schemes, seeing in them a way of checking that children are progressing systematically through the subject and identifying areas of difficulty.

Maths schemes can work well when they are used to reinforce the work already introduced and developed by the teacher, and where children are encouraged to apply these skills to practical activities. Problems arise when teachers rely too heavily on a scheme to cover all their mathematical activities. The temptation to send children off to do the next three pages in green book three when they keep racing through the material is often too strong for an overworked teacher to resist. Children may then fill in page after page of 100s, 10s and units exercises, without ever realizing the point or applying the skill mastered on paper.

Modern schemes often look very attractive, full of glossy pictures and cartoons, but this is no guarantee of quality content. The introduction of the **National Curriculum** spawned a rash of new schemes, each proclaiming that this was the one to fulfil new requirements. What lies under the gloss is often the same content with a different format and colour illustrations.

Parents often become over-anxious if their children are not sailing through the scheme or keeping pace with their friends. Many of the maths schemes used in schools are available in bookshops. Be wary of rushing out to buy a copy thinking that this is the best way of helping your child at home. Repeating exercises already struggled over at school may turn your child off completely.

(See **How to help with maths, teaching methods.**)

mature students

Students who begin courses of **Further** or **Higher Education** at a later age than most of their colleagues.

Most universities and colleges look favourably on mature students because they bring to their studies a wider range of experience than the average school-leaver. A great many institutions will consider modifying or waiving formal entrance **qualifications** for mature students. So if you are thinking about studying again, perhaps with a view to changing career or getting back into the job market, do not be discouraged if you have not got a string of **GCSEs** behind you.

Access courses, which prepare students without traditional academic qualifications for entry into Further or Higher Education, are an option worth considering.

As a mature student you may be eligible for a grant, but the amount of money involved is likely to be small.

For further information, contact

Education Counselling and Credit Transfer Information Service (ECCTIS) 2000 Ltd
Fulton House, Jessop Avenue, Cheltenham GL50 3SH

medical schools

Institutions of **Higher Education (HE)** for the training of doctors. Medical schools are attached to major hospitals and some universities. Competition for places on these six-year courses is fierce.

middle schools

In some local authorities in England, middle schools cater for primary-aged children between the ages of 8 and 10 until they are 12, 13, or 14.

Middle schools developed in the 1960s and were designed to smooth the transition from the one-teacher-per-class system found in **primary schools** to more formal subject teaching characteristic of **secondary schools**.

Middle schools have a lot to offer and are well worth considering if you have a choice in your area. There are, however, some potential pitfalls with the **National Curriculum** which you will need to discuss with the headteacher. Middle schools straddle key stages two and three. It is therefore very important for middle and secondary schools to liaise closely.

mixed-ability teaching

See **teaching methods**

modern languages

Languages such as French, German and Spanish taught as individual subjects.

A modern language must form one of the seven foundation subjects of the **National Curriculum**. It was originally envisaged that all children would study a modern language until they were 16. However the government has retreated from this position and now the subject will be compulsory only between the ages of 11 and 14. This change has drawn criticism from many quarters—particularly in view of the linguistic demands that will be made on British companies operating in the new, open **Europe**.

The most popular modern language in schools is still French (studied by 90 per cent of pupils), with German second and Spanish a poor third. In some schools it is possible to study languages from further afield, such as Russian or Japanese.

There is a national shortage of language teachers. This shortage, together with the demands of the National Curriculum (designed to occupy students for 80 per cent of their working week), is making it increasingly difficult for some schools to offer individual students two or more languages.

(See **direct method**, **shortage subjects**.)

modular courses

Courses made up of individual sections or modules, each complete in itself, which can be assembled to form a single qualification.

Perhaps the best-known modular courses are the degrees

offered by the **Open University** but they can be found in all parts of the educational spectrum —from vocational courses, such as **BTEC,** to **GCSE** and beyond.

Usually students are assessed as they complete each section of the course, either through an exam, assignment work or **continuous assessment**, or sometimes a combination of all three. If students fail to finish the course for any reason, they can still be credited for the modules they have completed. More importantly for some, the outcome of two years' work is not decided in a three-hour all-or-nothing exam. (See **A-level**.)

There have been criticisms that the modular approach can lead to a watering down of a course's content. Nevertheless, they are popular with many educationalists who point to the way they enable students to monitor their own progress and discourage last-minute cramming. Students too can find it helpful to see the long haul of a major qualification marked off in manageable sections.

Modular courses also offer the first real opportunity for breaking down the division between academic and vocational **qualifications**. There is no reason why a core of basic skills such as literacy, numeracy and communications skills could not be supplemented by both academic and vocational modules leading towards a single qualification. As yet no such courses exist, but the Business and Technician Education Council (BTEC) is showing the way forward with its range of courses available at **Colleges of Further Education**.

(See also **vocational education**.)

Montessori school

See **alternative education**

mother and toddler group

See **pre-school provision**

multi-cultural education

An approach to education which encourages awareness of, and respect for, the cultural and racial diversity of modern Britain.

Britain has always been a multi-racial society. By the time the Normans arrived in 1066 it was already home to Celts, Picts, Angles, Saxons, and Danes. Since that date the racial mix has been increased by representatives from almost every cultural and religious grouping throughout the world. Schools clearly have a special responsibility here to develop an approach to education that will increase tolerance and understanding of different ethnic groups and cultures.

While some schools have sections of the timetable given over to 'multi-cultural issues', this is not always the best way to go about things. Projects on Chinese weddings, Caribbean cook-ins, and visits to the local mosque can all be useful, provided they are part of a whole-school policy. Treating multi-cultural issues as a separate part of the curriculum reinforces the notion that the cultures they come from are exotic and strange.

Far more useful is a response in which multi-cultural issues can be integrated into mainstream subjects. There are plenty of opportunities even outside the obvious topics in **geography** and **history**. A **mathematics** project might include a look at the contribution made by Arabs and Chinese to our number system. A **science** lesson on the human body could provide opportunities for positive discussions about skin colour and facial characteristics. An **English** lesson could be used to trace the origins of our cosmopolitan vocabulary.

Clearly, a multi-cultural policy is essential if schools are to prepare their pupils to enter today's multi-racial society. Parents, through contacts with **teachers** and **governors**, should make sure that their school is not neglecting this responsibility. Schools which have no ethnic minorities—and thus no ready resources to draw on among their pupils—will need to take special steps to make up for this deficiency.

(See also **bilingualism, language differences, racial discrimination**.)

music

Music is one of the seven foundation subjects of the **National Curriculum**. Music can be studied at **GCSE, A-level** and beyond.

Music has a low status compared with other foundation subjects such as **technology** and **modern languages**. In common with **PE** and **art** it will not be formally tested. The curriculum does not have to be followed by all pupils—it acts as a series of guidelines rather than a legal framework.

In **primary schools** music is often in the hands of staff with little musical training. Hymn-singing may be the only form of music-making available to young children. Pressures to fulfil cur-riculum requirements in more prestigious subjects mean there is little time left over for something which is increasingly being seen as an educational frill.

In **secondary schools** the picture is complicated. Some schools have excellent musical provision and see the National Curriculum as an opportunity to capitalize on pupils' natural enthusiasm for making and listening to music. However, even the best schools are being forced to weigh the value of a musical education against the need to provide for the full range of academic subjects.

In many schools instrumental tuition is provided by **peripatetic teachers**, visiting the school to teach in small groups or on a one-to-one basis. In most cases this service is provided by the **Local Education Authority (LEA)**. In the current economic climate, when budgets are under pressure, the music service has been seen as a soft target. Some LEAs have dropped the service altogether, others have introduced fees.

What this means for parents is clear. If you value the contribution music makes to your child's education, you might have to take steps to supplement the service offered by your local school—particularly if your child is interested in learning to play an instrument. The school or LEA should be able to put you in touch with a reputable music teacher. If not, most music shops carry adverts from musicians offering tuition.

(See also **How to help with art and music**.)

N

National Certificate

Work-related courses offered by the **Scottish Vocational Education Council (SCOTVEC)** principally in Colleges of Further Education. (See **Further Education (FE)**.)

These **modular courses** are continually assessed. Some pupils in Scottish Sixth Forms study **link courses** leading to the National Certificate at local Colleges of Further Education.

National Council for Vocational Qualifications (NCVQ)

A body set up in 1986 charged with creating a consistent national framework for work-related **qualifications**.

(See also **National Vocational Qualifications (NVQs)**.)

National Curriculum

The National Curriculum sets out what must be taught to children between the ages of 5 and 16 in all state schools in England and Wales. It does not apply to **independent schools**, or **City Technology Colleges (CTCs)**. Schools in Scotland and Northern Ireland have their own versions of the National Curriculum. (See **UK education systems**.)

The National Curriculum was introduced in 1988 as part of a programme of reforms designed to raise overall educational standards. It will not be fully operational until 1995.

What is it and How does it Work?

The National Curriculum specifies 10 subjects which must be studied and sets out what children must learn in each one. Originally it was designed for all children in state schools between the ages of 5 and 16 but recent developments mean it has all but been abandoned for 14–16-year-olds.

These 10 subjects are:

English;	**design and technology;**
mathematics;	**music;**

science;   art;

history;   physical education (PE);

geography

A modern foreign language—for example, French or German. (See **modern languages**.)

In addition to these 10 subjects all pupils must study **religious education (RE)**.

Some subjects are considered more important than others, particularly English, mathematics and science. These are called the core subjects. They must be studied by all children to **GCSE** level. The other seven subjects are called foundation subjects.

Dividing the subjects into two groups like this is a little misleading. Just as there are differences between core and foundation subjects there are differences within the foundation group itself. For example, technology and modern languages have a higher status than art or PE. See below for more details about how these subjects might work in your child's school.

National Curriculum Jargon

Many parents are confused by the **jargon** associated with the National Curriculum. The following are the main terms that you are likely to come across as your children progress through the system.

Key Stages

The end of each Key Stage marks the point at which your children will be formally assessed:

Key Stage one: ages 5–7

Key Stage two: ages 7–11

Key Stage three: ages 11–14

Key Stage four: ages 14–16.

Attainment Targets

The content of each of the 10 National Curriculum subjects is broken down into a set of Attainment Targets. They are simply statements of what children are expected to know or be able to do at each Key Stage.

Levels of Attainment

Each Attainment Target is further divided into 10 levels. Each level becomes progressively more demanding. At the age of seven most children are expected to have reached level two; the brightest children will have reached level 10 by the age of 16. For example, Attainment Target five in maths deals with number. Children performing at level two should be able to distinguish between odd and even numbers. At level 10 of the same Attainment Target things get a little more tricky. Here they might have to be able to solve equations like this:

$$x_{n+1} = \frac{((a/x_n) + x_n)}{2}$$

In theory, a child of any age can perform at any level. A child with difficulties in say, maths or English, may never achieve more than level three or four. Exceptionally able children might be working towards level eight by the time they are 11. In the mid-1990s it is proposed that these levels will replace the familiar GCSE grading system.

Standard Assessment Tasks (SATS)

These are the set tasks used by teachers for formal assessment at the end of each Key Stage. (See **SATS**.)

Profile Components

SATS results have to be reported to parents. There are too many results to be reported individually so to simplify the process they are bundled together in groups known as Profile Components.

The National Curriculum in the Classroom

In many schools the working day is not divided into sections which correspond with the subject divisions of the National Curriculum. Some parents find this confusing. In **primary schools**, for example, pupils might spend a good deal of time doing project work. This does not mean the National Curriculum has been abandoned. It is quite possible—even desirable—to cover the Attainment Targets for different National Curriculum subjects in one exercise. A project on the Romans might cover part of the history curriculum, the science curriculum (looking at the materials which have survived from the period), and the maths curriculum (measuring the length of a Roman road on a map). (See **teaching methods**.)

At secondary levels—where most children work to a fixed timetable—the subjects might have different names. Geography, history and some aspects of English might be taught under the name humanities. Art and music might be called the performing arts. Many familiar subjects might disappear from the timetable altogether. These might include computing ing, **health education**, business studies, home economics, and and media studies. Under the National Curriculum these are expected to crop up as themes within the 10 core and foundation subjects. (See cross-curricular themes below.)

Official figures suggest that 70–80 per cent of the whole timetable should be taken up by the National Curriculum. This leaves a fairly small proportion of the available time to tackle other subjects such as economics, theatre studies or a second foreign langauge. This can have the effect of reducing a pupil's choice of subjects for GCSE. (See **options**.)

Cross-curricular Themes

These are themes which cut across the subject boundaries of the National Curriculum. While they are not treated as subjects in their own right, these themes are seen as an important part of every pupil's education. They should be covered within the framework of the 10 core and foundation subjects.

Economic and Industrial Understanding

An introduction to the world of business and commerce. Ideally all pupils are expected to be given direct experience of industry through **work experience** by the time they are 16.

Careers Education and Guidance

Designed to help pupils assess their own weaknesses and strengths and make informed decisions about their future beyond school.

Health Education

A look at the way our quality of life can be improved through basic health care. It will cover such issues as nutrition, safety, the abuse of alcohol and drugs, and **sex education**. (See **health education**.)

Education for Citizenship

Designed to help pupils understand their place in a democratic society. It will focus on areas such as the law, the electoral process, leisure, community, and public services.

Environmental Education

Aimed at promoting a positive approach to the world around us, and recognizng the environmental consequences of economic decisions. (See **environmental education**.)

Testing and Assessment

The National Curriculum made testing and assessment compulsory for all children at 7, 11, and 14. These arrangements are commonly referred to as SATS which stands for Standard Assessment Tasks—not tests as most people assume.

The tasks are designed to find out what individual pupils have achieved in relation to the prescribed Attainment Targets for a particular age group. It is argued that in this way **standards** can be monitored across the whole country. The tasks are in two parts:

> Teacher assessment: this is the teacher's considered opinion of pupils' achievements during the course. Individual assessments have to be moderated—checked and compared against other schools in the area and measured against national standards.

> The Standard Assessment Tasks (SATS) taken at the end of each Key Stage.

Amid great controversy, the first SATS were carried out on 7-year-olds in English, mathematics and science in the summer term of 1991. For more on this, see **SATS**.

National Curriculum and Children with Special Needs

Under the terms of the 1988 Education Reform Act, **headteachers** are allowed to modify on a temporary basis, the National Curriculum for children with special educational needs. In some instances this may mean that children with a **statement** of special educational needs are excluded from all or part of the National Curriculum. (See **special needs**.)

The exact nature of these modifications or exclusions is left to individual headteachers to decide. For example, a child with special difficulty in reading or written work may receive extra help during modern languages lessons.

If your child has special educational needs and the school wishes to change the requirements of the National Curriculum in some way, it is essential that you discuss these with the headteacher and any other members of staff involved as soon as you know. By the same token, if, as the parent, you feel that the demands of individual subjects, or testing procedures are too much for your child, you should ask the head to help you work out a sensible alternative. Try to include your child in these discussions too, listen to his or her opinions of his or her strengths, weaknesses and areas of interest.

For further information, contact

The Advisory Centre for Education (ACE) Ltd
1b Aberdeen Studios, 22–24 Highbury Grove,
London N5 2EA

National Union of Students (NUS)

A national body made up of local students' unions. Individual unions are funded by the colleges, polytechnics and universities where they operate. The NUS is especially active in areas of student welfare and in the campaign for better grants.

For further information, contact

National Union of Students (NUS)
461 Holloway Road, London NJ 6LJ

National Vocational Qualifications (NVQs)

Qualifications endorsed and graded by the **National Council for Vocational Qualifications (NCVQ)**. NVQs provide a framework for standardizing the levels of a wide range of work-related courses.

NVQs are an attempt to bring order to a chaotic picture. At the moment vocational qualifications are awarded at various levels by a large number of different bodies. This makes it difficult to compare the level of a qualification gained in engineering with one in catering or occupational therapy. NVQs will get round this problem by providing a common framework that cuts across subject boundaries.

Each qualification will be graded level one, two, three or four—where level one corresponds to a basic-skills level, two to general competence, three to supervisory level and four to managerial level.

Eventually the system is to be extended to take in degrees and professional qualifications.

It is hoped that people will be able to transfer credits for their NVQs from one area to another as well as using them to gain access to further qualifications.

A unified national system of vocational qualifications is also an essential first step in bringing into line work-related qualifications throughout **Europe**.

NCVQ

(See also **Business and Technician Education Council (BTEC)**, **vocational education**.)

NCVQ

See **National Council for Vocational Qualifications**

news

A topic popular in **primary schools** where children are encouraged to record their daily experience beyond the classroom. Children might keep a news book where they regularly write down and illustrate their weekend activities. You could try this at home if your child seems keen. Keeping holiday diaries with lots of drawings and cartoons are fun to do and encourage children to share their experiences with others once school starts again.

The term 'news' is sometimes confusing to parents who associate it with social and political events in the wider world.

Northern Ireland

See **UK education systems**

nursery classes

A nursery class is a separate class for 3–5-year-olds which forms an integral part of a primary school.

(See also **pre-school provision**.)

nursery nurse

A nursery assistant who has qualified with the Nursery Nurses Examination Board (NNEB).

Nursery nurses are employed in day nurseries, and as assistants to qualified **teachers** in **nursery schools** and classes. Holders of the NNEB qualification are often employed privately as nannies.

(See also **pre-school provision**.)

nursery schools

Separate schools for 2–5-year-olds which employ trained **teachers** and assistants. Some **Local Education Authorities (LEAs)** provide free nursery education but they are under no obligation to do so, except where children have special educational needs. (See **special needs**.) There are rarely enough places to go round and most parents have to look towards private nurseries.

There is a huge variety of private nursery schools, some charge high fees and expect their children to wear **uniforms**, others charge a minimal fee and put the emphasis on **play**. Spend some time looking around before you make your decision and generally follow the advice in **choosing a school**. Bear in mind that high prices and an orderly appearance do not necessarily guarantee quality. (See **pre-school provision**.)

nursery teacher

A qualified teacher who has specialized during his or her training in the education of children between the ages of 3 and 5.

Nursery teachers are usually employed in **nursery schools** and classes. Many of them have also been trained to teach 5–7-year-olds, and may teach the youngest groups of children in primary and infant schools.

(See also **pre-school provision**.)

NUS

See **National Union of Students**

NVQs

See **National Vocational Qualifications**

O

occupational therapist

A specialist who is trained to help people overcome physical co-ordination difficulties—perhaps the result of disability or illness.

Occupational therapists are usually based in a hospital but they do make home visits where necessary. They do not usually work in schools, but the advice of an occupational therapist may be sought by **educational psychologists** as part of an assessment of **special needs**.

The input from an occupational therapist can be very useful for those children who have problems with hand–eye co-ordination (which may hinder **reading** and writing, etc), or those children who have spatial difficulties (working out how shapes fit together, etc). Referral to an occupational therapist, therefore, does not necessarily mean that your child has a serious disability: the problem may be only temporary and rectified through a series of structured exercises.

ombudsman

See **complaints**

Open College

The Open College offers correspondence courses in vocational subjects such as health care, **information technology (IT)**, accountancy, and retailing. It also offers a Training Consultancy Service for employers.

The Open College was originally formed to try to build on the success of the **Open University** using broadcast lessons supported by correspondence materials. Unfortunately, the 'Open College of the Air' failed to meet its enrolment targets. High costs have forced it to trim broadcast support and appeal to corporate bodies rather than individuals.

The Open College operates through regional offices in London,

Manchester, Glasgow and Belfast and a network of local centres.

For further information, contact
The Open College
101 Wigmore Street, London W1H 9AA

(See also **open learning**.)

Open College of the Arts

The Open College of the Arts offers home-based practical courses in subjects such as **art** and design, textiles, **music**, photography, and creative writing. It also offers an arts foundation course for primary school **teachers**.

Students on some courses have to attend a local centre for advice and guidance.

For more information, contact
The Open College of the Arts
Freepost, Barnsley, South Yorkshire S7O 6BR

open enrolment

The system under which parents can choose the school they want their child to attend rather than accept the one allocated to them by the **Local Education Authority (LEA)**.

(See also **choosing a school**.)

open evening

An evening where parents and **teachers** meet at school to discuss the progress of individual pupils and view some of the work that has been done during the year.

Most schools arrange open evenings at least once a year. Schools which are anxious to establish good home–school co-operation are also likely to hold meetings for the children of new school entrants before term starts.

Although they are useful for parents who cannot often get to the school, open evenings are not always the best times to discuss your child's progress in detail. It is not especially easy to express your concerns with a queue of other parents waiting at the door. If your child is having problems, it is better to make

How to help with science

All parents can help their children to enjoy science—even if they feel they know nothing whatever about the subject themselves. For young children there is little difference between science and magic; for them the world is still a new and amazing place. Building on this natural sense of curiosity and wonderment, and keeping it going as children become more sophisticated, is something parents are ideally placed to do.

Consider these four key points:

Science is not confined to the laboratory where technicians in white coats brew up concoctions in test tubes—it is everywhere and happens all the time.

Scientific investigation begins with looking closely at many of the things we take for granted in our daily lives: insects, the stars, soil, plants and animals.

Asking children (however old they are) open questions like 'What do you think will happen if . . .' or 'What do you think caused that?' is the touchstone of all science and something that parents can do quite naturally.

Do not be tempted to think that your daughters are less interested in science than your sons. This is not true and may damage their chances later on.

It is not necessary to spend a fortune on equipment—a cheap magnifying glass, and a collection of odds and ends is more than you need to get started.

Begin by collecting things: stones, shells, seeds, feathers, off-cuts of wood, shiny things, grasses, dead bugs, scraps of material, yogurt pots, cotton reels, string.

Use these to help your child to see that there are ways of sorting objects into groups so that we can find out more about them. Ask the sorts of questions that lead to other investigations: Which things are hard, soft, heavy, light? What happens if we put them in water? Do all the objects float? Are all the big things also heavy? Why do think it is this colour?

You can also use these odds and ends to help children to make things: bird-feeders, toy cars and moon buggies, simple machines with moving parts—anything that sparks the imagination and encourages careful observation and a degree of problem solving. Older children can be encouraged to make more complex toys like moving puppets or vehicles that steer for younger brothers or sisters.

While your children are still young, indulge them in lots of 'kitchen sink'-type activities. Ask questions like: How much water will this cup hold? Will the teapot hold more? Can you make a drink that can float/sink? How do we make bubbles? Make the inevitable mopping-up operation part of the activity: What mops up the mess best?

When you are out in the country with your children help them to become detectives. Look for clues as to who or what has been there before you: sheep wool on barbed-wire fences, foot prints and animal tracks. Look for owl pellets, flattened patches of grass, holes in fruit and leaves. Encourage questions and if you do not know the answers, do not be afraid to admit it—look it up together later on.

If you and your children are particularly keen, it may be worth investing in a book of experiments to try at home. There are several to choose from. Be wary of those which promise to get ahead with **SATS**.

Do not stop helping with science once your children reach secondary school. You may not know the difference between an electron and a neutron but you can encourage your teenager to get involved in real-life science activities, such as helping to fix things around the house, taking care of parts of the garden, and inventing their own games. These things all help support science lessons at school. (See **How to help with older children**.)

(For more on the general approach to take when helping your child at home, see also **How to help at home**.)

a separate appointment, when the teacher will have more time to talk to you. (See **home–school partnership**.)

open learning

A method of study in which tuition is provided through correspondence courses, sometimes supported (as in the case of the **Open University**) by **radio** and **television** broadcasts. It does not require regular attendance at school or college. Open learning sometimes involves limited face-to-face contact with tutors.

A wide range of subjects can be studied by this method from courses on garden design to **GCSE** to postgraduate degrees. The advantages of open learning's great flexibility have to be set against the lack of regular contact with fellow students and teaching staff.

If you are interested in open learning, your local **Further Education** college should be able to give you more information.

(See also **adult education, correspondence courses, Open College, Open College of the Arts**.)

Open University

The Open University was founded in 1969 to offer degree courses for students without formal **qualifications**. Seen as the university of the second chance, it allows students to study at home by correspondence course using lectures broadcast on **radio** and **television**.

Courses are organized into manageable units and there is no limit on the length of time taken to complete the whole course. Many courses completed in one programme of study can be transferred to count towards a qualification in another. Open University degrees have the same status as those offered by conventional universities.

The Open University has been an outstanding success story. Today it offers a whole range of shorter courses to supplement its degree programme in subjects as diverse as **art**, **music**, the environment, childcare, business, computing, **science**, and technology. There are also short development courses for professionals like **teachers** and social workers. The Open Business School provides a variety of courses for managers.

The majority of courses require no formal qualifications. For most programmes of study the only requirements are that you are over 18 and resident in Britain or a member state of the

European Community when you begin the course. Some courses are oversubscribed and have a waiting list.

For further information, contact

The Open University
Walton Hall, Milton Keynes MK7 6AA

(See also **adult education, Open College, open learning**.)

Opting-out

Most state schools have traditionally been financed and controlled by **Local Education Authorities (LEAs)** based at the Town or County Hall. Since 1988 it has been possible for schools to 'opt out' of this arrangement, bypassing the LEAs entirely and receiving their **funding** directly from central government. Schools which have opted out are called **grant-maintained schools** (self-governing schools in Scotland).

Parents play a central role in the decision to opt out. If you are asked to vote on the issue, it is important to be clear what your school hopes to gain from the change. The issues here are not straightforward. Whether or not Opting-out is a desirable option depends very much on local circumstances and—often—your own political preferences. If you do not approve of the LEA and their policies (and you have complete confidence in your school management team), then freedom from outside control will seem a good thing. On the other hand, if you feel the LEA is doing a good job and providing a valuable service, the picture will look very different. Before you make a final decision, below are the most common reasons schools make the choice and some points to bear in mind.

To Improve the Financial Position of Schools

The situation here is complicated. First, there are short-term financial benefits to consider. When a school opts out it receives a grant to cover the administrative costs of transition. It can also apply for a capital grant to improve facilities. The government is anxious to support the grant-maintained sector and has been generous with these grants.

Beyond this, grant-maintained schools have access to a larger budget than they would have got from the LEA. This is because the LEA holds back some of the money allocated to its schools in order to provide things like educational welfare and advisory services. By opting out, schools can get their hands on this portion of the budget. Unlike the establishing grants, this money would be available every year. However, the school will still need specialist services such as **educational psychologists**, **advisers**, library services and transport and might have to use their extra money to buy them back in—probably from the LEA. In the long run, this might severely limit the financial advantages of Opting-out.

To Escape LEA Policies with which Schools do not Agree

Some schools have taken this route in order to preserve their status—for example, **grammar schools** under pressure from the LEA to become comprehensives. Others may welcome the opportunity grant-maintained status allows them to change the nature of their school, perhaps by introducing **selection**. Your opinion on this issue will largely depend on your feelings about selective education, though it is important not to overlook the implications for other schools in the area (see below).

To Forestall Closure

Some schools—particularly small schools—have applied for grant-maintained status when they have been threatened with closure by the LEA. This has the effect of putting the closure notice on ice until the application has been considered. As a delaying tactic it has some effect—but it is not a foolproof way of saving a school. (See **village schools**.)

In addition, the greater freedom offered to grant-maintained schools must be set against the following:

Some LEAs have closed ranks against schools which have opted out. This can lead to LEAs charging high prices for professional services, and refusing to allow pupils of opted-out schools to use facilities—such as outward-bound or holiday centres—available to local authority schools.

Grant-maintained schools—like **independent schools**—can employ teachers without formal teaching qualifications.

Procedures for monitoring **standards** are at the moment unclear. With the changing role of **HMIs** it seems likely that grant-maintained schools will have to buy in inspection and monitoring services.

Schools opting out can have an adverse effect on other schools in the area by throwing into confusion plans to produce co-ordinated local provision. At best this can make life difficult for the LEAs; at worst there are fears it might lead to the creation of **sink** and **magnet schools**—a development that favours some pupils at the expense of others.

How Schools can Opt Out

It is the **Secretary of State for Education** who decides if a school can opt out, but this cannot be done unless a majority of parents have voted in favour. The decision is made by secret ballot which can be called in two ways:

The school **governors** can vote to call a ballot. If they decide to go ahead, there must be a second vote to confirm this. The second vote must take place between a month and six weeks after the first (that is, not before 28 days and not after 42 days).

Parents can call for the ballot. So long as parents of 20 per cent of the pupils sign a written demand for a ballot, the governors must agree.

Once the ballot has been called, all that is needed for the application to go ahead is a simple majority. (If less than half the parents vote, there must be a second ballot within 14 days. However small the turn-out second time around, the majority decision counts.) It is important to note that this vital decision on the long-term future of the school can therefore be taken by a small minority of parents—most of whom will have no contact with the school once their child has left.

If parents vote to go ahead, the school governors have six months to put detailed proposals to the Secretary of State. These will then be considered—along with any objections that have been raised—and a final decision taken.

(See also **funding**.)

options

At the end of the third year of secondary school your children have to make a series of choices about the subjects to be studied over the next two years. These choices are usually referred to as options. Some or all of the subjects chosen may be taken for **GCSE**.

All children, regardless of ability, are expected to take GCSEs in the three core subjects of the **National Curriculum**. These subjects are: **English, mathematics** and **science**. All children are also expected to study the other so-called foundation subjects, for a 'reasonable amount of time'. Pupils who are more academically inclined will sit a range of these foundation subjects at GCSE level. There may be some modification to the requirements of the National Curriculum for children with **special needs**.

Although it might seem very early to be making decisions about the future, the options children take at 14 will have a serious impact on the rest of their career, both at school and eventually at work. Try to encourage your children to keep as many options open as possible at this stage, without making them feel unduly pressurized. It is wise to keep a balance between arts and science subjects. Find out about the new vocational courses which are slowly being introduced in some schools. (See **Business and Technician Education Council (BTEC)**.)

If you have daughters, you will need to make sure that they are not being pushed towards the arts subjects simply because of their gender. There is still a tendency to see science, technology and mathematics as subjects for boys, while girls gravitate towards arts subjects such as English or **history**. These stereotypes seriously undermine the chances of many able pupils. (See **hidden curriculum, sexism, single-sex schools**.)

The school should inform you when it is time to chose options. Talk to the **teachers** about your children's abilities in the various subjects on offer, and how you can help at home. Ask about the sort of **careers advice** offered by the school. Include your children in these discussions and help them to see the connections between the options that they take now and any plans they may have for the future.

For further information, contact

The Equal Opportunities Commission
Overseas House, Quay Street, Manchester M3 3HN

(Ask for their free leaflet called 'Get Your Future Right Now'.)

For guidance on making decisions as your child comes to the end of compulsory schooling, see **beyond 16**.

Oxbridge

A popular term for the universities of Oxford and Cambridge.

P

paired reading

See **How to help with reading**

parental guilt

Feelings of guilt about the upbringing of their children are widespread among adults.

Parents of shy children worry they have been over-protective; working parents worry they are not giving enough time to their children; parents of children with learning difficulties wonder if they are somehow to blame; parents are concerned they are doing less for their children than their neighbours and friends.

These feelings are natural but they need to be put into perspective.

Every family has a different style of parenting. Comparisons are nearly always misleading. There is no foolproof recipe that will produce the perfect, well-adjusted, academically able child. So long as your children are loved, listened to, and allowed space to grow in a caring atmosphere, you will be giving them the start they need.

Parents who want to do something practical about their feelings on the educational front can start by looking at ways of contributing to the **home–school partnership**. Beyond this, the best answer of all is finding ways to put in more **quality time** with your children—periods when all other issues are set on one side leaving you free to concentrate on working together. Provided this time is there, children will be ready to accept a lot of other things—such as the fact that parents have lives too.

Parent's Charter

In 1991 the Conservative government published its *Parent's Charter* as part of a wider move designed to make public services and institutions more accountable to ordinary people.

Under the *Parent's Charter* schools are required to provide certain information to parents to help them choose and evaluate individual institutions.

Schools will have to buy in inspection services at four-yearly intervals and make the results available to parents. They will also have to publish test and exam results and make public their **truancy** rates. It will be up the **Local Education Authorities (LEAs)** to make sure that comparative tables based on this information are available to parents in each locality.

At the same time as the government published its *Parent's Charter*, it announced a major shake-up of the **Her Majesty's Inspectorate (HMI)**. The effect of this will be to privatize the service and reduce the number of inspectors by more than half. How this will help them to undertake the increased numbers of inspections remains unclear.

While greater openness has benefits for parents, there are dangers that these moves will give exaggerated importance to exam league tables. Exam results are not the only measure of educational success to consider when **choosing a school**. More important for many children is the school's commitment to a fully rounded education and provision for pupils with **special needs**.

(See also **holism, SATS**.)

Parent–Teacher Association (PTA)

An organization which brings parents and **teachers** together for social, educational and fund-raising activities.

These fund-raising activities are increasingly important as schools feel the financial pinch. Without the efforts of parents to raise funds fewer children would have access to **computers**, for example.

(See also **home–school partnership**.)

part-time education

Part-time education is increasingly common in **Colleges of Further and Higher Education**. These courses cover a wide range of academic and work-related subjects. The great flexibility they offer allows many people to gain or improve **qualifications**—even degrees—while juggling other commitments such as work or families.

If you are interested in part-time courses, try contacting the College of Further Education in your area.

(See also **Further Education (FE), mature students.**)

pastoral care

Arrangements made by a school or college to look after the welfare of its pupils.

In **primary schools**, pastoral care is usually the responsibility of the class teacher—often the only adult, beyond parents, with whom the child has regular contact. This relationship is a valuable one. **Teachers** are usually very quick to pick up signs of a child in difficulties.

With the transfer to secondary school the issue becomes more complicated. Here pupils are faced for the first time with a series of specialist teachers rather than one class teacher. This might mean dividing their time between 10 or more members of staff. Under these conditions it is important that pupils and parents alike are clear who holds the responsibility for keeping an eye on the welfare of individuals. This will usually be the form tutor or year head.

These people have the task of helping children deal with the initial shock of moving from the intimate surroundings of a primary school to the often intimidating world of the average secondary school. Beyond this they are responsible for the emotional, academic and social well-being of pupils throughout their school career. They should be the first point of call for concerned parents. Parents should also keep them informed of any circumstances—such as bereavement or marital break-up—likely to affect their child's performance at school.

Very few schools can now afford to employ a full-time counsellor—though most will have allocated special responsibility for pastoral care to a senior member of staff. Parents should be sure to ask about provision when **choosing a school**.

(See also **post-trauma stress syndrome, separation and divorce, Sex 'n' Drugs 'n' Rock 'n' Roll.**)

PCAS

See **Polytechnics Central Admissions System**

PE

See **physical education**

peripatetic support at home

Help provided at home by visiting **teachers** for children who have been incapacitated either as a result of accident or disability.

Peripatetic teachers are employed by **Local Education Authorities (LEAs)**. Limitations on educational spending have resulted in reductions in their numbers in many areas. It may not be easy to get peripatetic support at home but it is worth fighting for. It may be possible to persuade the LEA to pay for the help of someone you have found yourself, as long as that person is suitably qualified. It may also help if you get your doctor or consultant to write a letter on your behalf to the **Chief Education Officer (CEO)** in your area requesting help at home.

For further information, contact

The Education Department at County or City Hall (listed in *Yellow Pages*)

Advisory Centre for Education (ACE) Ltd
1b Aberdeen Studios, 22–24 Highbury Grove,
London N5 2EA

peripatetic teachers

Teachers employed by **Local Education Authorities (LEAs)** to travel from school to school giving lessons in specialist subjects such as **music**.

Some LEAs provide peripatetic teachers for children with learning or behavioural difficulties (see **special needs**), where a school is too small to employ a special needs teacher of its own.

Severe limitations of educational spending, and the increasingly uncertain role of LEAs, have resulted in reductions in the number of peripatetic teachers across the country.

phonics

See **reading**

physical education (PE)

Physical education (PE) is one of the seven foundation subjects of the **National Curriculum** to be followed by all pupils between the ages of 5 and 16. PE is designed to promote fitness, physical self-confidence, an awareness of the benefits of healthy exercise and co-operation with others as part of a team.

The inclusion of PE in the National Curriculum has not been enough to stop the subject from dwindling on the timetable. In fact many schools blame the work-load caused by the arrival of the National Curriculum and the new **GCSE** exams for its decline. PE has a low status among other subjects and it is claimed that as a result many PE teachers are being used to support other subjects at the expense of their own.

Team games, such as netball, hockey and cricket are suffering the same decline in state schools as other aspects of sport and physical education. In some parts of the country, schools still keen to promote team games find it increasingly difficult to find leagues for their teams to compete against.

The cash squeeze felt by most schools under **LMS**—which makes schools responsible for balancing their own budgets— is partly to blame. In some schools sports fields and **playgrounds** are being sold off and groundsmen made redundant. Hard-pressed and demoralized teaching staff, reeling under the impact of introducing GCSE and the National Curriculum, may also be less willing to give up evenings and weekends. On crowded timetables, traditional team games are under pressure from activities such as dance and aerobics.

Swimming as part of the timetable is also under threat although it is well known that one in five children cannot swim.

Within the foreseeable future it is entirely possible that some pupils in **secondary schools** will do no PE at all—it is no longer to be compulsory at key stage four (14–16). This is a cause for concern at a time when research suggests there is a decline in the general level of fitness amongst school children. As a result parents may have to find other ways outside school to ensure that their children have adequate physical education: enrolling them into swimming and sports clubs perhaps or simply by going for cycle rides and long walks. If you feel that your child's school does not offer enough in the way of physical education, talk to the headteacher and your parent governor if necessary, and offer to help if you can.

(See also **after-school activities, football**.)

picture books

These are **books** for young children which have few, if any, words, where the story is conveyed through the pictures.

Surprisingly, sharing picture books with young children is an excellent introduction to the **reading** skills needed later on. Encourage your child to talk about the pictures, and offer suggestions about what the story is all about. Let older, more competent readers browse through picture books too: there is no such thing as a book that is too easy.

Helping your children to make their own picture books is also an excellent way of establishing the reading and book habit. Having picture books amongst your child's playthings need not cost a fortune. You can borrow them from the library, or pick them up second hand at jumble sales.

(See also **How to help with reading.**)

play

Play is a very important learning tool. It is through exploring, experimenting and fantasy that children learn to make sense of the world.

Before a child starts school, there is no natural separation between work and play—digging in the sand pit or building a den is a serious business for a 3-year-old. Yet when young children start full-time school they are suddenly expected to work all day and play when they get home. These artificial distinctions do not really help at this stage. Young children learn most when they are excited by an idea and can get involved themselves. Sharing in your child's play; suggesting ways to develop ideas; asking questions like, 'What do you think might happen next?', is the best way of supporting his or her learning.

Many of the activities in today's infant school classrooms may not look educational to parents brought up on rote learning and passive acceptance of facts, but be reassured—children at play are also learning. When your $5\frac{1}{2}$-year-old comes home and tells you that big school is easy because you do not have to do much work, do not be unduly alarmed. Playing at restaurants in the home corner, for example, introduces young children to many of the concepts developed later in say **mathematicss**, **science**, or language. (See **teaching methods.**)

Facilitating play activities is also a useful way for teachers to observe individual pupils. They may pick up on potential language, developmental or social problems, for example.

(See also **home–school partnership, How to help with the under-fives.**)

playgrounds

Areas of tarmac where generations of school children have attempted to relax between lessons.

The word playground is not a very accurate description in many schools. For the most part children spend their playtimes in flat, featureless areas; braving the elements, dodging footballs and attempting to stay out of the way of older, rougher children. Far from being the best antidote to a morning spent under the tight control of adults, children often find playgrounds intimidating and dangerous places. Most incidents of **bullying** occur in the playground.

Supervising large groups of children all charging around in different directions is a major headache for **teachers**. Minor accidents and torn clothing are commonplace. In calmer playgrounds children often complain that there is nothing to do—playtime becomes an endurance test rather than a form of relaxation.

With some thought and co-operation school playgrounds can be transformed into controlled yet stimulating places for children to be. Many schools, particularly in the primary sector, have enlisted the help of children and parents to paint games on the tarmac, build structures to climb on and hide in, set aside conservation areas and designated areas for ball games. Children who are involved in the planning and design of playground activities are also practising many of the skills outlined in the **National Curriculum**.

Some children, especially as they progress through secondary school, hate going outside to play—and who can blame them when it is minus two and blowing a gale? A few schools acknowledge this and provide facilities for children to do something quiet indoors, although supervision is difficult.

Talk to your child about playtimes and have a look yourself. A glance over the playground fence at lunch times can be a very enlightening experience for parents. If you think you could help to improve play areas, or have ideas about indoor playtimes, talk to the headteacher, the **Parent–Teacher Association** and your parent governor. Offer to help, you will learn a lot too.

How to help with art and music

Art and **music** are under pressure in the modern curriculum, squeezed out by the more urgent demands of the industrial and commercial world. If you value the contribution the expressive arts make to the all-round education of your child, you might find you have to take steps to compensate for this at home.

Encouraging your child in these areas is not the same as pushing them through graded hoops, or trying to give them a head start on a concert career. The intrinsic value of art and music as a means of self-expression and creativity have long been recognized. Beyond this, when you help your child at home, you are also helping to develop other essential skills: physical co-ordination, the ability to listen and observe closely, self-discipline and co-operation. It is extremely important to be sensitive in your responses. Find something positive to say about a model, a picture or a song. Make a point of displaying their masterpieces and listening to their songs and compositions. This does not mean you are encouraging children to be uncritical. Get them to talk about what they have done. Ask them if they are happy with it.

Art

You can help your child with art in the following ways:
It is not necessary to spend a fortune on expensive equipment. Make use of the backs of computer print-outs for drawing and painting, use old rolls of wallpaper, scrapbooks, old Christmas and birthday cards. Try to have a variety of drawing and painting tools. These need not be the best squirrel-hair paint brushes—use sponges, cotton buds, sticks, hands, fingers, feathers, wax crayons, etc. Not all children (or their parents) enjoy messy activities. Do not push it, there are plenty of cleaner activities to try.

Talk about the different effects produced by various materials. What happens if we soak the paper first? What happens to the colours? Talk about different textures. What happens if you put your paper on, for example, concrete or tree bark and then draw?

Do not worry too much about accurate copying. Use the opportunity to encourage your children to show how they feel about a story or a piece of music. Encourage the have-a-go technique, if you are painting, encourage them to do without a careful pencil outline first.

Use different shapes of pasta, rice, pebbles, scraps of material to make jewellery or collage pictures. They can be painted, threaded on strings, etc.

Older children often go through phases of very stylized art work—minute attention to detail, frustration if it does not work perfectly first time. Try to encourage then to keep experimenting with different techniques and to express themselves. Have a go yourself.

Music

You can help your child with music in the following ways:

Encourage an awareness of sound from an early age. Talk about everyday sounds: birdsong, the clatter of feet on pavements, music on the **radio, television**, in shops. If you have a cheap tape recorder help your children to record these sounds and experiment with others: the scrunching up of paper, a stick dragged along railings, a whistling kettle. Try building up these sounds into stories. Use them for special effects in space adventures or ghost stories.

Make a variety of simple musical instruments: bottles containing different amounts of water, yoghurt-pot shakers with beans or pebbles, biscuit tins to bang, cardboard tubes, comb, sandpaper on wood, and so on. Again, these can be built into stories or mini dramas to perform to friends or other members of the family.

As your children get older, try not to dismiss the music they listen too as rubbish because you do not happen to like it. Encourage them to have a go themselves: writing and recording raps, composing lyrics . . .

If your children show an interest in learning to play a musical instrument, look around for a teacher who is sympathetic to the ideas outlined above. Do not pressurize your children into performing or taking graded tests if they do not want to—this is likely to put them off altogether.

playgroups

Playgroups provide basic care and an opportunity for young children to socialize with other children before compulsory schooling begins at 5.

Playgroups are run mainly by volunteers (although some receive a very small wage) and usually operate out of rented accommodation—the Town Hall or Scout hut or surplus classrooms. A small fee is charged to cover running costs.

The playgroup movement grew in the 1960s out of the acute shortage of nursery school places, and has been the spearhead of **pre-school provision** in Britain. In 1991 there were 17 000 playgroups catering for some 600 000 children. The movement seems set to increase its standing and assistants are likely to qualify for **National Vocational Qualifications (NVQs)**.

playing fields

School playing fields are a valuable resource. Rising land costs and shortage of money have led some schools and local authorities to consider selling off part or all of their playing fields to raise much-needed funds. While this might have some short-term financial benefit, it has to be set against the permanent loss of an important facility. Once playing fields have been built on, they cannot be re-acquired once the financial climate improves.

(See also **funding**.)

play schemes

Play schemes operate in some areas of the country to cater for children during school holidays. Some schemes are financed and run by **Local Education Authorities (LEAs)**, using their own staff, others are run by voluntary organizations. Most play schemes are held in school **buildings**, often in inner-city areas.

For information on play schemes in your area, contact either your local library or the education department of your local Town or County Hall.

police

A late amendment to the 1986 Education Act resulted in the bizarre requirement that police chiefs are now required to be consulted on the curriculum in schools. How this consultation between police and governors will work in practice is unclear.

Direct contact between the police and the classroom is maintained through the schools' liaison officer, a police officer with special responsibility for schools.

More significant than the familiar advice on road safety and crime prevention is the opportunity this contact provides—particularly in the inner cities—to defuse the sometimes difficult relationship between police and young people.

Unfortunately, recent research suggests that the effectiveness of this public-relations exercise is sometimes limited. Older pupils readily draw a distinction between the schools liason officer (who they see as harmless and friendly) and the rest of the force (who appear to have a rather different image).

polytechnics

See **Higher Education (HE)**

Polytechnics Central Admissions System (PCAS)

The system which governs entry to degree courses in polytechnics.

Pupils apply for polytechnic places through PCAS during the final year of their **A-level** courses. Those who get the required grades have their positions immediately confirmed. Students who narrowly miss out with their final exams should contact the admissions office at the polytechnic to see if their grades are acceptable. If a place is not confirmed, students can contact other polytechnics direct as well as registering with the PCAS clearing system—a system which tries to match up students with untaken places.

The **University Central Council for Admissions (UCCA)** performs a similar function for universities.

For further information, contact

Polytechnics Central Admissions System (PCAS)
PO Box 67, Cheltenham, Gloucs GL5O 3AP

(See also **Higher Education (HE)**.)

Portage scheme

A scheme designed to help children of pre-school age who are having learning or developmental difficulties. Under the

Portage scheme parents and **teachers** work together to support the child in the home.

Schemes vary slightly from place to place, but generally a teacher will visit children and their parents on a regular basis—usually once a week. A carefully structured programme of learning tasks is worked out and explained to the parents. The programme is broken down into small, manageable sections and tailored to meet individual needs. Parents are given instructions on how to teach individual sections. They are also reassured that they do not need to be educational experts to help their children with the tasks set—moral support is very much a part of the process.

The Portage scheme, developed originally in Portage, Wisconsin, came into Britain in 1978. It is an excellent example of the value of active co-operation between home and school. Unfortunately not all **LEAs** operate the Portage scheme, but if you have a child who has been diagnosed as having **special needs**, you are entitled to some support at home. For further information contact your Local Education Authority first.

For further information, contact
The Advisory Centre for Education (ACE) Ltd
1b Aberdeen Studios, 22–24 Highbury Grove,
London N5 2EA

(See also **home–school partnership**.)

postgraduate studies

A course at a university taken after students have passed their first degree. Some of these courses may be taught, others may require original research by the students.

(See also **Higher Education (HE)**.)

post-trauma stress syndrome

Stress carried by a person following a traumatic experience, such as a road accident, bereavement, or major disaster.

Until recently it has been the accepted wisdom that children involved in traumatic events recovered quickly. They were seen as more resilient than adults and less likely to suffer permanent psychological damage. This may not be the case.

The small amount of research done in this area suggests that many children do not like to worry **teachers** or parents with their concerns. These adults in their turn assume nothing is wrong. As a result children are denied the vital post-trauma counselling which might be their best chance of coming to terms with their experience.

For additional support, contact

The Disaster Staff Network
Roselyn House, 93 Old Newtown Road, Newbury, Berks RG14 7DE

(See also **pastoral care**.)

pre-preparatory schools

Independent schools which prepare children aged between 5 and 8 for entry to preparatory schools. Some pre-prep schools are single-sex institutions others accept both boys and girls. Emphasis is usually placed on academic excellence in a highly competitive system. Fees vary.

pre-school provision

A general term used to describe a range of options available to children under 5.

Some services are funded by the state and administered through **Local Education Authorities (LEAs)** but the vast majority are privately run, either on a voluntary basis or as commercial concerns. Not all of the services available to the under-fives have an educational aim. Some are there to provide basic care.

There is no obligation on LEAs to provide pre-school education except for those children identified as having **special needs**.

A report on Britain's pre-school provision, conducted under the auspices of the European Commission in 1990, showed that, with the possible exception of the Netherlands, Britain is the worst pre-school provider in Europe.

Although politicians have consistently committed themselves to the idea of increased nursery provision, there has never been a central body to actualize it, nor the money to provide it. Recommendations in the 1944 Education Act, the cornerstone of the British education system, that LEAs should provide nursery education for children between the ages of 3 and 5, were never taken seriously. Margaret Thatcher announced in

1981 that free nursery places would be available to all by the end of the decade. This has been quietly forgotten.

Responsibility and funding for pre-school provision are shared between the **Department of Education and Science (DES)** and the Department of Health. Moves towards a single administrative body were quashed in 1991, despite recommendations from the government's own representatives.

The result of all this is that pre-school provision is patchy in the extreme. In some LEAs there is no state provision at all, whilst in others there are places for over 80 per cent of under-fives. There is a steadily widening gap between supply and demand as more women elect to re-enter the labour market after childbirth. This has increased the pressures on **primary schools** to take more pre-school age children into reception classes. (See **rising fives**.)

The backbone of pre-school provision has been provided by voluntary bodies and the private sector. Tax incentives, for private companies offering workplace nurseries and the parents who use them, are likely to mean that pre-school provision remains piecemeal for some time to come.

(To help you decide which of the various pre-school options to go for, see **childminders, crèche, day nurseries, How to help with the under-fives, mother and toddler groups, nursery classes, nursery schools, playgroups, working parents.**)

> *For further information, contact*
> The Advisory Centre for Education (ACE) Ltd
> 1b Aberdeen Studios, 22–24 Highbury Grove,
> London N5 2EA

preparatory schools

Independent schools which take children between the ages of 8 and 13. They prepare pupils for entry to private **secondary schools** through the **Common Entrance Examination**.

primary schools

Primary education covers children aged 5–11 years in England, Wales and Northern Ireland, and 5–12 years of age in Scotland. Primary education refers to:

infant schools (for children aged between 5 and 7);

junior schools (for children aged between 7 and 11);

combined junior and infant schools (sometimes called junior mixed infants JMI) (for children aged between 5 and 11).

Some areas in England operate a three-tier system of **first**, **middle** and **secondary schools**.

(See also **choosing a school**.)

prison education

Most prisons offer some educational facilities. Teaching staff are usually provided by local universities and Colleges of Further and Higher Education. (See **Further Education (FE)**, **Higher Education (HE)**.)

A wide range of academic and vocational courses can be studied in this way. New open-learning methods, where students can study by correspondence, have increased this range even further.

However, there are limitations. Most prisons do not provide ideal conditions for study. Overcrowding is a major problem, made worse by a shortage of supervisory staff. More significantly, educational provision is still seen as a soft option by some prison officers. These difficulties are particularly acute among the remand population where large numbers of young people between the ages of 14 and 20 are held with little or no educational provision.

(See also **open learning, young offenders**.)

private coaching

Tuition provided outside school on a fee-paying basis to supplement formal education.

In an increasingly competitive education system, private coaching is a growth area. Cost and quality vary enormously and parents need to be aware that anyone can set him- or herself up as a tutor, regardless of **qualifications**. Coaching starts early—sometimes with pre-school children.

Most tutoring is geared to particular exams: the **Common Entrance Examination**, **GCSE**, and **A-level**. Tutors claim to be able to make the difference between a borderline pass and a fail, or to improve grades by one or two places. Perhaps, surprisingly, this kind of help is not always to the pupil's advantage. Intensive coaching to pass an entrance exam, for example, might push children into an academic environment where they are out of their depth.

In cases where children have **special needs** which cannot be met satisfactorily at school, or where they have been deprived of schooling through illness, tutors can have an important role to play. Extra tuition that is simply geared to giving children a head start in the academic steeplechase is less easy to justify. School is a demanding experience for most young people— they need time away from formal study to be children again rather than pupils.

If you are tempted to hire a tutor for your child, talk to the school first. It is usually far better to deal with academic problems with your child's **teachers** than by buying in outside help. If you do decide coaching is the answer, contact a reputable agency and ask to see evidence of your tutor's qualifications.

(See also **peripatetic support at home.**)

private schools

See **independent schools**

probationary teachers

Teachers who have finished their college-based studies and are serving their first full year in the classroom. Probationary teachers are closely supervised and must complete the year satisfactorily to become qualified.

With the growing pressure on school budgets probationary teachers are sometimes sought after as a cheaper alternative to experienced staff. (See **funding.**)

Some parents worry that their children might suffer through having a probationary teacher. This is not necessarily the case. What many probationary teachers lack in experience they more than make up for in enthusiasm and new ideas.

Profile Components

See **National Curriculum**

profiles

See **records**

programmed learning

A method of self-study in which the course is closely structured and often allows pupils to correct their own mistakes and assess their progress.

(See also **correspondence courses, open learning.**)

project work

See **teaching methods**

prospectus

Every state school is required by law to produce a brochure or prospectus setting out basic information about the school. This can range from a few photocopied sheets stapled together by the school secretary to lavishly illustrated brochures containing samples of children's work, photographs of facilities, and profiles of teaching staff.

With increased competition among schools and the growth of **school marketing** brochures and prospectuses are assuming a greater significance. The best of them will tell you a good deal about the school and its philosophy. However, the prospectus can have more to do with the world of advertising than the world of education. Above all, when **choosing a school** do not allow a glossy brochure to become a substitute for a proper look round and a talk with the headteacher and staff.

PTA

See **Parent–Teacher Association**

public schools (England and Wales)

In England and Wales, another name for the more prestigious **independent schools**.

public schools (Scotland)

State schools in Scotland are known as public schools. While this is perfectly logical, it can be confusing for people in the rest of the Britain, where the term public school is used to refer to certain élite private schools.

punishment

Punishment in schools usually takes one of the following forms:

Detention: in which a pupil is kept behind after school. This is not popular with staff who have to supervise the activity. Parents will also have to be informed in good time in case they need to make alternative arrangements for transport, etc.

Extra work: to be carried out at home or in school. This has the merit of being a useful activity—unless of course it is merely writing out lines. But too much extra work can be counter-productive. If children see work as punishment, this will do little for their enthusiasm for the subject.

Loss of privileges: which might be free time, games periods, or playtime.

Exclusion from school either on a temporary or permanent basis. Exclusion is covered by complicated rules laid down in the 1986 Education Act, and supplemented by local rules drafted by **Local Education Authorities (LEAs)** and **governors**. In the case of permanent expulsion, pupils and parents have a right of appeal. (See **exclusion and suspension**.)

Physical punishment in the form of beatings has been illegal in state schools (though not **independent schools**) since 1987. (See **corporal punishment**.)

There is no real evidence to suggest punishment has by itself any lasting effect on improving behaviour. It is just as likely to reinforce the disaffection between pupils and school which led to difficulties in the first place. Most schools—and most **teachers**—recognize that giving pupils support and encouragement is generally more productive than a punitive regime.

If you find your child is being repeatedly punished, it is important to talk to him or her and to the school to find out why. If there is an underlying cause for a pupil's misbehaviour, it is important to tackle this quickly.

(See also **discipline, hidden curriculum**.)

pupil–teacher ratio

See **class sizes**

Q

qualifications

For qualifications see individual entries on: **A-level, A/S level, Baccalaureate, Business and Technician Education Council (BTEC), Certificate of Sixth Year Studies (CSYS), City and Guilds, eleven plus, General Certificate of Secondary Education (GCSE), Higher Grade, National Certificate, National Vocational Qualifications (NVQs), Scottish Vocational Education Council (SCOTVEC), Standard Grade**.

quality time

A period when parents and children are actively and creatively engaged in sharing time together.

It is quite possible to spend days in the company of your children without managing to fit in any quality time at all. The endless distractions of running life and home can easily squeeze out opportunities which allow you to respond at their pace to their concerns. Let them take the lead—the most important thing you can do is listen. Quality time is not time spent supervising your children, or in seeing they have something to occupy themselves—it is being with them and allowing them the luxury of your full attention.

The full involvement of parent and child in quality time makes it extremely valuable. It boosts **confidence**, makes the child feel valued, allows you to be fully in touch with what he or she is thinking and feeling, and creates an opportunity where the experience of learning can be shared.

If you manage to fit in some quality time each day, it will not matter that you are a working parent with a schedule that fully occupies you the rest of the time. It can make up for all sorts of other imperfections in your routine. Quality time is also the best possible antidote for **parental guilt**.

(See also **How to help at home**.)

R

racial discrimination

Unfavourable treatment on the grounds of a person's race, colour, nationality, or ethnic origins.

Under the terms of the 1976 Race Relations Act, schools and colleges must not discriminate directly or indirectly: on admissions; in applications; in access to any benefits, facilities or services; or by excluding them from the establishment. This applies to educational institutions in both the state and independent sectors.

Direct discrimination may take many forms in schools and colleges. It may vary from crude racist remarks, to subtle differences in **assessment**, expectation, provision and treatment. The fact that this kind of discrimination may be unconscious, or even well intentioned, does not prevent it from being illegal.

Indirect discrimination is a more complex and insidious concept. A requirement to wear a school cap as part of a school uniform might seem innocuous enough—but it would discriminate against Sikh boys, required by their religion to wear a turban.

In 1990 the government decided that the Race Relations Act could not be allowed to prevent parents from exercising their right to choose a school for their children. In other words, the parent's right to choose a school overrides race-relations legislation. In a market-led education system this is a potential source of difficulties for schools with high ethnic populations.

In some cases racial discrimination takes the form of racial violence or abuse. The incidence of such attacks is on the increase. Many take place in and around school. The seriousness of the problem should not be underestimated. (See **bullying**.)

If your child has been the victim of racial discrimination or abuse, you should take up the matter with his or her **teachers** and the headteacher. Schools should have a policy on dealing with such incidents. If yours does not, talk to your rep-

resentatives on the school **governors** and ask them to consider
drafting one.

For further information, contact

The Commission for Racial Equality
Elliot House, 10–12 Allington Street, London SW1E 5EH

(See also **multi-cultural education.**)

radio

Radio has played an important role in schools for many years
providing material for use in the classroom across the whole
age range. Even today facing competition from its more glam-
orous cousin, **television**, and at a time when broadcasting is
undergoing radical change, BBC radio retains a firm commitment to schools' programmes.

At home, the radio is a still largely untapped resource for many
children. Most are familiar with its music output, but there are
speech networks with a great deal to offer—particularly Radio 5,
which carries a range of magazine programmes, dramatiza-
tions, plays and readings all aimed at young listeners.

Parents who can persuade their children to turn off the television for a while and explore the radio output will be helping
them develop the listening skills which are an important part of
the **English** curriculum. Radio encourages children to exercise
their imagination in the same way that reading does. It does
not define the images of what the listener hears—it encourages
individuals to create their own. That is why there is a good deal
of truth in the often-repeated remark that radio's real advantage
over television is that the pictures are better.

RE

See **religious education**

reading

Reading is one of the first major landmarks in a child's educational development. It is one of the ways children learn to
make sense of the world. Reading is also an essential skill in
all areas of the curriculum.

This skill, like all others, takes time to develop, it does not
suddenly just happen. Like playing the piano, or learning to
drive a car, to be good at it you have to practise. Despite general

agreement on this, people still talk as if reading is something that all 6-year-olds should automatically be able to do for themselves. As adults it is easy to forget that the squiggles on the page are not self-evident to a child. Reading has for so long been part of our lives we can no longer remember a time when we could not do it.

Reading does not just happen in books, it is all around us—on road signs, in shops, on the ice-cream van. Good **teachers** use the language that is all around us to help teach children to read. Parents should do this too. At a time when headlines are full of scare stories about falling standards in **primary schools**, parents are understandably confused about what goes on in the classroom and how best to help. Much of this confusion is unnecessary.

Contrary to popular rumour there is no real disagreement in schools about the best way of teaching children to read. Very few teachers use only one method. Most schools use a combination of the following methods to teach reading skills.

Phonics

A system of decoding words through matching letters to sounds. Children are taught the sounds corresponding to the letters *S, T, O* and *P,* for example. Then as they become more proficient they are taught to blend these sounds together to construct whole words (*'s-t-o-p* says *stop'*). Increasingly complex blends of sounds are taught over time. The major problem here is that **English** is not a phonetically regular language—children have to remember that *C-O-U-G-H* says *cough*.

The Apprenticeship Approach

The apprenticeship approach is often referred to as the real book method. This is based on the theory that children learn to read in the same way they learn to talk—by reading alongside experienced readers. Teachers using this method encourage their pupils to use context and other clues, such as illustrations and rhymes,to work out the words and to make sense of the story. The **books** used may be graded according to their level of difficulty, but are not part of a fixed scheme.

Look and Say

In this method children learn to read by recognizing the shape of whole words. This works better for some words than others. For example, the word 'aeroplane' is easy to recognize, but words like 'than' and 'then' are easily confused; many of the most common words are of this second type.

During a typical day your child will be involved in a whole range of reading activities: labelling objects on the nature table, following written instructions, completing punctuation exercises, researching the leisure pursuits of the ancient Greeks and deciding what to have for lunch. Do not assume that because the teacher has not signed the reading record for three days, he or she is failing to teach the class to read. The best way of helping your child is to share in the adventure of learning to read. Introduce your child to books as part of the toybox— even babies enjoy dribbling on plastic **picture books**. Sharing a picture book with your 2-year-old introduces him or her to the pleasure and the mechanics of reading a book (turning the pages, holding the book the right way up, moving from left to right, etc). Once your child is at school, make sure you understand how the school organizes its reading programme and support your child at home. (See **home–school partnership**.)

Read to your children every day, even if it is only for a few minutes. Do not suddenly stop reading aloud once they know how to do it for themselves—it is easy to convey the impression that reading aloud is something only beginners do.

Adults often withdraw their support from the reading process once children reach secondary age. However, there is still a lot you can do to help improve reading skills at this stage. Instead of answering all their questions yourself, try encouraging them to look things up in reference books. Join a library and have a look at your own example: do your children see you reading? (For more on the sorts of things you can do at home, see **How to help with reading, reading age, reading difficulties, reading schemes, reading tests**.)

reading age

Reading ages are calculated from standardized reading tests. These usually compare a child's actual age with his or her reading ability.

A child of average ability (according to the standardized test) will have a reading age which roughly matches his or her actual age. A child with a reading age significantly lower than his or her chronological age is generally considered to need special

How to help with geography and history

Although the words **geography** and **history** might mean very little to young children, the concepts which lie at the heart of these subjects will come quite naturally to them. Do not worry if you know nothing about foreign mountain ranges or the dates of kings and queens. Both geography and history can be approached using your children as the starting point.

Geography can begin with maps and plans of the home. From here you can move outwards to take in your child's immediate surroundings: garden, neighbourhood, countryside, towns.

Your own children can also provide the starting point for an exploration of the past. Take your cue from questions like 'What was I like when I was small?' Use this as a stepping stone to questions about other members of the family, and what life was like when they were young.

Geography

You can help your child with geography in the following ways:

Make maps of your house, your street. Look at a map of the country. Show where Grandma lives, aunts and uncles.

Play games with memory maps. Ask your child to describe the route to school, to the shops, to a friend's house, remembering as many features as possible. Draw pictures.

Look at the contents of your shopping basket. Where does everything come from? Can you find it on a map? Why can't we grow bananas in the garden?

Compare man-made features of the landscape with natural ones. Which are which? Why aren't roads straight? What are houses made of? Is there a local material for walls, or roofs? Where is the nearest river? Ask them to think why it was sensible to build a village or town in a particular location.

Make a weather chart. Where does the rain come from? Where does the water go?

Older children will be interested in the social and political issues: links with environmental concerns; the work of Greenpeace, the Worldwide Fund for Nature; pollution, etc.

History

You can help your child with history in the following ways:

The concept of time is a difficult one for children to grasp. Try to encourage an awareness of change and the passage of time; trousers that no longer fit or a plant that grows, flowers and dies are useful starting points.

Look at family records—not just photographs but letters, diaries, certificates, pictures, furniture handed down through the family. Talk about the way appearances have changed—hair fashions, clothes, beards and moustaches.

Make a time line. Make one toy brick represent 10 years. Three bricks will take you back to when parents were young. Ten bricks to the turn of the century. A hundred bricks would take you back to before the Norman conquest. To find the last of the dinosaurs you would need a line of bricks over 40 miles long. You can do the same with knots in a piece of string: one knot for every year of your child's life. Talk about the sorts of things they were doing when they were only one 'knot' (ie year) old.

Make a family tree. Are there family names that recur? Are the Christian names still popular today?

Explore recollections of parents and grandparents. What was it like when you were young? (Be specific:) We didn't have Biros® or **calculators** . . . What was school, the classroom, your teacher like? What were the shops like?

Encourage them to speculate. What do you think we did before cars? Before electric light? Before glass? What would it be like living in a house without central heating/television/carpets?

Look out for everyday features that were once familiar but are now disappearing—boot-scrapers, for example. What are they? Why were they important in Victorian times? Why don't we have them now?

Keep this sense of investigation going as your children get older. Talk about news bulletins (for example, the impact of the Gulf War or the attempted coup in Russia); help them to see that history is made every day.

(See also **How to help with green children**.)

help. Very able readers may have a reading age which is several years ahead of their chronological age.

(See also **dyslexia, reading tests**.)

reading difficulties

A collective term applied to children who have problems learning to read—an estimated 20 per cent of the population.

(See also **dyslexia, reading, special needs**.)

reading schemes

These are graded reading books, through which children progress while they are learning to read.

The use of reading schemes in schools is a controversial issue. Parents generally like them because they find it easier to keep track of their children's progress. Most schools have a reading scheme but some stick more rigidly to it than others. Make sure you know how the school uses its reading scheme so that you can support your child at home.

Some Points to Bear in Mind

Books which do not contain genuine stories, but are simply exercises in reading practice are dull:

'Look, Ben, look.
Come, Ben, come.
Come and look, Ben.'

will be alien to your child and boring. Reading may become a chore rather than a pleasurable experience. If your school uses a scheme like this, you will have to work hard to provide your child with more stimulating reading material.

Although a very structured approach may suit some children, reading schemes tend to generate competition, not only amongst the children but in parents too sometimes. Success is defined in terms of getting on to the next level. Getting stuck on a low level creates feelings of failure.

(See also **reading, special needs**.)

reading tests

These are generally standarized tests which are used to work out a child's **reading age**.

Results can be misleading. It is dangerous to assume that a child who does not perform well on a reading test is of generally low ability—he or she may, for example, do better in a test where reading for meaning is given higher priority.

Equally, a child who has mastered reading without any apparent effort may be good at deciphering the words on a page but have little understanding of what they mean—this is sometimes called 'barking at print'.

Many reading tests were designed during the 1950s by psychologists to diagnose reading difficulties. The same tests with some slight modifications are still used in schools today. They often contain words which have been rendered obsolete by the age of technology (references to the milkman's horse, pantry, wireless) and pose particular difficulties for those children whose first language is not **English**.

The introduction of **SATS (Standard Assessment Tasks)** as a compulsory part of the **National Curriculum** may in time replace older tests.

(See also **reading**.)

real books

See **reading**

reception classes

Classes in primary school which receive pupils who have reached compulsory school age (5 in England and 6 in Scotland).

Children under compulsory school age—the so-called **rising fives**—are also admitted to reception classes in some education authorities.

Children may attend school for part of the day for the first term or so before starting full time. This gives them a chance to get used to the set-up in manageable doses.

(See also **choosing a school, pre-school provision**.)

record of achievement

See **reports and records**

religious education (RE)

In Britain religious education (RE) aims to introduce children to the beliefs, values and morals of a society which considers itself fundamentally Christian.

Religious education can be studied as a subject at both **GCSE** and **A-level**.

In accordance with the 1988 Education Reform Act the basic curriculum must include provision for religious education for all students—including Sixth Formers and those in **Sixth Form Colleges**. This must be broadly Christian in character, though the teachings and practices of other main religions in Britain can be taken into account.

In addition, all pupils in state schools, including **grant-maintained schools** (but not **nursery schools**, **CTCs**, or **independent schools**), must take part in a collective act of worship each day. (See **assembly**.)

While the act of worship should be wholly or mainly of a broadly Christian character, the **Standing Advisory Council on Religious Education (SACRE)** (to be set up by individual **Local Education Authorities (LEAs)**) has the power to override this requirement.

Parents have the right to remove their child both from the daily act of worship and religious education only if they object strongly on the grounds of conscience.

(See **Church and denominational schools**.)

remedial teaching

A rather old-fashioned term for teaching which is intended to support children with **special needs**.

The expression has spawned other terms you might hear. **Teachers** sometimes talk of remediation programmes, for example—by which they mean a programme of work designed to help overcome a child's difficulties. (See **jargon**.)

reports and records

By law all schools must provide parents with a yearly written report on their children's progress.

It is up to individual schools to work out the exact nature of these reports but they must include a comment on subjects tested as part of the **National Curriculum**. This may be no more than comments on **English, mathematics,** and **science** for the 5-year-old, but can cover up to 10 separate subjects for a 15-year-old.

Children are increasingly encouraged to record their own views on individual subjects covered during the year and how well they think they have done. Self-evaluation of this sort tells teachers a lot about their pupils' **confidence** and gives individual children a chance to see progress not so much as a competition with classmates as a question of improving their own performance.

Parents generally like to receive a written report at the end of a school year, even if the content is not what they were expecting. Those which attempt to offer far more than 'A satisfactory year's work' or 'Daisy should concentrate more' are clearly the most helpful. If there is anything you do not understand on the report and most of it seems to be written in a foreign language, go and talk to the **teachers**. Reports are never a satisfactory surrogate for face-to-face discussion. Do not be fobbed off with words you do not understand. (See **jargon**.)

A new kind of record, called 'The National Record of Achievement' (NRA), is available for everyone reaching the age of 16. This is a document which tells future employers or colleges what a person has achieved in education as well as listing any jobs held and achievements in other areas such as sport, hobbies or travel. Since the NRA is a national scheme, it should be useful everywhere in the country—a sort of travelling testimonial. Older people can use the NRA if they and their school, college or employer wish. It can also be updated regularly.

Since the **National Curriculum** puts increased emphasis on **assessment** and **testing** and the government is keen for parents to compare one school's results with another, there is the danger that reports will contain little more than the results of these tests.

(See also **choosing a school, home–school partnership**.)

resources

When **headteachers** talk about being short of resources they usually mean money. However, the term also covers a school's tangible assets—everything from pencils, **textbooks** and **computers** to **teachers** and **buildings**.

As a result of serious underfunding—made worse by recent

developments such as **LMS** (where schools are responsible for their own budgets) most schools are forced to operate with inadequate resources. Signs are visible everywhere: in the poor condition of many buildings, large classes, lack of textbooks and equipment, and in the poor provision for children with **special needs**.

(See also **funding**.)

rising fives

A popular term for children who are just below compulsory school age.

In some **Local Education Authorities (LEAs)** rising fives are admitted to the first class of an infant or first school. There is often no additional funding for them. **Village schools**, often threatened with closure, are under pressure to take more rising fives because there is an acute shortage of nursery places.

Infant school teachers do the best they can for very young children in their classes but are struggling with inadequate resources (large-scale play equipment, for example). If you are thinking of sending your child to school full time before compulsory school age, it is important to visit the school, talk to the **teachers** about the sort of provision they can offer and compare it with other childcare facilities in the area.

(See also **pre-school provision**.)

Royal Society of Arts (RSA)

An examining body offering work-related **qualifications**, particularly in the commercial field.

(See also **vocational education**.)

RSA

See **Royal Society of Arts**

S

SACRE

See **Standing Advisory Council on Religious Education**

sandwich courses

Sandwich courses combine a period of academic study at a college or university with time spent working in industry.

These technical and vocational courses are popular with employers who will sometimes provide financial support for students.

Details of suitable courses are available from colleges and universities.

(See also **vocational education**.)

SATS (Standard Assessment Tasks)

Standard Assessment Tasks (SATS) form one part of the complex procedure which is used to monitor children's progress as they work through the **National Curriculum**. Teacher **assessment** forms the other part.

Although the *T* in SA*TS* stands for *tasks*, it is commonly confused with the word test—a word people associate with passing or failing; but you cannot fail an assessment. It is merely a summary of the teacher's judgment on how well children are progressing. It also highlights areas of difficulty so that action can be taken to improve them. Unfortunately 'tests' have lodged in the popular mind and this is the word you are likely to meet.

From the outset, SATS caused more anxiety and controversy amongst **teachers** and parents than any other aspect of the National Curriculum.

Teachers were told that assessment must now form part of their work. Good teachers were insulted by this. Teachers worth their salt want to know that their class has understood the material they have been teaching all year. Beyond this, most schools make at least some attempt to liaise with the teacher taking over next year, paying particular attention to the strengths and weaknesses of individual children and also involve parents in the education process. SATS, teachers argued, would tell them nothing they did not already know.

Parents, encouraged by a good deal of media hype, began to worry about their children somehow failing SATS (even though this is not technically possible). Commercial interests lost no time in producing material for parents to help their children through SATS. They sold like hot cakes.

It became obvious that somewhere between the conception of SATS and their delivery into the classroom, things had gone badly wrong. Many felt that the huge sums of public money involved could more usefully have been spent on other priorities: more teachers and resources, provision for the under-fives and on school **buildings** in chronic need of repair.

Parental opposition to SATS was strongest in Scotland, where large numbers of parents made it impossible for schools to administer the tasks by keeping their children at home.

All the signs are that SATS will become much simpler in the future—they will probably be replaced by the famous pencil and paper tests. However, simplifying SATS will not solve all the problems, even though the tests will be much easier and cheaper to administer.

Suggestions for parents

Remember first of all that test results are not the only measure of a good school. Schools which put exaggerated emphasis on tests may be failing your children in other aspects of education. (See **holism**.)

You should be wary of using these results as the sole criterion for **choosing a school**, even though you may be encouraged to do so. (See **Parent's Charter**.) Talk to the school about its policy on SATS and ask to have all the technical terms explained to you. (See **jargon**.)

Do not attempt to cram your child for SATS, neither the school nor your children will thank you for it.

When the school sends home an end of year report full of SATS results, make sure there is an opportunity for you to discuss exactly what this means in terms of your child's educational needs. (See **reports and records, selection**.)

SCE

See **Scottish Certificate of Education**

scholarship

An award made by an educational institution to selected pupils to cover tuition fees. The award is usually decided through open competition.

Scholarships provide a limited means of access to fee-paying institutions—from **independent schools** to universities—for exceptionally able students who might otherwise not be able to attend.

(See also **bursary, grants and loans**.)

school boards

See **governors**

school closure

Local Education Authorities (LEAs) have to follow an agreed procedure before they can close a school. In principle this is quite straightforward and involves giving a period of notice and talking to the people most closely concerned. Before 1980 the **Secretary of State for Education** had to give his or her approval. Now he or she only has to give a ruling if the case is contested. (Or if the school involved is a voluntary school.) So if no one objects, LEAs can close a school as long as they have consulted parents, **teachers** and **governors** and given two months' notice.

It is not easy to save a small school threatened with closure. LEAs do not like them because it costs so much more to educate a child in a village school catering for just a few pupils—particularly when there are unfilled places in larger schools. (See **baby booms and bulges**.) Some LEAs are also claiming that small schools are less likely to be able to deliver the **National Curriculum**.

Parents who want to save a small school from closure have three main avenues open to them:

Make sure the closure is opposed. Organize local opposition. Make a vociferous and clearly argued objection to the LEA.

Band together with other local schools to provide a united

front to the LEA and demonstrate that sharing resources and expertise can overcome the limitations of size. (See **consortia**.)

Apply for grant-maintained status. (See **Opting-out**.)

Grant-maintained schools cannot be closed by LEAs.

None of these provides a foolproof answer to a notice of closure. Objections can still be overruled by the Secretary of State (though parent power has succeeded in saving small schools in the past). Consortia are not easy to set up and co-ordinate—particularly at short notice. Even then they do not address the problem of **funding**. In the case of small schools, opting out is unlikely to be effective in the long term, although an application for grant-maintained status will put a temporary stop on a closure notice while the matter is decided.

For further information, contact

Small Schools Network
University of Exeter, School of Education, St Lukes, Exeter, Devon EX1 2LU

National Association for the Support of Small Schools
Mrs Molly Stiles, The Cottage, Little Barrington, Norwich NR11 7LN

school councils

A body made up of **teachers** and pupil representatives—usually elected from each class- or year-group—designed to give pupils a voice in their own schooling.

School councils were very popular in the 1970s but their popularity seems to have faded. This is a pity—school councils can provide a valuable and much-needed channel of communication between pupils and staff. Today, where they survive, their activities are often limited to marginal issues, such as deciding where to put the soft-drinks machine, or what flavour crisps to sell at break. This actually suits most schools who can claim to support pupil-power without exposing themselves to its consequences.

(See also **children's rights**.)

school day

The length of the school day in state schools can be decided by the **governors**. The **Local Education Authority (LEA)** sets the school terms.

While there is no legal minimum school day, the government has offered the following guidelines:

Years	Hours
5–7	21
8–11	23.5
12–16	24

These hours are to include religious education but not the statutory act of worship.

This increased flexibility means that schools are free to adopt the so-called Continental day in which lessons start and finish earlier. Under this system, more time is available for **after-school activities**.

Some schools might also choose to lengthen the school day in order to cope with the demands of the **National Curriculum**—particularly for pupils in the Fourth and Fifth Years.

Before any changes can be made to the existing school day, parents have to be consulted, given the opportunity to voice their opinions, and allowed three months' notice. Changes can only be made at the beginning of term.

school marketing

A public relations exercise designed to sell the school to the parents of potential pupils.

School marketing—long a feature of private education—has now entered the state system. Developments such as increased parental choice, **open enrolment** and the arrival of **Local Management of Schools (LMS)** have all led to increased competition among schools for pupils and resources. The growth of school marketing is the inevitable response.

The chief marketing document is the brochure or **prospectus** which each school must produce by law. Other marketing initiatives range from selling T-shirts bearing the school's crest, and hiring out school facilities to private companies and fully-fledged partnerships with industry.

Many people are uneasy about these developments. Marketing is a concept drawn from the commercial sphere and is not always appropriate for the world of education. Clearly there is a need for schools to present themselves well so that parents can make informed choices about the services that are available. However, there is a danger that the marketing exercise becomes an end in itself—more concerned with style than substance. Money used in a market-led scramble for pupils and extra resources could be more usefully spent in the classroom where it is really needed.

Some schools and colleges are going to the lengths of appointing full-time fund-raisers and marketing teams. The money they generate will be welcome for **headteachers** trying to balance the books, but with this development comes the added danger that fund-raising becomes an acceptable substitute for proper government **funding**.

(See also **education and the market place**.)

school meals

Local Education Authorities (LEAs) are legally obliged to provide free school meals for children of low-income families; they can offer meals to other children if they wish. This can be a considerable drain on resources in areas of high unemployment. However, there is no longer any legal requirement to provide meals which are suitable as the main meal of the day: some authorities only provide sandwiches.

Before 1980 all schools were obliged to provide meals which provided up to a third of a child's daily nutritional requirements. The 1980 Education Act left the nutritional content and staffing levels to the discretion of Local Education Authorities. This was the beginning of the end for the traditional school meal.

The 1988 Local Government Act made it compulsory for Local Education Authorities to put their school-meals services out to **competitive tendering**. This means that private companies are invited to submit proposals to run services traditionally controlled by LEAs. This has lead to fears that commercial interests will ultimately override nutritional considerations. Many LEAs have replaced the traditional school meal with a cafeteria system.

Although catering companies may give some thought to dietary balance, the availability of chips and hamburgers is often too strong for children to resist. The reduction in the scale of school-meals provision coincided with research which suggested that many of today's school children are suffering from the effects of a poor diet. Deficiencies in key nutrients such as calcium and iron were highlighted. The high fat intake of many of today's school children is also a cause of serious concern. In practice many schools now operate a three-tier system, in which children either eat school meals, packed lunches or are given money to go to the chippy.

Although both major political parties are ostensibly concerned about the state of school meals, neither of them is prepared as yet to re-introduce statutory provision.

All things considered, it is probably better to provide your child with a packed lunch every day. At least that way you know what your child is eating at lunch times and you can ensure that there is some dietary balance. Children given a cash allowance to get themselves something to eat are unlikely to give much thought to the nutritional value of what they choose. Many will be quite willing to settle for a portion of chips every day.

(See also **funding**.)

school milk

The **funding** for **Local Education Authorities (LEAs)** to provide free school milk for children, including those on Income Support, was removed by the 1988 Education Reform Act.

Although children under five in state schools are legally entitled to free school milk, the government no longer provides the money to pay for it. Instead, individual LEAs who wish to provide milk must pay for it themselves, then apply for a refund from the European Community—a process that takes at least four months. As a result many local authorities, especially those which have been charge-capped, can no longer afford to provide free school milk. (See **rising fives**.)

school nurse/school doctor/school dentist

The team which makes up the school health service.

The school health service is now part of the National Health Service (NHS). Local health authorities appoint a doctor with special responsibility for school health. He or she heads a team which goes into schools to carry out medical inspections.

The service is patchy and varies from region to region. Some schools have regular check-ups for all pupils, others offer a more limited and selective service. Parents can ask for their child to see a school doctor or nurse.

In general, parents have the right to refuse to allow their child to attend a medical inspection. Their permission is not required to examine a child suffering from head lice or someone believed to be a victim of **child abuse**.

It would be wrong to see the school health or dental services as an alternative to mainstream provision. Talks in **assembly** about, for example, dental care are useful, but they are no substitute for regular check-ups with your own dentist.

school phobia

An acute aversion to school.

This condition is more serious than the common reluctance to attend school which all pupils feel at one time or another. Professional help is usually needed to overcome the problem.

If you feel your child might be suffering from school phobia, the Children's Home-based Education Association runs a School Phobics Helpline from Monday to Friday between 12.15 pm and 1.00 pm (tel: 0302 833596).

school secretary

A person employed by the school to help the headteacher with administration.

Besides their official duties many school secretaries, especially in small schools, are frequently called upon to administer first aid, supervise children who have become unwell, and deal with the bruised emotions of pupils, parents and staff. Since the introduction of the **National Curriculum** and **Local Management of Schools (LMS)**, where schools become responsible for controlling their own finances, school secretaries have faced a much greater work-load. Without extra training many have found themselves having to take on part of the role of an accountant or **bursar**.

Some **Local Education Authorities** are beginning to acknowledge the increasingly important and complex role of secretaries. In the London boroughs, secretaries can now earn more than new classroom teachers although this is more a reflection of poor pay rates for **teachers**, rather than overblown wages for the secretaries. Secretaries in **secondary schools** usually earn more than those in primary schools.

Many infant and **primary schools** however, can only afford to employ secretaries on a part-time basis. It is worth finding out when your school secretary is available to avoid having to disturb teachers during lesson times. (See **funding**.)

school trips and visits

Visits to places of educational interest organized by a school as part of the curriculum. These may be a day trip to a stately home as part of a **history** project or a more extended stay in a field study centre as part of the **geography** course.

There has been a reduction in the number of school visits offered by many schools. This is due to a squeeze on school budgets and new charging policies for certain activities—both the consequence of the 1988 Education Reform Act. This is a pity. The importance of taking children out of the classroom and into the real world where they can apply their knowledge and skills is recognized by the great majority of **teachers**.

Parents must give their consent before a child can be taken out on a visit or residential trip. Special arrangements can be made for those parents who cannot afford to pay for trips and visits. Talk to the headteacher or the school secretary if you are in this position. This information must be treated in confidence.

(See also **funding**.)

science

Along with **mathematics** and **English**, science is one of the three core subjects of the **National Curriculum**. All children between the ages of 5 and 16 are expected to study science up to **GCSE** level.

In today's science classroom there is a much greater emphasis on a hands-on approach than there was 20 years ago. Children have experience of the scientific method from the outset. They are encouraged to formulate their own theories, find suitable ways of testing them, and to draw conclusions which can be applied to real situations. (See **teaching methods**.) The skills involved have a growing importance in a modern highly technological society.

The introduction of a compulsory science curriculum in **primary schools** caused a great deal of unease among **teachers**. On the one hand there were those who felt they had been doing a good job in teaching science already and felt the National Curriculum, far from broadening their approach, would actually restrict it. Many other primary-school teachers felt they lacked the experience or the background to teach the subject effectively. This need not have been a serious problem if enough money had been made available for the sort of **in-service training** the new reforms required. This money was not forthcoming.

A recent report by **Her Majesty's Inspectorate (HMI)** showed that science is still taught badly in 20 per cent of primary schools and 15 per cent of **secondary schools**. The report highlighted a serious shortage of qualified teachers and inadequate equipment and facilities. (See **buildings, shortage subjects**.)

A further point of controversy is the effect of the so-called 'balanced' science now studied at GCSE level. There has been a move away from the separate sciences—physics, chemistry and biology—into an approach which combines the three. Supporters of this approach say that it stops pupils specializing too early, and helps to develop a wider range of skills. Critics see balanced sciences as a watered-down version of each subject. This, they argue, leaves prospective **A-level** candidates at a disadvantage.

(See also **arts/science divide, How to help with science, sexism**.)

Scotland

See **UK education systems**

Scotland: 5–14 Development Programme

The **National Curriculum**, which prescribes what pupils must study in schools in England and Wales, does not apply to Scotland. The equivalent north of the border is the 5–14 Development Programme.

The curricular guidelines of the 5–14 Development Programme have a good deal in common with the National Curriculum. They have introduced **teachers** and pupils to an unfamiliar world of **Attainment Targets**, programmes of study and **testing**. However there are important differences between the two systems. In Scotland the 5–14 Development Programme is only advisory—it offers guidelines rather than a statutory straitjacket.

In primary school the programme is based on five main areas: language, **mathematics, environmental studies**, expressive arts, and religious and moral education.

In secondary school these areas are expanded to eight modes:

language and communication, mathematical studies and applications, scientific studies and applications, social and environmental studies, technological activities and applications, creative and aesthetic activities, physical education and religious and moral education.

(See also **testing**.)

Scottish Certificate of Education (SCE)

The most important Scottish **qualifications** at secondary level.

Standard Grade of the Scottish Certificate of Education is taken at 16 and is the equivalent of the English **GCSE**. **Higher Grade** is taken at 17 or 18.

(See also **Certificate of Sixth Year Studies (CSYS)**, **National Certificate**.)

Scottish Office Education Department (SOED)

The government department responsible for education in Scotland.

For information on all aspects of Scottish education, contact

Scottish Office Education Department (SOED)
New St Andrew's House, St James Centre, Edinburgh EH1 3SY

Scottish Vocational Education Council (SCOTVEC)

The Scottish Vocational Education Council is the principal examining body for **Further Education (FE)** in Scotland. **SCOTVEC** offers **National Certificate** courses in a wide range of work-related subjects. These courses are built up of continually assessed modules of around 40 hours each. At the moment there are 2000–3000 modules to choose from.

SCOTVEC is restructuring its **qualifications** so that at advanced levels they will lead to the Higher National Certificate or Higher National Diploma.

There is also to be a Scottish Vocational Qualification (SVQ), analogous to the **National Vocational Qualifications (NVQs)** offered in the rest of the United Kingdom.

(See also **Sixth Year Studies (Scotland)**.)

SCOTVEC

See **Scottish Vocational Education Council**

secondary modern schools

Before the introduction of **comprehensive schools** in the 1960s and 1970s, secondary modern schools provided a general education for pupils aged between 11 and 16 who were not selected for entry into **grammar schools**.

Scottish equivalents were known as junior secondary schools but have now been replaced entirely by comprehensive schools. In Northern Ireland where the **eleven plus** examination is still used, these schools are called secondary intermediates.

(See also **selection**.)

secondary schools

Secondary schools provide education for pupils between the ages of 11 and 18. In Scotland pupils begin secondary education at 12.

(See also **comprehensive schools, independent schools**.)

Secretary of State for Education and Science

The government minister responsible for the education system in England and Wales.

(See also **Department of Education and Science (DES)**.)

selection

The process in which schools choose the pupils they wish to admit.

Selection of pupils by ability is one of the most contentious issues in the educational scene. For 20 years it practically disappeared from the state system, but current educational reforms have seen the stage set for its return.

Until the 1970s it was standard practice to select secondary pupils on the basis of a single exam. The **eleven plus** was used to decide which children would go to **grammar schools** and which to **secondary modern schools**, or their equivalents. Although the approach was extremely popular with parents of brighter children, its limitations were widely acknowledged. The system failed to take account of the fact that children develop at different rates. It also meant that a large proportion of pupils began their secondary careers branded as failures. The comprehensive system largely did away with this kind of selection.

There are fears that recent developments such as **Opting-out, open enrolment** (giving parents the right to choose a school for their child) and the publication of National Curriculum assessment results will lead to the re-introduction of selection by the back door. There is nothing in the current legislation, for example, to prevent **grant-maintained schools** from introducing selection procedures—in fact, the concept is entirely in keeping with the government's support of competition as a tool for improving **standards**. The use of **National Curriculum** assessment results at Key Stage two (11 years old) would even provide a direct equivalent of the eleven plus.

It is not difficult to imagine the effects of selection in a market-led system. Schools will be judged on their examination results. The surest way of guaranteeing success in this area—as many **independent schools** have long been aware—is to screen pupils as they enter the school and select only the most able. Successful schools with bright pupils will thrive, those catering for pupils most in need of help will be left with dwindling resources.

(See also **magnet schools, sink schools.**)

self-governing schools

See **grant-maintained schools**

separation and divorce

Over a third of marriages end in divorce. This means that in any school there is likely to be a sizeable minority of pupils whose parents are experiencing a traumatic separation.

The possible long- and short-term effects on children are well documented. Feelings of confusion, anxiety, depression and guilt can all lead to learning difficulties and **behavioural problems**. These signs might not be immediately visible to parents who are under considerable strain themselves.

If parents are going through the process of separation and divorce—or any other traumatic event, such as bereavement— it is a good idea to inform the member of staff responsible for

pastoral care at their child's school. This will be the class teacher at a primary school and either the year head or form tutor in **secondary schools**.

service children

Children whose parents are members of the armed forces posted overseas.

The Service Children's Education Authority (SCEA), run by the Ministry of Defence, administers more than 100 schools overseas for service children and children of MOD employees.

The schools are staffed by civilian **teachers** and closely modelled on schools in the UK. Secondary education is co-educational and run on comprehensive lines. Schools have full support services such as **HMI**'s inspection, **advisers**' visits and a careers service. SCEA also offers an advisory service for service personnel who want their children to attend boarding school in the UK. The MOD usually pays an allowance to cover most of the **fees**.

Planned reductions in the size of our armed forces are likely to lead to a corresponding reduction in the numbers of service schools.

For further information, contact
The Service Children's Education Authority (SCEA)
HQ Directorate of Army Education, Ministry of Defence, Court Road, Elthem, London SE9 5NR

(See also **state boarding schools**.)

setting

See **banding, streaming**

sex education

Sex education attempts to teach children and young people about reproduction and their own sexuality and the possible effects on their adult lives.

Sometimes sex education is left until children reach secondary school, where it is often subsumed into the **science** syllabus. **Primary schools** may incorporate it into other projects such as 'How the Body Works' or 'Life Cycles'. This is largely a matter for individual schools and **governors** to decide, although there are some legal requirements which all schools must meet.

School governors must have a written policy on sex education even if they decide against including the subject in the curriculum. If sex education is provided, the subject must be taught: 'in such a manner as to encourage . . . pupils to have due regard to moral considerations and the value of family life' (1988 Education Reform Act). The 1988 Local Government Act prohibits local authorities from promoting homosexuality or suggesting that it can form the basis of family life. (See **Clause 28.**)

Governors are not allowed to limit the teaching of biology by claiming the right to have the last word on sexual matters within the curriculum. They have no control in this area if the teaching forms part of a syllabus leading to a public examination.

The validity of leaving sex education to the science curriculum is open to question. Even if this deals with the mechanics of reproduction, you might argue that a science lesson is not the ideal place for discussion of the wider social and moral issues.

More worrying is the fact that teenagers are often sexually active before they receive any organized sex education at all. This is something that many parents and **teachers** would prefer not to think about. As a result, sex education in schools has tended to be negative in tone: abstinence or monogamy being held up as the healthiest form of sex. This has not worked. Recent research has shown that despite all the publicity about **AIDS**, for example, teenagers still see safe sex in terms of avoiding pregnancy rather than avoiding AIDS.

So while parents generally agree that sex education should form part of the school curriculum, particularly at secondary level, there is no guarantee that it will. Most of it will be left up to you and will depend upon your own attitude to the subject. Trying to keep an open mind and allowing the possibility of free and frank discussion are probably the best policies. Answer your children's questions (however young they are) as honestly as you can. If you are concerned that more sex education should be provided at school, talk to the headteacher and your parent governors. Arrangements can usually be made for your child to be withdrawn from sex-education lessons if you have strong objections.

(See also **health education, Sex 'n' Drugs 'n' Rock 'n' Roll**.)

sexism

Discrimination against a person on the grounds of gender.

Sexist attitudes can be found operating at all levels of the education system—in this it is no different from the rest of society. Sexism is about attitudes and stereotypes and it is often insidious—it will not be stated or even acknowledged in most schools but it may well be felt by both **teachers** and pupils alike.

Clearly an extra responsibility falls on educators to make sure the structure of their institutions and their **teaching methods** do not reinforce sexual stereotypes.

Most discussion of sexism in schools has concentrated on the lack of equal opportunities for girls at secondary level. Despite the passing of the Sex Discrimination Act 1975, which made it illegal to exclude pupils from a subject purely on the grounds of sex, many discriminatory practices survive throughout the school system.

In mixed schools, girls tend to receive less teacher attention than boys. Boys tend to monopolize **computers** and other technical equipment, while encouragement for girls to take **science** subjects is often seriously lacking. The number of young women going on to take engineering degrees remains relatively low. This is a waste of talent, especially since girls who do opt for subjects such as technology usually do well in them. Teenage girls tend to take their work more seriously than boys. **Headteachers** of independent boys schools, forced for financial reasons to open their doors to girls, have found that academic standards have improved as a result.

During the heyday of the **eleven plus**, the results in some local authorities had to be adjusted to allow more boys to pass the exam. As a result, some girls often missed out on grammar school places for reasons that had nothing to do with intelligence and ability.

Meanwhile, much of the literature that children are exposed to still portrays girls in a passive role while boys make decisions and have all the adventures.

The way most schools arrange their **physical education** programmes and **sports days** also reinforces sexist attitudes. **Team games** have traditionally been organized along gender lines with girls taking netball and hockey while boys play **football** or rugby. At school sports days single-sex races are still commonplace even in **primary schools** where there is no real physi-

cal justification for the division. This division is being
challenged in some schools by the arrival of sports such as
New Image Rugby (called Dragon Rugby in Wales) where the
rules stipulate that at least two members of the team must be
girls. The sport is fluent and fast moving and avoids the physical
aggression which is an integral part of conventional rugby.
However, there is still a long way to go in this area.

All this has lead an increasing number of teachers and parents
to believe that girls in mixed schools should be taught
separately—particularly in such subjects as **science** and technology. Girls schools are currently enjoying something of a
revival as more parents recognize the need for greater opportunities for their daughters.

With the focus of attention on equal opportunities for girls it is
easy to forget that boys too can experience sexist attitudes.
Boys with an interest in **music** or fine **art** rather than **computers**
or **sport** can have a tough time in the playground. Lugging a
bulging sports bag around generally earns them more respect
than carrying a clarinet case.

Sexism in schools does not stop at the children, it effects the
teachers too. It is rare to find a primary school staff room with
equal numbers of men and women. Where there are some
male teachers they often get promoted ahead of their female
colleagues. Throughout the system, there are still far more
male headteachers than female. Women teachers often find
themselves playing second fiddle to men on **in-service training**
courses.

(See also **equal opportunities, single-sex schools**.)

Sex 'n' Drugs 'n' Rock 'n' Roll

'Sex 'n' Drugs 'n' Rock 'n' Roll' do not exhaust the sources of
parents' concern for their children, but they do form a con-
venient shorthand for the kinds of problems that leave them
lying awake at night.

Youth culture has a curriculum of its own quite independent of
the wishes of parents and the stated aims of schools. The
counter-culture is real, and so too are its dangers, but the
message must be: do not panic. **Adolescence** is a time of experiment and exploration for most teenagers. Growing up often
takes the form of rebellion against the values of school and
home. Parents are likely to disapprove but taking a high moral

line is generally counterproductive. It is also important not to lose sight of the fact that most teenagers negotiate this period of their lives without any long-term damage.

The crucial factor here is communication. Talk to your teenager. Make sure both of you have access to information about contraception, **AIDS**, drugs, and other issues that tend to be inadequately covered in the school curriculum. (See **sex education**.) Adjustments need to be made on both sides. Adult refusal to acknowledge the sexual activity of teenagers can act as a block to successful communication.

If you are worried your child is getting into serious difficulties, the most pressing need is to talk sensitively and openly to him or her. If this fails, the member of staff responsible for **pastoral care** at school may be able to offer help. Beyond this, help is available from a number of support groups which can be contacted through your local Citizens' Advice Bureau (CAB).

shortage subjects

There is a serious shortage of **teachers** in key subject areas such as **mathematics**, chemistry, physics, technology and **modern languages**.

These shortages represent two-thirds of the core subjects of the **National Curriculum** and almost half the curriculum overall. Recent research has shown that almost a third of classes in **secondary schools** were being taken by teachers without a post-**A-level** qualification in the subject they were teaching.

Government initiatives to attract new recruits into shortage subject areas have only scratched the surface of the problem. The situation is unlikely to improve until the underlying causes of disaffection among teachers—poor pay, low prestige, and a heavy work-load—have been addressed.

single-sex schools

Schools which cater exclusively either for boys or girls.

Since the introduction of **comprehensive schools** in the mid-1970s the number of single-sex state schools has declined significantly. More have survived in the private sector. (See **independent schools**.)

All state primary and middle schools are now co-educational (catering for both sexes).

Single-sex comprehensives still exist, particularly the **voluntary-aided schools**, but in many areas single-sex education is no longer an option. This may change in the near future as the rules about **Opting-out** are eased, and schools are allowed to change their status.

In mixed schools fewer girls succeed in scientific and technological subjects—partly because boys tend to monopolize the equipment and partly because expectations for girls in the sciences remain low. (See **sexism.**) For this reason, parents of girls will sometimes consider a single-sex school if one is available. The drawbacks here are that, first, it is generally agreed that educating both sexes together provides a more normal social environment; and, second, some girls schools, in both the private and maintained sectors, have fewer resources to teach technical subjects.

If you send your daughters to co-educational **secondary schools**—and most people do—you might have to work hard through discussions with the school and through support activities at home, to ensure they get a fair bite of the technological cherry. (See **home–school partnership.**)

sink schools

An informal name for the schools that might be left with dwindling resources in an increasingly competitive system.

Sink schools are not yet a feature of our education scene, but all the mechanisms for producing them are in place.

New **funding** arrangements favour schools which publish the best test results and therefore attract the largest number of pupils. Since schools are in competition with each other, individuals who fare less well academically are increasingly unattractive to **headteachers** and governing bodies. If **selection** procedures can identify these children, schools can exclude them. The end result is that children who need the most help will find themselves in schools which, because of their poor academic results, no one wants to go to. These schools would then be on a downward spiral. As results get worse, fewer parents will want their children to go there and their funding would contract further. The result is a sink school.

(See also **choosing a school.**)

Sixth Form Colleges

See **beyond 16**

Sixth Year Studies (Scotland)

Pupils in Scotland have a wider range of courses open to them in the upper years of **secondary schools** than their counterparts south of the border.

Scottish **Higher Grades (Highers)** can be taken at 17 after a course lasting only a year. Successful pupils can then move on to universities or **Higher Education (HE)** at 17 rather than 18. In order to take advantage of this most Scottish degree honours courses run for four years instead of the three which is the norm in the rest of the United Kingdom.

Not all pupils choose to take their Highers at 17 or, if they do, leave school. Many choose to stay on. These pupils might take their Highers over two years and perhaps supplement them with the **Certificate of Sixth Year Studies (CSYS)**, or work-related **National Certificate** courses. There are also short courses suitable for study in the fifth and sixth years developed by the Scottish Examination Board. It is becoming increasingly common for schools to form **consortia** so that, alongside their Highers, pupils can study **link courses** for the National Certificate at a **College of Further Education**. (See **Further Education (FE)**.)

This choice gives Scottish pupils a far broader range of **qualifications** than those provided by traditional **A-levels** studied in English schools.

social services

The local government department responsible for the welfare of children in need.

In recent years social services departments across the country have had a bad press. Nevertheless they do an extremely difficult and valuable job on limited resources.

Their involvement in the education process extends across the whole age range, from **day nurseries** for pre-school children to **community homes** for persistent **young offenders**. They may also take over the care of children considered to be in physical or emotional danger (the so-called children at risk).

The marriage between education and social services departments has not always been a happy one; precise areas of responsibility are difficult to draw and communication is sometimes poor. As a result, parents of children with problems often complain of endless red tape and delay. It remains to be seen whether the major changes to local government structures laid out in 1991 will ease the situation.

If you feel you need the help of the social services department it is probably best to contact them through the **Education Welfare Officer (EWO)** with responsibility for your child's school.

(See also **children in care**.)

SOED

See **Scottish Office Education Department**

special needs

Until comparatively recently only children who were obviously disadvantaged—the physically handicapped, the deaf, the blind or the mentally ill—were classed as having special educational needs. All this changed in 1981 when the definition was widened to include children who have significantly greater difficulty in learning than the majority of their peers. This new definition included up to 20 per cent of all children—a figure which might represent five or six pupils in each primary classroom.

Once children with special needs have been identified it is—in theory—up to the **Local Education Authorities (LEAs)** to provide special help to enable them to overcome their difficulties.

The LEAs' formal response is contained in a document called a 'statement of special educational needs' ('record of needs' in Scotland). The statement is legally binding and contains a summary of the child's difficulties together with the steps the LEA must take in order to help with them. The kind of help it provides will depend on the nature of the individual child's difficulties. Schools are not legally obliged to provide help for children without statements. (See **statement**.)

Officially there is a policy of integrating those with special needs alongside other children, but in the most severe cases children will attend **special schools** where specialist help is available that will not be found in ordinary schools. Some schools run **special units** where children can be coached intensively for a period with the aim of returning them to the mainstream classes as progress is made. Others have specialist teachers or helpers working unobtrusively with the class teacher.

In theory then, the system is straightforward. The child is identified, assessed, a statement of needs is made and the appropriate help is provided—with LEA, **teachers**, relevant specialists and parents all working alongside each other to overcome the child's educational difficulties. In practice the picture is bleak: the system is cumbersome, fraught with difficulties, slow to respond and seriously underresourced. As a result, few children with special educational needs receive the help they need, when they need it. Children without a statement are particularly vulnerable.

There is the very real prospect of an already gloomy situation becoming worse. New **funding** arrangements for schools are tightening the squeeze on budgets. While **governors** have a statutory duty to help children with special needs, there is not much they can do if the money is not available. Moreover, with schools competing with each other for pupils—and the importance of published **assessment** results as a measure of a school's effectiveness—there is a growing disincentive for schools to accept children with special needs. They eat up precious resources and seldom return the sort of results schools want to see.

The message for parents then should be clear: if you have a child with special educational needs, you will have to struggle to get the necessary help. Look carefully at the statementing process before you begin. Be persistent in making your problem known, and keep all channels of communication open with the school—particularly with your child's class teacher.

Here are some further points you might consider:

It is natural for parents to be concerned about their children's progress but many worry unnecessarily. Remember that all children learn things at different rates and in different ways. It is alarming to watch your 7-year-old struggling with **reading** or number work, while all his or her friends seem to be forging ahead. However, do not automatically assume that there is a serious long-term problem.

Try not to convey your anxiety to your child. This never helps, and may lead to a loss of **confidence**. A child who has lost his or her confidence is at a serious disadvantage in the learning process. (See **parental guilt**.)

It is, however, crucial to pick up any problems early so that there is plenty of time to help before children begin to see themselves as failures. You are more likely to get help for your child while he or she is in the primary-school sector. It is a sad fact that many **secondary schools** offer inadequate help to children who are low attainers.

As soon as you feel worried, make an appointment to see the class teacher. He or she should be able to advise you about what you can do to help at home and in all probability will put your anxieties into perspective.

If both you and the school consider that it is time your child had some extra help, think very carefully about subjecting your child to assessments by **educational psychologists**, the medical services and the like.

(See also **dyslexia, hyperactivity, speech therapist**.)

special schools

Special schools cater for children with special educational needs who cannot be educated in a normal school.

Special schools tend to be much smaller than ordinary schools, with a lower **pupil–teacher ratio**, and they often take children across the whole age range from nursery to 16 plus. Some special schools are residential but the majority are day schools.

Since 1990 special schools have been required to implement the **National Curriculum**. Most welcomed this in principle, seeing it as an opportunity to answer the criticism—often levelled at special schools—that the range of opportunities for pupils was very narrow. However, there are also fears that the demands of the National Curriculum may make life difficult for those special schools which have worked hard to develop programmes to meet the needs of individual pupils.

If it has been suggested that your child should attend a special school, or indeed if you think this might be the best solution, here are some points to consider:

Evidence suggests that children with special needs thrive best when integrated into ordinary schools, supported by specially trained staff and sympathetic **teachers**. In the current economic climate such specialist help is difficult to find and could be withdrawn at any time.

You have the same rights as other parents to choose a school for your child. However, if you are considering the possibility of integrating your child into an ordinary school, it would be wise to make sure that what is on offer is at least as good as he or she would get at a special school.

Special schools are more likely to offer the specialist staff and equipment that can make your child's life easier—there are still very few ordinary schools with wheelchair ramps and bathrooms for the disabled, for example.

Schools may not be available in your immediate area. If your child has to go to a residential school, will visiting be a problem? Will your child be able to cope with the potential stress of separation from home?

In the end the choice between special school attendance or mainstream schooling will very much depend on the nature of your child's **special needs**, and the policy of **Local Education Authorities (LEAs)** and individual schools.

(See also **parental guilt**.)

special units

Units provided by some schools to cater for children with special educational needs. (See **special needs**.)

Special units are designed to provide extra learning support for those children with problems, such as physical handicap, difficulties with academic work or emotional disturbance. Ideally, attendance in a special unit should be temporary so that when progress is made, children can be re-integrated into the classroom.

Many special units work well, especially in the primary sector where children with learning difficulties can be picked up early and given a period of sustained expert help. However, there is an acute shortage of special needs teachers and there can be no guarantee that all special units can offer the sort of high-level teaching they were designed to give.

Unfortunately, there is a tendency, especially in **secondary schools** (both among **teachers** and pupils), to regard these units as 'sin-bins'. Children who have not had the support they needed early on, often become totally disillusioned as the spectre of public examinations looms and the prospect of failure becomes impossible to avoid. This may lead to disruptive or disturbed behaviour. Such children are very difficult to teach in large classes with teachers under pressure to achieve good test and examination results. However, consigning young people to the special unit for longer and longer periods, is unlikely to improve their self-esteem—or their academic progress.

Some special units go by more picturesque names such as 'the sanctuary'. There has been controversy over the way some of these units have been used as punishment centres for isolating individuals, both children in local authority care, and pupils at boarding school in the independent sector. It is illegal to lock up children who are in the care of the local authority. New laws designed to protect children in **independent schools** stipulate that independent **boarding schools** must now be inspected by local authorities. (See **children's rights**.)

If it has been suggested that your child would benefit from some time in a special unit, it is wise to have a careful look at what is on offer. Do not be afraid to ask the headteacher about the qualifications of the staff involved and long-term aims for special needs provision in the school. Many children, especially younger ones, benefit from a temporary period in a special unit for part of the normal school day; others do not. Confidence is the crucial factor. If attendance in the special unit seems to be undermining your child's **confidence** this may be detrimental in the long term. It will be very important to work closely with the school so that you can support your child at home. (See **home–school partnership**.)

Of course you may not have a choice: special needs provision is very patchy generally, and schools with special units may not be available in your area.

speech therapist

A specialist who helps people overcome speech defects.

Local Education Authorities (LEAs) have to provide speech therapy for any child who has had a speech defect since birth. Until recently some LEAs were challenging this ruling and arguing that speech therapy was a matter for the health department and not the education department.

The issue was finally decided in the Appeal Court in 1989. This decision was good news for parents, but it did not solve their problems—or those of their children. The real difficulty is that, first, money for **special needs** is short and, second, there are not enough speech therapists to go round. So even if you can persuade the LEA to provide help, it is unlikely that the speech therapist will be able to spend enough time with your child to make a real difference.

So what can you do? In the present economic climate any help you do get will have to be fought for. It is probably wise to look beyond the LEA. Most speech therapists are employed by the health authority and you can approach them directly—it is not necessary to be referred through your GP. The telephone number can be found in the phone book.

Beyond this, you could contact one of the following organizations offering help and advice to parents:

Association of Speech-Impaired Children
347 Central Markets, Smithfield, London EC1A 9NH

Voluntary Organizations for Communication and Language (VOCAL)
336 Brixton Road, London SW9 7AA

spelling

See **How to help with spelling**

sponsorship

Businesses are sometimes prepared to offer financial support to educational establishments and individual students through sponsorship deals.

Schools and colleges feeling the financial pinch may turn to the business community for help. Students on **Higher Education (HE)** courses are looking increasingly to sponsorship in the face of a notoriously poor grant system. Private companies may respond by giving money or equipment to particular school departments or subjects—technology or business studies, for example. Or they may offer financial assistance to individual students entering Further or Higher Education. Some big companies also offer top-up bursaries to promising students in their final year.

Although most money goes towards supporting engineering and business studies, the range of courses available for sponsorship is steadily increasing as more companies get involved. For example, up to 30 per cent of university engineering students are now sponsored. This trend is likely to continue into the next century as the business world is encouraged to forge stronger links with education.

There are mutual advantages in sponsorship: educational establishments manage to stay afloat or gain valuable extra resources; students may be better off and companies have the opportunity to hand-pick future employees—and have a greater say in course content. However, sponsorship is no real substitute for adequate central government **funding** on education.

It is worth talking to the teacher in charge of **careers advice** about local companies offering sponsorship. Alternatively contact the personnel officer of some large companies in your area.

(See also **education and the market place, grants and loans**.)

sport

See **physical education (PE), sports day**

sports day

An annual event—to which parents are usually invited—where children take part in a range of athletic activities.

The school sports day has been a focus of a good deal of disagreement in educational circles. The question at issue is whether or not the element of **competition** is good for children.

It is quite possible to devise sporting activities which, instead of rewarding pupils for beating someone else, give them credit for improving their own individual performance. What matters is not jumping higher than everyone else in the school, but jumping higher than you have ever jumped before. In this kind of non-competitive sports day the benefits of physical activity can be made available to all—even those who would not normally excel in games.

Opponents of this approach argue that non-competitive sport is a contradiction in terms, that competition forces an improvement in overall **standards** and gives non-academic pupils a chance to shine in at least one area of the curriculum.

These issues are more hotly debated at primary level, where even some supporters of competition feel it can be introduced into children's lives too early.

standard English

Standard English is the version of the English language used in the education system, professional life, and in print.

However, the **National Curriculum** recognizes standard English is not the only version of **English** in use today. It is seen as one dialect among many—though one with a particularly high status.

How to help with green children

On green issues the challenge for parents is not so much creating a sense of environmental awareness in their children as trying to keep up. Children are usually extremely well informed about the importance of conservation. This is not just because they meet the subject in school—though we do owe the high level of awareness among the growing generation of children to good teaching. More significantly perhaps, children have none of the world-weariness that adults often develop as they grow older. The world is still new to them, and the damage we are causing is keenly felt. It might seem hard to be lectured by our children, but we would probably be wise not to discourage it. It might be our best hope for the future.

Two closely related issues lie at the heart of most green questions: the first is the fact that we are using up natural resources which cannot easily be replaced; the second is that we are making a mess of our world along the way. There are plenty of opportunities to introduce these ideas through the following activities:

Go on an un-nature trail. Follow a local walk and make a list of all the features that are not a natural part of the countryside: crisp packets, beer cans, discarded mattresses, tin kettles, abandoned cars.

Ask how nature disposes of its rubbish. What happens to dead trees, animals, leaves, etc? Find some leaf litter in woodland. Look for leaf skeletons (leaves that have decayed to leave only a network of veins).

Investigate some man-made rubbish—litter. (Use protective gloves.) Collect some litter. Make a list of the different kinds. Where does it gather? Why? What can be done about it? Take different materials (paper, crisp packets, tin foil, plastic, etc) and bury them in the ground. Leave for a month or so. Dig up. Which have broken down? Explain biodegradable materials (ie materials that break down naturally).

Look at the waste produced by the household: water, sewerage, rubbish, etc. Find out where it goes. What happens to it when it leaves the house?

Can you sort your own household waste? Bottles for the bottle bank, waste paper, organic waste for the compost heap. Your local council will have information about recycling schemes in your area.

Look at different kinds of packaging. A box of chocolates or a new shirt is a good place to start. Do we need so much packaging? If you buy a shirt, what do you get to go with it? Make a list (pins, cellophane, cardboard, plastic, paper, etc). Producing all these bits and pieces takes energy and uses up resources such as fuel. Look closely at the packaging itself. Most will simply be thrown away. Which will be easy to dispose of? Which are biodegradable? Write a letter to the manufacturer explaining what you think is wrong.

See how much water we waste each day. Ask children to clean their teeth under a running tap. Collect the water and measure it. Ask them to find a way of cleaning their teeth that uses less water.

Capitalize on children's natural interest in animals—look at endangered species. Bring it closer to home. What can you plant in the garden to improve the habitat for animals/birds/butterflies? Build a bird table, or put food on a window sill, plant a buddleia, leave some grass uncut. Keep charts of the species seen.

(See also **How to help with science**.)

The idea that there can be more than one version of English will be unfamiliar to most of today's parents. In fact there are many versions of the language—each with its own vocabulary and **grammar**. Some of these versions are formal (like the language of the law courts), some are informal (like the language of agricultural workers in Norfolk). What makes standard English so useful is that it can be used anywhere and in any situation. This makes it a very powerful tool and one all pupils need to master.

Standard English should not be confused with the sort of pronunciation which turns 'out and about' into 'ite and abite'. You can speak standard English in any accent and it will still be standard English.

(See also **accent and dialect**.)

Standard Grade

The Scottish equivalent of **GCSEs** taken by secondary pupils at 16.

Standard Grade of the **Scottish Certificate of Education (SCE)** replaces the former Ordinary Grade exams in the same way that GCSE replaced O-levels south of the border.

The new exams are designed to suit every level of ability. Most courses offer three papers at the end of the final year. These are at Credit level (which lead to passes at grades one or two), General level (grades three or four) and Foundation level (grades five or six). Usually pupils take two of these exams to give them the best chance of gaining an award which reflects their abilities.

Assessment can be by a folio of work submitted to the Scottish Examining Board (SEB), final exams, **continuous assessment** or a combination of these. SEB certificates can also show results of short courses taken at the school and assessed internally.

(See also **Higher Grade**.)

standards

Parents are told at every turn that standards in our schools are falling. Banner headlines proclaim that this generation of school children is getting worse at **reading**, **spelling** and **mathematics**.

This has been the cry since the 15th century, when writing and reading ceased to be the exclusive preserve of monks and scholars. However, as Britain entered the 1990s and **Europe**, the standards debate received an unprecedented amount of media attention. Education moved up the political ladder and was nudged to the top of the political charts in the middle of 1991, with speeches by Prince Charles on Shakespeare's birthday, and by the Prime Minister, John Major, a month or so later. Education is now a vote-catcher—something to bear in mind as you read all the stories and listen to the news broadcasts. There is certainly nothing sophisticated about the level of debate. It has become fashionable in some political quarters to blame new-fangled teaching methods for this supposed decline. There has been much mud-slinging and more than a few, frankly, ridiculous stories. (See **Zulu**.)

All this has added to the serious and prolonged bout of low-morale amongst **teachers**. It has also created widespread confusion and dismay amongst parents, who no longer know what to believe.

The fact is nobody knows whether standards in our schools are rising or falling. There has as yet been no systematic survey which could prove the point one way or the other. When the reading debate was in full swing during 1990–1, for example, it was a little reported fact that there had been no serious attempt to measure reading ability across the whole age range since 1979.

Local Education Authorities (LEAs) do not always keep records of tests or indeed attempt to conduct them in the first place. Statistics are, however, more often kept about children with **special needs** (those having problems) and because there has been some attempt to improve provision for these children, there appears to be more of them. It is often these figures which are used to fuel the debate about falling standards. For the rest of the school population, there is no benchmark against which to measure progress on a national scale.

Many teachers and educationalists favour the setting-up of a General Teaching Council, rather like the General Medical Council (GMC) in the medical profession, to monitor standards and act as an advisory body on all aspects of education. It is only possible to check standards of educational achievement through long, careful and impartial monitoring.

The **National Curriculum**, with its emphasis on assessment and testing, might provide this measure. However, it will be years before such tests, which are still fraught with controversy, can reasonably provide this benchmark. The government is very keen on these assessments, which were first used in 1991 amidst a storm of protest from teachers and parents. Parents will be able to compare the results of these standardized assessments when **choosing a school** in their area. You should bear in mind that the results of tests alone do not make a good school.

One point that is frequently overlooked here is that schools in the 1990s have to prepare to enter an increasingly complex world. They have more to teach. The National Curriculum is a very demanding and radical piece of legislation. Many schools feel that there is now so much content to get through and so many tests to prepare for that the whole thing has become overloaded.

In answer to those employees who lament, 'that's all very well but the fact is my secretary cannot spell', teachers might well reply that the chances are that their secretaries will know how to use a word processor with a spell-check facility. This does not mean that teachers have forsaken the basics like **grammar**, **spelling**, **handwriting** and arithmetic, it is simply that these things must sit alongside all the other aspects of contemporary classroom practice. (See **teaching methods**.)

These arguments may not convince parents. The standards question remains central. Statements like 'Yes, but when we were at school we all knew our tables and when to use an apostrophe' flow freely whenever groups of parents talk about their children. There is the feeling that things were much better before the new age of **SATS**, New Maths, **integrated days** and **continuous assessment** dawned in our schools. This has in turn led people to believe that there should be a return to the old system of **grammar schools** and **selection** at 11.

So where does all this leave parents? What are you to believe? There is undeniably a lot wrong with our school system, some even talk of a crisis in the classrooms. However, this is not new. The crisis has been a long time coming and will continue into the foreseeable future. The story of British education is one of long-term underfunding and a lack of clear direction. (See **funding**.)

The only long-term solution is to invest more money into the system. Politicians like to quote figures and are fond of telling us how much more they spend than their opponents. Often these increases are rhetorical—sometimes less is put back in than was taken away in the first place. (See **training**.) This means that you may have to provide some of the things you want for your child's education yourself—perhaps extra learning support, learning to play a musical instrument or even basic **books** and resources.

If you are worried about the standard of your child's education, use the channels of communication that are now open to you to do something about it. Visit the school, talk to the teachers, watch what goes on and offer to help if you can. Complain to your parent **governors** and the LEA if need be. You do not have to sit quietly and say nothing. The law is geared in your favour.

Supporting your child at home is one of the best ways of helping to improve standards. (See **How to help at home.**)

(See also **complaints, home–school partnership, jargon, Parent's Charter.**)

Standing Advisory Council on Religious Education (SACRE)

A statutory body set up by **Local Education Authorities (LEAs)** to advise on **religious education (RE).**

Local SACREs contain representatives from the Church of England, other denominations and faiths, **teachers** and the LEA.

Since 1989 local SACREs have the power to lift or modify the legal requirement that a school's daily act of worship should be 'wholly or mainly of a broadly Christian character'.

state boarding schools

Schools in the state sector which provide accommodation— usually for a limited number of pupils.

While most **boarding schools** are in the independent sector, there is a small but significant number of state schools which offer the same facility.

You do not have to be wealthy to send your children to state boarding schools. As a result boarders are drawn from a wide range of social backgrounds. Much of the boarding population is made up of children whose parents are in the armed forces, or who have difficult home lives. In most cases the **Local Education Authority (LEA)** pays the fees but well-off parents might be asked to make a contribution.

The number of state boarding places has declined over the last 10 years. The main reason has been pressure on already stretched LEA budgets. This has led in some cases to a backlog of repairs and poorly maintained buildings.

The same considerations apply to choosing a state boarding school as to those in the independent sector. Make sure you are satisfied with the standard of accommodation and the provision for boarders out of school hours—particularly as the majority of pupils at these state schools are likely to go home at the end of the school day. (See **boarding schools**.)

You can get information about state boarding places from:

The Clearing House for Maintained Boarding Provision
75a Claypath, Durham DH1 1QT

statement

A statement of special educational needs is a legally binding document, drawn up by the **Local Education Authority (LEA)**. It must define the authority's view of the nature of a child's **special needs**, and specify the kind of additional support it is able to provide.

Schools are not legally obliged to provide extra help for children without statements.

In essence the process of statementing is straightforward. A child with difficulties is referred to an **educational psychologist** for an assessment. After initial testing, the educational psychologist may decide to bring in other experts for further advice, such as **occupational therapists**, **speech therapists** or social workers. The LEA—which has a legal obligation to involve parents as fully as possible in the process—then responds by issuing the statement detailing the extra help it is going to provide.

Although obtaining a statement seems a logical way to get special help if your child is having problems, the operation is fraught with difficulties. Statementing is a long, bureaucratic process. The inevitable delays invariably leave the child without help when he or she most needs it. Even when the process is complete and the LEA has reached a decision, there may not be adequate **funding** available to provide the recommended help. Parents also relinquish some rights over their child's education once the statement is in place. As if this was not bad enough, some educational psychologists have complained publicly that the LEA has instructed them to tailor their statements to the amount of money available to pay for extra help. Some have been sacked for refusing to comply.

Bearing these drawbacks in mind, you should not enter into the process lightly. It might be wise to take specialist advice from an organization such as the following:

The Advisory Centre for Education (ACE) Ltd
1b Aberdeen Studios, 22–24 Highbury Grove,
London N5 2EA

(See also **alternative education, National Curriculum.**)

story time

Most primary school teachers, especially in the early years, try to set some time aside every day to read a story to the class. This is popular with children, especially if teachers are prepared to make fools of themselves by putting in all the accents and expressions.

As well as being fun, story time provides opportunities for all sorts of learning activities. Through discussion of the story children are encouraged to listen carefully (an essential skill), look at how language is put together and express some of the emotions explored in the story. It allows them to experience a range of emotions (ie the scary or sad bits) in a secure setting. Many valuable educational projects started life as a chapter from a story.

With the increased emphasis on group work and self-discovery which are features of modern **teaching methods**, story time also provides an opportunity for teachers to bring their class together at the end of the day.

Unfortunately, as children progress through the system and the demands on the timetable increase, the practice of story time dies away. Parents, too, tend to assume that once their children have mastered the art of **reading** for themselves, they no longer need to be read to. The dominance of **television** and video in our lives has also contributed to the demise of story time. Read to your children long after they have learned to do it for themselves—children can easily be left with the feeling that reading aloud is something that only beginner readers do.

(See also **books, How to help with reading.**)

streaming

The division of children of the same age into ability groups for the purposes of teaching.

In **infant** and **primary schools**, it is standard practice for **teachers** to organize their classes into groups for at least some of their activities. At this level, these groups are usually not fixed and children of different abilities will often work together. It is rare for a primary school to divide a whole year-group into separate streams.

Most **secondary schools** operate some kind of **streaming** system. Sometimes a whole intake year is assessed then put into classes according to ability. Many secondary schools operate a modified version of streaming. Sometimes this means dividing a year-group into broad bands of ability: above average, average or below average. This is known as **'banding'**. Other schools organize children into ability groups for different subjects. This is called 'setting'.

The major problem with streaming in its various guises is that it may become too rigid. Not all children develop at the same rate: those who do badly on assessment tests at 11 may well blossom by the time they are 13. Being confined to a group that does not extend a child's new-found abilities may lead to serious motivation and **behavioural problems** later on. Sensitive teachers recognize this and allow for some movement between ability groups.

Some **GCSE** courses are effectively streamed. Different coursework is set for children of different abilities. One consequence of this approach is that not all pupils are given access to the higher grades. It is up to the teacher to decide which version of the course each pupil will follow. This is particularly worrying for girls. There is a danger of them losing out because they are still often seen as inherently weaker at mathematical and **science** subjects than boys. (See **hidden curriculum, sexism.**)

If you feel that your child has been incorrectly placed, discuss this with the class teacher or head of year. Be wary of pushing your child beyond his or her natural capacity: a child under pressure rarely thrives at school.

(See also **National Curriculum, selection.**)

stress

A disease of 20th-century living that has become a fact of life for many **teachers**.

It has been estimated that as a direct result of stress-related conditions the education service in England and Wales is losing more than £230 million a year. This is hardly surprising.

Research shows that teachers are more stressed than other professionals who work under pressure, such as GPs, tax inspectors, and nurses. Teaching is not the soft job it appears to many outside the profession. Beyond the physical and emotional demands of classroom teaching, factors such as poor pay, low prestige and the additional burden involved in implementing the **National Curriculum** have all been cited as major causes of stress.

Although it is rarely acknowledged, children can also suffer from stress. Teenagers face their first public exams at a difficult age, both emotionally and physically. (See **adolescence**.) In extreme cases, stress amongst examination candidates can affect physical health. Younger children often suffer their stress in silence or express it as naughtiness. Common causes of stress amongst primary school children are: feelings of failure perhaps as a result of a slow start in reading or number work, **bullying**, and lack of support.

(See also **home–school partnership**.)

structural apparatus

This is the technical name for equipment used in schools to help children understand basic number.

The most commonly used types of structural apparatus are Cuisinaire® rods, Unifix®, Stern® and Dienes® blocks; but there are many others on the market.

Through using structural apparatus, children in the early stages of mathematical development learn how numbers relate to each other. Wooden cubes may be used to represent units, while rods of units joined together show 10s. Use of such equipment boosts children's confidence because there is less chance of miscounting and getting things wrong.

If you can afford it, it is worth having some structural apparatus at home. You will probably find it will be used for building roads and houses too—children find all sorts of ingenious uses for wooden blocks. This is fine, it all helps your child's confidence in handling mathematical equipment. If buying your own structural apparatus seems above and beyond the call of duty, use everyday objects, such as stones or segments of fruit, to help your child understand how numbers are made up.

(See also **construction toys, How to help with maths**.)

student accommodation

Halls of residence at universities and colleges provide accommodation for a limited number of students. The majority have to rely on their own resources.

There is something of an accommodation crisis for students. The situation became particularly acute during the late 1980s and early 1990s. Although Britain's **Higher Education** population is low compared to many other European countries, numbers are rising. A prolonged squeeze on spending has meant that Higher Education establishments have been unable to keep pace with demand for accommodation. In 1990 and 1991 the media ran many stories about new recruits arriving at universities and polytechnics only to find that there was nowhere for them to live.

The situation has recently been made worse by the ruling that students are liable to pay the community charge; by inadequate student grants and the unpopular loans scheme and the shrinking rental sector of the housing market.

Before beginning a full-time course it is worth spending some time checking the accommodation situation with the institution concerned. Find the time to check the local housing situation so that you know the kinds of rents to expect. (See **grants and loans**.)

student grants

See **grants and loans**

supply teachers

Teachers employed on a temporary basis to fill in for absent school staff.

Supply teachers are a very important part of the school system. They keep schools running as permanent members of staff spend time away either as a result of ill-health or on training courses. In some **Local Education Authorities (LEAs)** teacher shortages are so acute that supply teachers are increasingly used to fill vacant posts. Although most schools keep a list of the supply teachers they use regularly to minimize disruption, as many as 60 phone calls may have to be made to find emergency cover. (See **shortage subjects**.)

Since supply teachers are not automatically entitled to attend staff meetings or **in-service training** courses, it is very difficult for them to keep pace with new developments in education, although good ones try hard to keep themselves informed.

Children of all ages are unsettled when they are taught by a series of supply teachers. If it becomes obvious that your child is frequently being taught by supply teachers, you should find out why. It may be that there are problems with staffing levels at the school, which may in the long run be disadvantageous.

suspensions

See **expulsion and suspension, punishment**

T

tables

See **How to help with maths, mathematics**

teachers

Employees of governing bodies popularly supposed to finish work at 3.30 pm and have enough holidays to run a second career.

Ask a teacher in the 1990s to describe the job and you will get a very different picture. You will probably be told that teaching should carry a government health warning. There will be descriptions of evenings spent marking, preparing, record-keeping, attending meetings, talking to parents. Strongest of all will be the feeling that what teachers do is constantly scrutinized, criticized and undervalued.

Teachers have always had an image problem. School children have traditionally struggled with the idea that teachers might also be human beings when school is out. Parents understandably take their own bad memories of school days with them when they meet their children's teachers. Politicians find them easy scapegoats for hidden inadequacies in the system, but pressures on teachers reached unprecedented levels during the late 1980s and early 1990s. A staggering array of new, often hastily implemented legislation has left teachers reeling under the work-load. Persistent proclamations by politicians about the decline and fall of **standards** in our schools, and years of poor pay and career prospects have resulted in a seriously demoralized teaching force. In some areas teachers are in such short supply that fully implementing the **National Curriculum** is virtually impossible. Problems focus on:

Pay: teachers' salaries have been allowed to fall behind other white-collar workers during the last 20 years. Morale was lowered further in 1987, when, after a long and acrimonious pay dispute, teachers in England and Wales lost the right to negotiate their own salaries. Negotiating rights are still in place in Scotland. By 1991, when government could no longer ignore the impending crisis in teacher recruitment, the idea of setting up an independent pay body, similar to that which operates for nurses and doctors, was offered to teachers on the condition that they lose the right to strike. Whether this will be acceptable to teachers remains to be seen.

Poor career prospects: this has been due to pressure on school budgets resulting from new **funding** policies, many teachers in mid-career have little or no prospect of increasing their salaries or improving their positions. It is cheaper to employ younger, less experienced teachers.

Insufficient **in-service training**: in recent years, pressure on budgets and the demands of new legislation has reduced the sort of professional development needed to boost career prospects. Professional development has had to take second place to stop-gap courses which help teachers to cope with new policies and classroom practice.

Government reforms: the National Curriculum was imposed on teachers in 1989, hard on the heels of changes to **GCSE**, **governors** and school funding. Many teachers felt that they were never seriously consulted on these changes.

Teacher appraisal: in response to the much-publicized decline in school standards (for which there is as yet no real evidence) a system of teacher appraisal is to be introduced by 1995. Under this system teachers will have their classroom performance assessed by a senior colleague, either the headteacher or head of department, every two years. Teachers are concerned that appraisal will be linked to financial reward, and see the move as potentially divisive.

Changes to the nature of teacher training: two new breeds of teacher will operate in schools in the future: the articled teacher and the licensed teacher. Both come from schemes designed to attract new recruits and shift some of the responsibility for teacher training away from **Higher Education (HE)** to the schools themselves. Articled teachers must already have a degree and spend 80 per cent of their time training in the classroom under the supervision of a mentor, and 20 per cent in college. Licensed teachers are not required to have a degree but must have spent at least two years in Higher Education. Although parents have no need for alarm, such schemes must pose the question: have schools really got time to add training to an already overcrowded schedule?

Threats and violence: teachers are three times more likely to be threatened in the line of duty than other workers. The Elton Committee, a government appointed body, found in 1988 that one in 200 secondary teachers had suffered violence and one in seven had been verbally abused by pupils or parents.

Clearly something needs to be done to staunch the flow of teachers away from the profession and ways have to be found to attract more high-calibre recruits. The only long-term solution is to invest more money into the system for teacher salaries and resources in the classroom. The signs are not good.

(See also **headteachers, stress, supply teachers**.)

teacher shortages

See **shortage subjects, teachers**

teaching methods

Teaching methods have changed significantly since parents were themselves at school. Comments such as, 'I don't understand how they teach **reading** these days' or ' Maths isn't like it was in our day' can be heard every day amongst groups of parents as they wait to collect their children.

The best way of finding out what happens in your child's classroom is to visit the school and talk to the teacher. Provided that you exercise some tact and are helpful in your approach, most teachers are glad to talk about what they are trying to achieve and how parents can help at home.

The most significant change in teaching methods has been the move away from the idea of children as empty vessels into which so much knowledge can be poured, towards the view that children learn best when they are active in the process. A major shift from passive to active participation. Across the whole age range there is now much greater emphasis on group work, discussion, project work and problem-solving.

Although there is never a substitute for face-to-face discussion between teacher and parent, an understanding of at least some of the educational **jargon** may help you to work out what is going on.

The following is a quick guide to some of the terms you are likely to hear.

Child-centred: this is a term which is frequently mis-represented by politicians eager to point out that new-fangled teaching methods are the scourge of the education system. As a result, much confusion surrounds the idea. Child-centred means that the teacher takes the child rather than the subject matter as the starting point. Contrary to popular myth, teachers using this method (and most teachers of young children these days do) do not simply leave their pupils to do whatever they fancy all day, rather they try to capitalize on the interests and capabilities of individuals to make learning both more stimulating and relevant. There is much to recommend this method of working.

Discovery learning: closely linked to child-centred teaching methods, discovery learning enables children to test their ideas and find things out for themselves. For example, it is possible to discover the conditions necessary to sustain plant life from a book or from the teacher, but children are far more likely to remember the lesson if they have planted two seeds in separate pots, one containing sand the other containing soil and monitored the outcome. Again, this method has a colourful reputation. Parents may think it means that their children are left to their own devices, floundering around in areas they know nothing about. The opposite is true. Tea-chers using discovery methods have to structure the activities carefully without the children being aware what the outcome will be. You can help your child to understand the way things work by asking, 'I wonder what will happen if . . .' This question is the cornerstone of discovery learning in schools.

Project work: this is work which attempts to integrate various subjects into a more meaningful whole. Previously, it was often difficult to see how a subject like, for example, **mathematics** might have any relevance to subjects like **history** or **science**. The feeling that what was done at school had little or no bearing on the world of home or work was hard to avoid. Teachers keen on project work focus on a particular area of interest and make sure that pupils' practise a whole range of skills. For example, a project on dinosaurs in the primary school can include science, mathematics, language, history, geography, **art**, design and many more. A project on statistics in the secondary school harvests a similarly large crop of skills and experiences.

Integrated day: this is a method for organizing classes without rigid adherence to a timetable. Teachers using this method usually arrange their classes into smaller groups and each group works on different things. The teacher divides his or her time between the groups and gives individual attention where it is needed. The class will be gathered together inter-mittently throughout the day so that children can share their experiences with others.

Child-centred teaching methods, project and group work have all been ridiculed at various times by those who insist, without concrete evidence, that **standards** are falling in our schools. They have an excellent educational pedigree, and are implicit in most of the **National Curriculum** guidelines.

(See also **home–school partnership, How to help at home.**)

team games

See **physical education (PE)**

Technical and Vocational Education Initiative (TVEI)

A government scheme designed to improve links between the world of work and the education system. Under the scheme **Local Education Authorities (LEAs)** receive grants from central government via the local **Training and Enterprise Councils (TECs)** to fund approved programmes of a technical and vocational nature.

In the past TVEI money has been used to pay for additional teaching posts, to help schools acquire **computers** and technical equipment, and for establishing links with industry. How the scheme will develop in the future is unclear. Its **funding** is due to end in 1996.

(See also **education and the market place.**)

technical schools

Institutions which provide a general education but with extra emphasis on technical subjects.

Technical schools never existed in large numbers and are now almost extinct.

(See also **vocational education.**)

technology

See **design and technology**

Technology Academies

The Scottish version of **City Technology Colleges (CTCs)**.

teenage parents

Over 64 000 children are born to teenage parents every year. The outlook for many of these parents—and their children—is bleak. The failure rate for teenage marriages is high, children born to mothers under 20 are twice as likely to be taken into care, and when children of young parents grow up they are also likely to give birth early.

Most school girls who become pregnant find their formal schooling at an abrupt end. In theory they can stay at school until their confinement, but few do so. Some continue to study in a segregated group or at home with the help of visiting **teachers**. Once the baby is born, home visiting is the only alternative for most mothers, but this usually stops when the mother reaches 16.

An experimental unit in Scotland has shown that by using **crèche** facilities and integrating young mothers with adults it is possible to continue their education. Findings also suggest that providing this support dramatically cuts the incidence of second pregnancies among young mothers—which is running nationally at around 25 per cent. Unfortunately, this kind of innovative approach is available to very few.

Teenage fathers have traditionally been seen as irresponsible and incapable of looking after their children. Recent research challenges this view and suggests they are in fact no better or worse than any other group. Wherever possible they should clearly be given the opportunity to contribute to the new family group.

television

Over a year the average teenager spends as much time watching television as he or she does at school. This is not a habit teenagers are likely to grow out of: recent research suggests that by the time they are adults, they will be watching for longer still.

With statistics like this it is easy to see how in many people's eyes television becomes a leading candidate for the cause of all society's ills. It is blamed for increases in violence, a decline in moral standards—and accused of contributing to the alleged

How to help with older children

Many people who start off helping their children enthusi-
astically when they are small allow their interest to fall away
as they get older. This might partly be in self-defence. Older
children are often studying subjects parents know nothing
about. Do not be intimidated. There are more important
things you can contribute than a detailed knowledge of **mathematics** or **geography** or French. The practical things you
can do to help are essentially no different from those you
would do for a younger child. Be interested, listen to them,
value their opinions.

You might also need to acknowledge that as children grow
up there are rival attractions competing for their time and
attention. (See **adolescence**.) This makes it all the more
important to stop yourself being a stranger to your child's
world. You might not immediately take to the music they are
listening to, for example, but give it a try. They will accept
your not liking it, but not your dismissing it as trash.

Here are some further points to consider:

Make sure they have a suitable place to work—a flat
surface, a decent light and a measure of calm and quiet.
(See **homework**.)

Remember that for many 15–16-year-olds, the work they
bring home is likely to be part of their coursework for
GCSE.

Ask them to explain things to you, show you how to use
the computer, talk about the **books** they are reading, or
why they are not reading. Make sure you know what is
going on at school. Who their **teachers** are, who they
like and dislike. Find out their strengths and weaknesses.
Involve yourself in decisions over **options**.

Use their practical knowledge. Let them repair their own
bicycles, wire a plug, decorate their bedroom. Encourage

their expressive, skills which can easily be swamped in the pressure to conform to the identity of the group.

At some time during their academic career you will find your children facing the prospect of exams. The stress involved can be considerable for young people; besides recognizing this—and perhaps making allowances at home—you can do a lot to encourage a sensible approach to the business of preparation.

This is what your children should have been told:

The key to successful revision is planning. Organize your time. Do not leave everything to the last minute and expect to be able to fit it all in.

Adopt a positive approach to revision. That is, do not simply sit and stare at books trying to remember what you are reading. You will recall information much better if you have organized it in some way. Make summaries, checklists.

Revision does not have to be an isolated activity. Some can be shared with friends.

Develop a strategy for the exam itself. Look at past papers. Make sure you know what sorts of areas are likely to be covered. Make sure you answer the question they ask, not the one you want to answer. Allow time for planning and checking—it really makes a difference. Do not spend more than the recommended time on one question—you lose marks that way, even if you are very good. Remember that examiners are not trying to catch you out: they are giving you an opportunity to show what you can do. Do not worry too much about exam nerves—a little adrenalin is useful in the exam room. If paralysis does set in, tell the invigilator and ask to be allowed outside for five minutes to get your breath back. And finally, if you make a mess of things, it is not the end of the world. You can almost certainly have another try.

(See **home–school partnership**.)

falling-off in educational **standards**. TV has often been accused of leading to a decline in reading ability, for example. In fact it has yet to be proved that standards *are* falling. What can be said, however, is that with so much time taken up by television there is little time left over for other activities—**reading** among them. Perhaps more significantly, in houses where the television is on all the time it is difficult to find the conditions that are essential for private reading. Even so, the argument is not entirely one sided. Many children are introduced to books through television adaptations. The BBC's successful *Chronicles of Narnia*, for example, will have helped to sell thousands of C.S. Lewis's *Narnia* stories. It is also worth remembering that Britain has a television service that is the envy of the world—though many fear that with the deregulation of broadcasting the stage is set for this to change.

The issue then is not straightforward. Parents effectively have three choices where television is concerned: you can give in, and let them watch whatever they like; you can lock the TV away in the loft; or you can try to limit the amount they watch. The video machine is a great boon if you are trying to manage your children's viewing. Programmes can be recorded and watched later—either at the weekend or when homework is out of the way. Children can also be encouraged to discriminate, choosing the programmes they want to watch and taking on the responsibility of recording them.

Beyond this, you might encourage your children to explore the radio—particularly Radio 5, which has evening programmes designed for young people of all ages—and finally, consider what sort of an example you set yourselves.

(See also **radio**.)

tertiary colleges

Tertiary colleges cater for students of all abilities from the age of 16. They combine the functions of a Sixth Form College and a College of Further Education. (See **beyond 16**.)

Although there are still only a limited number of tertiary colleges, they offer a wide range of academic and vocational courses, some of which can be studied part time. It is not uncommon for a tertiary college to offer, for example, 30 or 40 subjects. The examination success rate is high.

Tertiary colleges are popular with students who enjoy the more mature atmosphere and the chance to combine vocational and academic subjects: **A-level English** with business studies perhaps, or **mathematics** and physics with an engineering course.

The future of tertiary colleges hangs in the balance. They are favoured by those who see in them a chance to bridge the gap between academic subjects and **vocational education**. Others see them as a threat to the more traditional Sixth Forms in **secondary schools** and **Sixth Form Colleges**, which are all vying for students in a more competitive educational atmosphere.

(See **education and the market place**.)

testing

See **National Curriculum**

textbooks

See **books**

toy libraries

Centres, run along the same lines as book libraries, which lend toys and games to parents of young children.

Toy libraries were originally developed to help parents of handicapped children, but many have now extended their activities to all families with young children, particularly those in deprived areas. If there is a toy library near you, it is well worth a visit, especially if money is tight.

For further information, contact
Play Matters
66 Churchway, London NW1 1LT

(Play Matters also publishes *What Toy.)*

(See also **construction toys, play**.)

training

Britain entered the 1990s with a large unskilled workforce, high youth unemployment, and almost a third of 16-year-olds joining the job market each year without **Further Education (FE)** or training. It also has a major skills shortage in industry. Yet, despite this, we spend less on training than our major competitors and have repeatedly cut our training budget. Perhaps more significantly, Britain has recently abandoned attempts to produce a coherent national training system in favour of locally led initiatives run through the **Training and Enterprise Councils (TECs)**.

The TECs are not just a rehash of the old Manpower Services Commission and Training Agency, which were government bodies staffed and led by civil servants. The TECs are run by boards made up largely of prominent people from the business community. Some TECs—though by no means all—have senior educational representatives on the board. These business-led bodies must deliver the **Youth Training (YT)** programme, Employment Training, have part responsibility for the **Technical and Vocational Educational Initiative (TVEI)**, and have a brief to stimulate small businesses and enterprise. Between them, the 80 or so TECs have a budget running into billions of pounds.

The TECs have also been given the responsibility of running the training credit scheme. Under this scheme young people leaving full-time education are given a training voucher or credit. The vouchers are presented to the employer and used to purchase an agreed programme of education and training. The scheme began as a pilot in 1991 and is to be extended to cover the whole country.

The TECs might yet prove to be a powerful training lobby. Their influence is certainly growing as more initiatives are devolved to the boards. However, it is too early to say whether they can do anything to improve the bleak picture of our national training provision.

If there seems to be no suitable training place for your 16-year-old, your best move is to contact your local **College of Further Education** and ask about vocational courses.

(See also **vouchers**.)

Training and Enterprise Councils (TECs)

See **training**

Training Days

Days when schools are closed for staff **training. Teachers** must attend a minimum of five of these each year. Training Days are also known as Staff Development Days or Baker Days (after the former **Secretary of State for Education**, Kenneth Baker).

transport

Local authorities have a legal obligation to provide transport to local schools for children under eight if they live more than two miles away. Over the age of 8, the distance is three miles. In some rural areas, such as Norfolk, transport costs eat up a sizeable proportion of the educational budget.

Local Education Authorities (LEAs) have no legal obligation to provide transport for children whose parents choose to send them further afield than their local schools. This means that under the government's new **open enrolment** policies you can send your children to the school of your choice so long as you undertake to get them there each morning and bring them home in the afternoon.

Local authorities have traditionally agreed to foot the bill for transporting children to **voluntary-aided schools** if there was not one in the immediate area. Children whose parents want them to attend Church of England or Catholic schools have benefited from this arrangement. With the growing pressure on LEA budgets this concession is under threat.

(See also **choosing a school, funding.**)

travelling children

Children of parents for whom travelling is a way of life.

Most **Local Education Authorities (LEAs)** make provision for the education of travelling children. **Teachers** either visit children at travellers' sites or arrangements are made for children to attend local schools. Special **funding** is available to cover most of the cost of educating children who are not permanent residents of any particular LEA area.

One of the biggest obstacles to the successful education of travelling children is the failure of local authorities to provide permanent sites for travellers to use. All authorities have to provide these sites by law but many have yet to comply. Without them it is difficult to establish regular contacts both with the children and with local schools.

trips and visits

See **school trips and visits**

truancy

The deliberate avoidance of school.

Traditionally, the **Department of Education and Science (DES)** does not keep figures on the level of truancy—though they do acknowledge it is a major problem. Research suggests that by the Fifth Form almost a quarter of pupils are skipping school regularly or intermittently. More worrying still, between one in four and one in five truants began the habit at primary school.

The government has recently highlighted the issue of truancy. As a way of tackling the problem it has suggested that all schools publish truancy rates to help guide parents when they are **choosing a school**. Keeping records is not as straightforward as this makes it sound: first, because it is not easy to tell genuine absences from truancy; and, second, because most truants are smart enough to sign in before doing their disappearing act.

As parents it is your responsibility to make sure your children attend school—if they do not, you can be taken to court. Local authorities can no longer take children into care for persistent truancy. Instead they must apply for an educational supervision order to be placed on the parents of a truant. This requires them to work together with an **Educational Welfare Officer (EWO)** to overcome the problem. Further fines can be imposed if this process is not successful.

If you discover your child has been playing truant, here are some things to think about:

Talk to your child. Is there a specific problem that is leading to truancy—**bullying**, racial tension, fear of failure, clashes with **teachers**?

Talk to the school. In particular, talk to individual teachers and try to find out what is going wrong.

How did you find out? If the first you heard about your child's truancy was a visit from the school or welfare services, were there signs you should have picked up earlier? A child seriously disaffected with school is unlikely to be doing homework, for example.

The key to identifying the problem early and working out a strategy to deal with it lies in improved links between school and home. (See **home–school partnership**.)

Is your child's truancy a response to a difficult situation at home? If long-term relationships are under strain or breaking up, are there ways that the effects on children can be minimized?

Pupils who see school as pointless are the most difficult truants to deal with. The best hope lies in parents and schools being able to provide a degree of motivation. This is not always easy. Young people are often immune to the sort of argument that insists long-term gain (in the shape of improved **qualifications** and life choices) is worth short-term dissatisfaction and boredom.

trustees

See **voluntary-aided schools**

tuck shops

Shops run by pupils or staff selling snacks on the school premises.

In **primary schools**, tuck shops are sometimes run by pupils to provide a realistic situation where they can practise managing money. In others, the tuck shop is run on strictly profit-making lines in order to provide funds for school equipment such as **computers** and minibuses.

Tuck shops have been criticized for raising funds at the expense of children's health. Most of the food they sell—crisps, chocolate bars and sweets—has a high fat and sugar content and limited nutritional value. Evidence suggests some schools are reluctant to sell healthier food because profit margins might fall.

(See also **health education, school meals**.)

TVEI

See **Technical and Vocational Education Initiative**

twenty-one-hour rule

A regulation governing the number of hours the unemployed are allowed to give to part-time study before their benefit is stopped.

In order to claim benefit, individuals must show they are actively seeking work. The Department of Social Security has argued that if people are studying, they cannot be out job-hunting. The result is that at a time when one government department is trying to improve the **qualifications** of its workforce, another is taking steps to limit educational opportunities for those who need them most. Against a background of over 2 million unemployed the 21-hour rule has led to the absurd situation of students being forced to abandon their studies under pressure from the employment services in order to search for non-existent jobs.

Some colleges are setting up job-search activities to fulfil demands that their students are actively seeking work.

(See also **adult education, dole**.)

U

UCCA

See **University Central Council for Admissions**

UK education systems

Northern Ireland

Educational reform in Northern Ireland is proceeding at a slower pace than in the rest of the United Kingdom. The social and political upheaval of the Troubles have created a climate where entrenched positions are common and consensus is difficult to reach in many areas.

Northern Ireland has its own version of the 1988 Education Reform Act which sets out curricular guidelines, provisions for assessment and arrangements for **Opting-out**, which are broadly similar to those in England.

Administration

Education in Northern Ireland is administered through five education authorities known as Education and Library Boards. These boards are funded in their entirety from central government, unlike their counterparts in England, which receive part of their funds from local taxation.

Central administration rests with the **Department of Education Northern Ireland (DENI)**.

Types of Schools

Controlled schools are mainly Protestant and might be **primary**, secondary intermediate, **grammar** or **special schools**. **Voluntary-maintained schools** are mainly Roman Catholic. There are a few integrated schools which actively seek to break down sectarian differences by educating Catholics and Protestants under one roof, but they cater for a tiny proportion of the school population. The **Department of Education and Science (DES)** has a statutory duty to encourage the development of the integrated sector.

Secondary Education

Though agreement has been reached on the principal of comprehensive education Northern Ireland's secondary education remains selective. Until recently the **eleven plus** exam has been the main means of **selection**. Selection procedures have been successfully challenged in the courts on several occasions and are still the source of much controversy. In recent moves the government has made it clear that the only academic criterion for selection will be the assessment at the end of key stage two of the National Curriculum. This would give primary teachers the responsibility of deciding who should go to grammar school. The root of the problem lies in the fact that the 52 grammar schools in the province can accommodate only 30 per cent of the school population. This leaves the majority of pupils attending secondary intermediate schools, whose level of **funding** and educational achievements are lower.

Because of the peculiarities of its secondary system the independent sector in Northern Ireland fulfils a rather different role from its counterpart in the rest of the United Kingdom. Rather than acting as a magnet for a social and academic élite, it caters largely for children who have failed to get into grammar school and whose parents do not want to send them to secondary intermediate schools. (See **independent schools**.)

Schools in Northern Ireland come under:

Department of Education Northern Ireland (DENI)
Rathgael House, Balloo Road, Bangor, Co. Down BT19 2PR

Scotland

Scottish education is entirely distinct from the system in the rest of the United Kingdom. It has its own legislation, its own education department and its own Secretary of State.

The 1988 Education Reform Act does not apply to Scotland; neither does the **National Curriculum**. However, many of the major developments in the rest of the United Kingdom have their counterparts north of the border. The 5–14 Development Programme, for example, shares much of the machinery of the National Curriculum—attainment targets, programmes of study, testing—although the curriculum remains merely advisory. (See **Scotland: 5–14 Development Programme**.) Many differences in terminology obscure the similarities between the two systems. (**CTCs** are called **Technology Academies**, a **statement** is called a record of needs, etc.)

Scottish pupils begin school at 5 and transfer to secondary level at 12.

Most **secondary schools** are co-educational and run on comprehensive lines.

At 16 secondary pupils take the **Standard Grade** of the **Scottish Certificate of Education (SCE)**. These resemble **GCSEs** in their approach, **teaching methods** and methods of **assessment**.

Scottish pupils do not sit **A-levels**. Instead they study for **Higher Grade (Highers)** exams of the Scottish Certificate of Education. These are taken by most pupils at 17 after only a year's further study beyond Standard Grade. It is not uncommon for pupils to take as many as five Highers and to supplement them with other exams such as the **Certificate of Sixth Year Studies (CSYS)** or **National Certificate**. The result is a much broader education between 16 and 18 than is normal in the rest of the United Kingdom.

Many Scottish university courses last for four years instead of the three that is common in England and Wales. Students who have taken Highers after only one year can enter university at the age of 17.

For further information, contact
Scottish Office Education Department (SOED)
New St Andrew's House, St James Centre, Edinburgh EH1 3SY

Wales
Schools in Wales are covered by the same educational legislation as those in England. The major differences in education in the two countries centre on the use of the Welsh language.

The Welsh language is a compulsory part of the National Curriculum for all children in Wales. In Welsh-speaking schools it is a core subject (in addition to **English, mathematics** and **science**). In schools where the medium of instruction is English, Welsh is a foundation subject, taught as a foreign language. Making Welsh a compulsory part of the curriculum has caused problems. In the Anglicized south of the country many schools lack Welsh-speaking teachers and have pupils who do not know a word of the language. This makes delivery of the curriculum difficult. There are also major regional differences in Welsh language competence—in the north, for example, many children are bilingual. Given this situation it is hard to see how standard assessment tasks **(SATS)** in Welsh can give a fair indication of a child's ability.

The future of assessment of the Welsh component of the National Curriculum has yet to be decided. (See **bilingualism**.)

Schools in Wales come under:

Welsh Office, Education Department
Phase 2 Government Buildings, Ty Glas Road, Llanishen, Cardiff CF4 5WE

uniform

A code of dress—which might include school colours or insignia—designed to reinforce a school's public identity. Decisions as to whether uniform should be worn rest with the headteacher and school **governors**.

Uniforms tended to fall from favour in the 1960s and 1970s, when individual expression seemed more important than social cohesion. Today in the corporate-minded 1990s they are making a comeback.

New **grant-maintained schools** and **City Technology Colleges (CTCs)** have taken to uniforms in a big way. These schools are anxious to present an image which stresses old-fashioned discipline and traditional educational values. Adopting a uniform is partly a way of forging a new visible identity, and partly a marketing device.

Parents tend to see uniforms as confirmation of an orderly well-run school. In some cases they may be right but uniforms are not a reliable guide to educational performance. They are part of the image, rather than the substance. Equally, schools without a uniform and a more relaxed, informal atmosphere can have very high educational **standards**.

Uniform codes vary in their strictness. Some schools stipulate the precise nature of all dress items and the way they are to be worn (no loose ties, top collars to be done up at all times, etc). This strict code can be reinforced by the awarding of colours and flashes for particular achievements—which might be sporting, academic or musical. Pupils themselves tend to take these things very seriously.

Other schools have a more relaxed attitude to uniforms and settle for a dress code rather than a strictly specified uniform. The code might suggest types of garment and a range of colours. This approach allows pupils some measure of individual expression in what they wear, while still offering some of the benefits of group identity.

Many schools relax uniform requirements for members of the Sixth Form.

For parents in receipt of benefits help with the cost of school uniforms may be available through the **Local Education Authority (LEA)**.

(See also **discipline, hidden curriculum, school marketing**.)

university

See **Higher Education (HE)**

University Central Council for Admissions (UCCA)

The system which governs entry to degree courses in universities.

Pupils apply for university places through UCCA in their final year of **A-level** studies. Those who get the required grades have their positions immediately confirmed. Students who narrowly miss out with their final exams should contact the admissions office at the university to see if their grades are acceptable. If a place is not confirmed, students can contact other universities direct as well as registering with the UCCA clearing system, which tries to match up students with spare places. PCAS (The Polytechnic Central Admissions System) performs a similar function for polytechnics.

For further information, contact
UCCA
PO Box 28, Cheltenham, Gloucs GL50 3SA

University of the Third Age

An American organization with administrative offices in London. The aim is to encourage older adults (a growing section of the population) to form self-help groups to develop educational activities and share experiences. In 1991 there were 100 such groups in Britain with around 15 000 members. For advice and support on setting up a group, contact:

University of the Third Age
c/o Bassac, 13 Stockwell Road, London SW9 9AU

(See also **adult education**.)

V

vandalism

Criminal damage to property usually associated with young people.

The annual bill for vandalism, arson and burglary runs into millions of pounds a year. Vandalism directed against school property is of such concern that the **Department of Education and Science (DES)** has set up a special Action Squad to deal with it. Following the introduction of **Local Management of Schools (LMS)**, **headteachers** are now having to pay for much of the cost of repairs out of already tight school budgets.

Ideas for tackling the problem include rethinking the design of school **buildings**, the introduction of Good Neighbour schemes and holding parents responsible for the actions of their children.

Holding parents responsible for their children's actions, in other words making them liable to pay compensation for damage caused, is a contentious issue. Critics argue that this is not in the best interests of the children concerned and puts further pressure on already troubled families.

Vandalism might be reduced by a combination of these approaches but it is unlikely it can be tackled effectively without addressing the underlying causes of disaffection among young people.

(See also **young offenders**.)

vertical grouping

Vertical grouping (sometimes known as family grouping) is the practice of arranging teaching groups in **primary schools** so that pupils of different ages are in the same class.

Supporters of vertical grouping argue that it is more natural for children of different ages to learn together (like a family) and that there is much that older children can learn from younger ones and vice versa.

Modern **teaching methods** make vertical grouping a viable alternative to class arrangements based on strict year-groups. In smaller schools vertical grouping might be forced on staff through small class sizes. (See **rising fives**.)

veterinary schools

Higher Education establishments specializing in the training of veterinary surgeons.

Careers in veterinary science are much sought after. There are six centres in Britain offering between 350 and 400 places each year. Entry requirements include at least three good **A-levels**, preferably in technical and scientific subjects. Applicants also need to show evidence of strong motivation, such as a period spent working in a veterinary practice. Courses will last five to six years.

For further information, contact

Careers Research and Advisory Centre
Shereton House, Castle Park, Cambridge CB3 OAX

Royal College of Veterinary Surgeons
32 Belgrave Square, London SW1X 8QP

village colleges

See **community schools**

village schools

In the present economic climate, village schools are having a thin time. With the drift away from villages into towns many schools face the prospect of numbers falling below even their current low levels. Despite—or perhaps because of—their small size, village schools tend to be popular with both the local community and with parents and staff. **Local Education Authorities (LEAs)**, however, take a different view.

It costs more to educate a child in a small school than in a large primary school. The overheads—in terms of **teachers**, equipment, ancillary staff and **buildings**—are much higher. **Local Education Authorities (LEAs)** are also faced with large numbers of unfilled places in many larger schools. (See **baby booms and bulges**.) Simply by closing small schools and bussing children to fill these empty places, they could save a great deal of money.

The situation is being complicated by the arrival of LMS (Local Management of Schools). (See **funding**.) This imposes a squeeze on many school budgets. In addition, more of the head's time has to be spent on administration rather than teaching. The end result is that the books become harder to balance. In their enthusiasm to close small schools some LEAs are suggesting that schools with only a handful of pupils might have difficulty implementing the **National Curriculum**. Some schools are banding together in **consortia** to get round this problem—sharing resources and expertise.

Other schools are applying for grant-maintained status. (See **Opting-out**.) An application to opt out of local-authority control takes priority over a notice of closure. However, even if parents are in favour, the proposal still has to be approved by the **Department of Education and Science (DES)**.

In the end, neither Opting-out nor banding together provides a foolproof response to the threat of closure.

Parents should also remember that not all small schools are good schools—the same advice applies to choosing your school whether it is in a small village community or a densely populated city. (See **choosing a school**, **school closure**.)

For further information, contact

National Association for the Support of Small Schools
Molly Stiles, The Cottage, Little Barrington,
Norwich NR11 7LN

violence

Acts of physical or psychological aggression towards another person.

In some schools the threat of violence is a constant additional burden for **teachers** to carry and one reason—together with low pay, low status and a steadily increasing work-load—why disaffection in the profession is running high.

The Elton Report, produced by a government-appointed body, found in 1988 that one in seven teachers had suffered verbal abuse and as many as one in 200 had been physically attacked. Teachers—at risk from both pupils and parents—are three times more likely to be threatened than other workers. The National Union of Teachers has called on the government to provide extra money for tackling violence in schools.

Violence at the hands of other pupils is also part of the school experience of many children, although this is rarely admitted by **headteachers**. In areas of racial uneasiness, this violence is often directed towards pupils from ethnic minorities. (See **bullying**.)

Violence against pupils in the form of **corporal punishment** is now illegal in state schools but is allowed in **independent schools** as long as the pupil's fees are not being paid by the state.

(See also **children in care**.)

vocational education

Education which is closely geared to the needs of industry and commerce. The term is usually contrasted with academic education.

Vocational courses are one of the main growth areas in education today. While academic **qualifications** (such as **GCSE** and **A-level**) show that pupils can undertake a sustained period of study, they do not tell prospective employers what an individual can actually do. Vocational qualifications on the other hand (such as **BTEC** or **City and Guilds**) provide evidence of particular skills that might be useful in the workplace.

Someone with an **English** A-level, for example, has shown an ability to use language to discuss and analyse the works of a number of authors. However, he or she may or may not be able to transfer those same skills to the writing of a business report. A student with a BTEC in a commercially related subject is likely to have studied the way business reports are put together as part of the course.

The structure of our education system separates academic and vocational education. In schools we have an academically based **National Curriculum** and an exam system which is designed to cream off the top 30 per cent who will go on to study A-levels. At 16, those who do not measure up to this demanding academic steeplechase—the majority—are faced with the option of leaving education altogether or turning to work-related courses in Colleges of Further Education. (See **Further Education (FE)**.) As a result, vocational courses have traditionally been seen as a second-class option fit only for academic failures.

Faced with a major skills shortage and the increased technological demands of the workplace the government is trying to raise the status of vocational education. The development of **National Vocational Qualifications (NVQs)** is an attempt to unify the huge range of vocational qualifications and provide direct equivalents to GCSE and A-levels.

By themselves, NVQs are unlikely to break down the academic/vocational divide. The only real way to bring about this change would be to bring vocational courses into school alongside GCSEs and A-levels and make them a realistic alternative. Pupils might then take a common core of key subjects such as language, **mathematics** and a foreign language and supplement these with a range of **modular courses** drawing on academic and vocational elements. The current slow pace of A-level reform suggests that developments like these are a long way off.

(See also **options**.)

voluntary-aided schools

State schools which are funded partly by the **Local Education Authority (LEA)** (85 per cent) and partly by the Church (15 per cent).

These schools—mostly Church of England or Roman Catholic—have a religious policy determined by a group of trustees. This allows them to give a greater emphasis to the religious teachings of the Church than would be possible in other maintained schools.

Some **independent schools** representing minority religious groupings in this country (such as the Evangelists and Muslims) are actively seeking voluntary-aided status.

voluntary-controlled schools

State schools with close links to the Church (usually Church of England or Roman Catholic) but funded entirely by the **Local Education Authority (LEA)**.

Unlike **voluntary-aided schools**, which are partially funded by the Church, voluntary-controlled schools have to follow the same policy on **religious education (RE)** as other schools under LEA control.

vouchers

Credits issued to 16-year-olds leaving full-time education which can be used to purchase a recognized course of **training**.

The scheme—run through the local **Training and Enterprise Councils (TECs)**—began as a pilot in 1991 and is being extended to cover the whole country. School-leavers present the vouchers or credits to their new employer to help fund a programme of training or **Further Education**.

W

Wales

See **UK education systems**

work experience

A scheme designed to bridge the gap between the classroom and the world of work in which pupils spend part of the school term in the workplace.

Work experience can involve a hands-on approach with pupils working amongst full-time employees. Sometimes a shadowing technique is used where pupils follow (or shadow) individual workers to get a fuller picture of what their job involves. The scheme works best when pupils are able to relate their workplace visits to school courses. The introduction of an academically based **National Curriculum** has made this more difficult.

Some major companies—while applauding the aims of the scheme—have criticized the lack of suitable preparation and follow-up work that would help pupils make sense of what they saw.

Work experience of up to two weeks a year is allowed for 14–16-year-olds. Government guidelines stress that it must not be seen as a preparation for any particular job or career.

(See also **vocational education**.)

working parents

Today the majority of children from two-parent households have a mother and father who both work outside the home.

Traditionally, men have provided the main source of family income while women shouldered most of the responsibility for childcare. While reversal of these roles is becoming more common, this pattern still holds good in most households. What has changed in these families over the last few years is the number of women going out to work—both full and part time. There are now twice as many working women as there were in the early 1980s. The pressures which have brought about this change are partly economic, partly social and partly political. As a response to the serious skills shortage the government and commercial companies are officially trying to encourage more women back into the labour market. Meanwhile, fewer women are prepared to accept a life which revolves exclusively around children and the home. Moreover, there is the general desire or need to earn more money.

The key issue for working parents is none of these things. What concerns them on a day-to-day basis is the availability of childcare facilities. Compared to many of their European counterparts, British families fare badly on this score. The promise of a free nursery place for every child—advocated by Margaret Thatcher in 1981—has been quietly set aside. The demand for childcare facilities far outstrips demand in most areas and will do so for some time to come. (See **pre-school provision**).

Many women who want to go back to work therefore find that the problems and expense involved make it impossible. The problem is often worse for single-parent families who must either depend on the state or find a job which pays enough to finance the childcare.

Yet, with the right childcare facilities there is no reason why the return to work should not be good for everyone concerned: parents, children and the economy as a whole. Research from Sweden (where childcare is better) suggests that children can benefit from being separated from their parents for part of the day. They tend to be more independent and confident, and do every bit as well at school. Consistency is the most important thing. Try to ensure that your child has a routine: this minimizes the chances of anxiety and uncertainty creeping in. Although it is probably the last thing you feel like doing when you come in from a hard day at work, try to set aside some time each day to spend exclusively on your child. (See **quality time**.) This is the best antidote of all for the **parental guilt** that comes from trying to juggle the responsibilities of work and children.

workplace nurseries

See **pre-school provision**

Y

young offenders

Young offenders are broadly defined as children between the ages of 10 and 14 and young people between the ages of 14 and 17 who have been convicted of criminal offences.

Over the last few years the damaging effects of custodial sentences on the young have been recognized, as a result there has been a major change in sentencing policy for young offenders. Rather than sending them to prison, courts have been encouraged to use the powers they already possess to hold parents responsible for the actions of their children. Parents can be fined, made to pay compensation, and told to impose evening curfews on their children. This approach has been criticized for putting undue pressure on already troubled families. (See **vandalism**.)

Young offenders who find themselves in custody are unlikely to receive much in the way of educational help. This is particularly true if they are on remand. The National Association for the Care and Resettlement of Offenders (NACRO) have long campaigned for educational provision at a time when it could minimize disruption to the lives of remand prisoners. However, provision remains patchy.

There are young offenders' institutes attached to some remand centres.

(See also **children in care**, **prison education**.)

youth service

An umbrella term covering the clubs and centres for young people run by voluntary organizations and local education departments.

In 1990 the government decided the youth service ought to be covered by its own **National Curriculum**. The core of this curriculum was to deal with issues such as drug abuse, homelessness, crime, anti-racist and anti-sexist work, physical and mental health, and political education. Organizations as different as local boys' clubs, Scout troops, and the Girls' Friendly Society were expected to incorporate this core curriculum into their activities. The proposal was greeted with derision by many youth workers.

The suggestion is unlikely to make serious inroads into the youth service. Beyond the small local-authority sector, most of the youth service is run by unpaid volunteers—people who would not easily be persuaded to deliver major reforms with which they did not agree.

Youth Training (YT)

A scheme administered by the **Training and Enterprise Councils (TECs)** designed to provide temporary on-the-job training for young people between the ages of 16 and 25. During the term of their Youth Training (YT) placement, young people are paid an allowance which is equal to the standard rate of unemployment benefit.

The scheme has changed radically since its introduction in 1983. Originally it lasted for a fixed time-span (a year, extended later to two years). Now the period is much more flexible and training is geared towards a specific qualification. (See **National Vocational Qualifications (NVQs)**.) It was thought that industry would put money into the scheme once it was running. This has not happened. Planned government spending on Youth Training was cut by almost a quarter between 1990 and 1993. The scheme was intended for employed and unemployed alike.

Though this idea was quickly dropped, the scheme's long association with unemployment has ensured its second-class status. In 1988 benefit rights were withdrawn for under 18s— turning the option of YT into the only option for many people.

YT has been dogged by bad publicity. Introduced at a time of high unemployment, it was accused of adding to the problem as companies replace full-time staff with a series of cheaper trainees. Trainees have no employment security and are not fully protected by legislation such as the Race Relations Act (1976) or the Sex Discrimination Act (1975). In many cases the quality of **training** has been severely criticized.

It remains to been seen if the newly empowered TECs can truly tailor the scheme to local needs and improve the quality of training.

(See also **beyond 16**.)

Z

Zulu

A survey compiled by a pressure group in 1990 claimed that a class of Zulus had performed better in English **spelling** tests than Sixth Formers from Britain.

The report was carried in many national newspapers. In fact, the story did not actually say that the Zulus could spell better than their British counterparts (the only thing that might have justified the story), only that they had done better 'in some aspects of spelling'.

The report with its misleading headlines and overtones of racism is a good example of what can happen to the **standards** debate when it is handled by sections of the popular press.